The Death of Jesus and the Politics of Place in the Gospel of John

The Death of Jesus and the Politics of Place in the Gospel of John

PETER CLAVER AJER

PICKWICK *Publications* · Eugene, Oregon

THE DEATH OF JESUS AND THE POLITICS OF PLACE IN THE GOSPEL OF JOHN

Pickwick Publications
An Imprint of Wipf and Stock Publishers
199 W. 8th Ave., Suite 3
Eugene, OR 97401

www.wipfandstock.com

Paperback ISBN 978-1-4982-7962-8
Hardback ISBN 978-1-4982-7964-2
Ebook ISBN 978-1-4982-7963-5

Cataloging-in-Publication data:

Names: Ajer, Peter Claver

Title: The death of Jesus and the politics of place in the Gospel of John / Peter Claver Ajer.

Description: Eugene, OR : Cascade Books, 2016 | Includes bibliographical references and indices.

Identifiers: ISBN 9781498279628 (paperback) | ISBN 9781498279642 (hardback) | ISBN 9781498279635 (ebook)

Subjects: 1. Bible. John—Criticism, interpretation, etc. 2. Jesus Christ—Crucifixion. 3. Bible—Geography.

Classification: BS2615.52 A5 2016 (print) BS2615.52 (electronic)

Manufactured in the U.S.A.

For the deceased members of my family:
Dad Salvatore Daii, siblings Armstrong Innocent Emuny and George Obong

Table of Contents

Foreword

The scholarly conversation on the significance of Jesus' passion in the fourth Gospel had, until recently, focused mostly on the historical, literary, and theological aspects of this narrative. Few studies had discussed its political and spatial aspects. The present study by Peter Ajer takes these less-travelled roads with a political reading of the passion narrative in John that is also sensitive to spatial questions.

The first parts of the book show Dr. Ajer's knowledge of previous studies on the Johannine passion narrative and of the approaches taken thus far to address it. On the one hand, these pages convey his expertise concerning contemporary political theories, especially those related to war, peace, and empire. On the other hand, they show how conversant he is with recent theories about space and place formulated by contemporary geographers.

The readers of Dr. Ajer's book will profit from his scholarship in many ways. First, readers will better comprehend the assets and liabilities of previous studies of the Johannine passion narrative. Next, they will understand the dynamics of power in the Eastern Mediterranean part of the Roman empire during the first century CE, enabling them to perceive what is at stake for the narrative's various characters. Readers will therefore be better able to appreciate the decisions that the characters make. Third, readers will observe a creative use of Chinua Achebe's masterful novel *Things Fall Apart,* which serves as an intertext to discuss some dimensions of an empire. Fourth, readers will discover the richness of recent discourses on space and place in contemporary geography, especially since few biblical scholars have paid attention to the evolution of contemporary geography, focusing instead on historical questions. Fifth, readers will discover a refreshing interpretation of the Johannine passion narrative that moves beyond the usual dualisms that oppose the world to the heavens and the literal to the symbolic. Dr. Ajer's expertise on the spatial theories formulated by Henri

Lefebvre and Edward Soja helps him to formulate a perspective that broadens our imagination when discussing the significance of the Johannine passion. He suggests that the passion shows Jesus' capacity at creating a new type of space by transforming the cross, the quintessential tool of imperial oppression meant to inspire terror among the subjected populations, into an attractive and inclusive space of glorification that unites and empowers those who had been powerless, standing non-violently against the empire.

Jean-François Racine
Associate Professor of New Testament
Jesuit School of Theology of Santa Clara University
and Graduate Theological Union

Abbreviations

AB	Anchor Bible
ABD	*Anchor Bible Dictionary*
ABRL	Anchor Bible Reference Library
AnBib	Analecta Biblica
BAG	Bauer, W., W. F. Arndt, and F. W. Gingrich. *Greek English Lexicon of the New Testament and other Early Christian Literature.* Chicago, 1957.
BETL	Bibliotheca ephemeridum theologicarum lovaniensium
Bib	*Biblica*
BibInt	*Biblical Interpretation*
BNTC	Black's New Testament Commentaries
BTB	*Biblical Theology Bulletin*
BZAW	Beheifte zur Zeitschrift für die alttestamentliche Wissenschaft
BZNW	Beheifte zur Zeitschrift für die neuetestamentliche Wissenschaft
CahRB	Cahiers de La Revue biblique
CBQ	*Catholic Biblical Quarterly*
CBQMS	Catholic Biblical Quarterly Monograph Series
CBR	*Currents in Biblical Research*

ConBNT	Coniectanea neotestamentica or Coniectanea biblica: New Testament Series
CTQ	*Concordia Theological Quarterly*
EDNT	Exegetical Dictionary of the New Testament.
EQ	*Evangelical Quarterly*
EThL	*Ephemerides theologicae lovanienses*
FRLANT	Forschungen zur Religion und Literatur des Alten and Neuen Testaments
FV	*Foi et vie*
HBS	History of Biblical Studies
HNT	Handbuch zum Neuen Testament
HTS	Harvard Theological Studies
HUT	Hermeneutische Untersuchungen zur Theologie
ICC	International Critical Commentary
Int	*Interpretation*
ITQ	*Irish Theological Quarterly*
JAAR	*Journal of the American Academy of Religion*
JBL	*Journal of Biblical Literature*
JJS	*Journal of Jewish Studies*
JSNT	*Journal for the Study of the New Testament*
JSOT	*Journal for the Study of the Old Testament*
JSNTSup	Journal for the Study of the New Testament: Supplement Series
JTS	*Journal of Theological Studies*
KD	*Kerygma and Dogma*
LCL	Loeb Classical Library
LS	*Louvain Studies*
NCB	New Century Bible
Neot	*Neotestamentica*

NIB	*The New Interpreter's Bible*
NJBC	*The New Jerusalem Biblical Commentary*
NovT	*Novum Testamentum*
NovTSup	Supplements to Novum Testamentum
NTAbh	Neuestestamentliche Abhandlungen
NTD	Das Neue Testament Deutsch
NTS	*New Testament Studies*
PIBA	Proceedings of the Irish Biblical Association
RB	Revue biblique
RivB	*Rivista biblica italiana*
RivBSup	Supplementi alla Rivista Biblica
RivSR	*Rivista die scienze religiose*
SANT	Studien zum Alten und Neuen Testaments
SBLDS	Society of Biblical Literature Dissertation Series
SBLRBS	Society of Biblical Literature Resources for Biblical Studies
SBLSymS	Society of Biblical Literature Symposium Series
Semeia	*Semeia: An Experimental Journal for Biblical Criticism*
SemeiaSt	Semeia Studies
SJLA	Studies in Judaism in Late Antiquity
SNTSMS	Society for New Testament Studies Monograph Series
STAR	Studies in Theology and Religion
TD	*Theological Digest*
TDNT	*Theological Dictionary of the New Testament*
TLZ	Theologische Literaturzeitung
TTS	Theologische Texte und Studien
TynBul	*Tyndale Bulletin*

USQR	*Union Seminary Quarterly Review*
WMANT	Wissenschaftliche Monographien zum Alten und Neuen Testaments
WUNT	Wissenschaftliche Untersuchungen zum Neuen Testament
ZNW	Zeitschrift für die neuestestamentliche Wissenschaft und die kunde der älteren Kirche

Acknowledgments

Much gratitude to my parents the late Salvatore Daii and Sidonia Daii for supporting, educating, and encouraging me at all times. As I look back, I recognize the immense sacrifices you made to sustain and educate ten children. Salvatore, you did not live to see this happen but I'm sure you smile as you rest in peace. To my siblings, your love and care at all times have sustained me through every moment of life. You made this work possible. To Monica Bland Ajer, you are part of this success in many ways. Thank you for your support throughout the writing process.

I am greatly indebted to Dr. Jean-François Racine, who has guided and advised me in every moment of my graduate student life at the Graduate Theological Union, from dissertation to classroom leadership to major knee surgery. I extend my gratitude to your family for their time and kindness during my recovery. I have learned so much from you as a mentor and feel most grateful for your time and sage advice.

Great thanks to Dr. David L. Balch (Graduate Theological Union) and Dr. Darren Zook (University of California, Berkeley), who have been kind and helpful guides during my research work. David, thank you for sending to me every material you considered useful for my research and for your critical reading of my writing as it was coming together. Darren, I appreciate the many times you put aside your own work so that we could have tremendous conversations about postcolonial theories.

To Franca D. Firinu, thank you for always finding solutions when challenges seemed overwhelming. You have my family's sincere gratitude.

To Richard Murray, thank you for making time amidst your busy schedule to proofread my work. Your generosity with your time is beyond compare. I am greatly indebted to you.

Last but not least, Dr. Eugene Eung-Chun Park, I had many conversations with you at the conception of this work. Thank you as well for your friendship.

Introduction

Studies on the death of Jesus in the Fourth Gospel have focused on its soteriological significance. While scholars have covered numerous aspects of this topic, they have not arrived at any universal consensus on the meaning of the death of Jesus. In the late twentieth century, scholarly investigation shifted from a focus on its salvific significance to assessing the significance of politics for understanding this event.

Heinrich Schlier's publication (1966) on John and Pilate in the Fourth Gospel inaugurated this new perspective by emphasizing the political aspect of the death of Jesus.[1] Schlier argued that each NT author was convinced that Jesus was not merely a private individual nor the church merely a voluntary association. Instead, these authors each narrated Jesus' encounter with the political world of the state and its authorities, with John presenting the most challenging interpretation of this relationship. Schlier distinguished the political world of "the state and its authorities," represented by Pilate, from "the world," represented by the Jews, with the latter seeking its salvation from Caesar. He claimed that by telling the story of the trial of Jesus, John intended to highlight the problem of the state, and to attain fundamental insight into the nature of the state as it appeared in the New Testament.[2]

Some scholars interpret John's interest in the death of Jesus as apologetic, aimed at protecting the Christians against the Romans (Dodd, 1953; Haenchen, 1965; Dauer, 1972; Hoskyns and Davey, 1981; Lindars, 1990). Others interpret John as putting before his readers a choice between the kingship of Christ and that of Caesar, meaning that the church need not be always apologetic (Meeks, 1967; Richey, 2007). These studies of the political aspects in John center on the various characters mentioned in the

1. Schlier, "Jesus und Pilatus."
2. Schlier, *Relevance of the New Testament*, 215–25.

narrative of the death of Jesus (Carter, 2003; Bond, 2004; Piper, 2007). They pay little attention to the diverse spaces mentioned in the story (Richey, 2007; Thatcher, 2009; Resseguie, 2001).

Postcolonial hermeneutics followed these initial analyses, arguing that the text was the product of an imperial Roman context; it has various political ideologies and diverse geopolitical ramifications. These texts carry the political ideologies of imperial Rome, of the oppressed population of Palestine of the first century CE, and of the minority Johannine community. This study will continue this postcolonial conversation, discussing the political aspects of the death of Jesus by concentrating on insufficiently studied contexts of its social and political geographies.

John describes the death of Jesus as a triumph, moving away from presenting Jesus in distress. In John 11:47–57, the council of Jerusalem's leaders decides to kill Jesus in an attempt to avoid the political risk of a Roman invasion. John remarks that this death will lead to the positive outcome of gathering together the scattered children of God. When Jesus foretells his death on the cross (John 12:20–36), he remarks that it will bring about the unity of all people. Finally, in the so-called Passion narrative (John 18:1–19:22), one reads only of Jesus' triumph in the various political spaces of his arrest, trial and death. John tells the story in a way that prevents the reader from sympathizing with Jesus or from fearing for Jesus and for oneself and thus seeking to avoid a similar destiny. What are the implications of John's presentation of the story as a triumph stripped of any suffering?

This study attempts to answer the above question by looking at the various social and political spaces in the Fourth Gospel's narrative of the death of Jesus. Basic political geographies include Roman space, Caiaphas' space, the Sanhedrin's space, the garden space, the praetorium space, Pilate's space and the crucifixion space. In each of the political discourses and activities of these spaces, the political elite look forward to crucifying Jesus, yet John convinces the reader that Jesus is the victor in each of these socio-political spaces. His triumph climaxes on the cross, when he gathers all people to him. I argue that in the Fourth Gospel, Jesus' crucifixion is a politically-charged space that critiques and resists the power of the Roman Empire, while constructing an alternate space of liberating interdependence.

To accomplish this, this study will bring together social and political theories of space as formulated by Henri Lefebvre and Edward W. Soja, approaches from the social sciences as they are laid out by, inter alia, Bruce

J. Malina and Jerome H. Neyrey, and a postcolonial approach inspired by Chinua Achebe.[3]

In chapter 1, I survey prior scholarship on John in order to uncover new paths of inquiry. In chapter 2, I review prior works on place in John's Gospel and elaborate on and expound the methodology for my study.

In the third chapter, I demonstrate how Jesus' signs construct social and political spaces and highlight the impact of these signs on his society and on the political authorities. I contend that John's Gospel redefines Caiaphas' and the Sanhedrin's spaces, and reveals these leaders as unknowing mouthpieces and pawns of God, thereby challenging and resisting the Jerusalem authorities and their Roman masters.

In chapter 4, I discuss Jesus' announcement of the defeat of the "ruler of this world" in his death on the cross. By constructing the cross as a space of glory, John defeats Rome's weapon of oppression, and by designating the cross as a place of unity of all people, John forms a community of oppressed people moving together towards greater liberation.

In chapter 5, I show that in various places of struggle, Jesus remains in control of every situation. He answers Pilate rudely, contradicts his words, and exposes him as a weak judge who does not know "truth." Pilate's weakness is also exposed in the many times the opponents of Jesus outside the praetorium respond to his questions with other questions. His movements inside and outside imply that he struggles to manipulate all affairs. When Jesus explains that his death is a fulfillment of Scripture, Pilate becomes a mouthpiece, an instrument to realize the divine plan. Pilate is the third victim of Jesus' divine politics. At the same trial, Jesus defines his followers as a truth community, an alternate community creating a new world order that challenges the Roman world's disorder.

---

3. Achebe, *Things Fall Apart*.

CHAPTER 1

Previous Studies On The Death Of Jesus

Introduction

Many individuals were crucified under Roman rule in first century CE Palestine, but no single death has influenced the history of the world more than that of Jesus Christ. This influence stems from Christian interpretation of Jesus' death on the cross, which made the horrible death acceptable. By interpreting it as an atoning sacrifice, the event took on salvific significance, and became the foundation of Christian faith.

An interweaving of John's story with that of the synoptic Gospels formed the basis for this interpretation of the death of Jesus, but critical scholarship uncovered the difference between John's narrative and that of the Synoptic Gospels. Craig Koester's observation that the "Synoptics tell of Jesus' suffering, John tells of Jesus' triumph" demands investigation into what are the effects of John's presentation of the story as a triumph, stripped of any suffering.[1]

Rudolf Bultmann ignited the probe into the significance of the death of Jesus in the Fourth Gospel with his provocative position that the Gospel of John is void of atonement terminology and therefore has neither atonement nor salvific significance.[2] Ernst Käsemann staunchly followed Bultmann, differing from him on certain aspects but reaching the same conclusions. Subsequent studies reacted to both Bultmann and Käsemann. While Pro-Bultmann scholars made minor modifications to the arguments

1. Koester, "Death of Jesus," 141.

2. Bultmann, *Theology of the New Testament*, 2:52–53.

in favor of the non-atonement character of John, opponents resisted Bultmann's conclusion and reclaimed the death of Jesus as atoning sacrifice. Later scholars focused on diverse motifs such as glorification and exaltation, sacrifices, ascent and lifting up, revelation, sign, cosmic war, and death of a "noble" shepherd.[3]

In the late twenty-first century, interpretations of the soteriological significance of the death of Jesus in John shifted to inquiry into the centrality of politics. Because no single explanation has been unilaterally accepted, this chapter will critically review scholarship that addresses the salvific significance of the death of Jesus in order to identify weaknesses in interpretation that are strengthened by interpretations focusing on politics.

Death of Jesus as Completion of Mission and Return to the Father

Rudolf Bultmann, along with Ernst Käsemann, pioneered interpretations of the death of Jesus as the completion of his mission and a return to his Father. Bultmann's polemic affirmation that the Gospel of John is of no soteriological significance sprang from his conviction that the Fourth Gospel lacks atonement terminology and cannot be interpreted as an expiatory sacrifice for the sins of others.[4] According to Bultmann, Jesus' coming into the world is central to understanding the person and works of Jesus. Jesus' arrival and departure "constitute a unity," wherein "the center of gravity" is the incarnation. Bultmann argues that any attempt to make Jesus' death central uses Paul's theology to interpret John's.[5] Jesus' death should be understood as part of his total revelatory work with no significance in and of itself because the release from sin is mediated not through Jesus' sacrificial death but through his word (8:31–35; 15:13).[6] Any allusions to atonement

---

3. For glorification and exaltation, see Müller, *Heilsgeschehen im Johannesevangelium*; for sacrifices, see Grigsby, "Cross as an Expiatory Sacrifice," 51–80; Carey, "Lamb of God," 97–122; for ascent and lifting up, see Nicholson, *Death as Departure*; for revelation, Forestell, *Word of the Cross*; for sign, see Dodd, *Interpretation of the Fourth Gospel*, 438–39; Senior, "Death of Jesus as a Sign," 271–91; on the rhetorical usage of signs, see Salier, *Rhetorical Impact of the Semeia*; Van Belle, "Death of Jesus," 3–64; for cosmic war, see Kovacs, "Now Shall the Ruler of this World," 227–47; and for noble death, see Neyrey, "Noble Shepherd," 267–91.

4. Bultmann, *Theology of the New Testament*, 52–53, 55.

5. Ibid., 52.

6. Ibid., 53.

in the Fourth Gospel such as in 1:29, 35, are "later accretions or remnants of earlier traditions."[7] Bultmann thus boldly concludes that the understanding of the death of Jesus as an atoning sacrifice "has no place in John."[8] Jesus' death is therefore "no offence, no scandal, and no catastrophe needing a resurrection to reverse or illuminate it."[9]

Instead, Bultmann understands Jesus' crucifixion—which John recounts under the force of tradition—as his "elevation" (ὑψωθῆναι) and "glorification" (δοξασθῆναι) whereby Jesus completes his mission of obedience to God and returns to the glory he had when pre-existent.[10] For this reason, Jesus is never portrayed as a worldly phenomenon, someone to be captured and domesticated in worldly categories. He is not depicted as the "passive victim" but as the "active conqueror."[11]

Like Bultmann, Käsemann argued that Jesus' death must be understood in the context of his total mission of "coming and going," as Jesus' death as the completion of his heavenly mission and his "going away" back to his Father. This "going away" (ὑπάγειν: 7:33; 8:14, 21–22; 13:3, 33, 36; 14:4–5, 28; 16:5, 10, 17) represents the end of the earthly sojourn that Jesus' incarnation began.[12] The return represents no real change in the person of the revealer, anymore than his incarnation does. He may change his location, but he always and everywhere exhibits and possesses the divine glory.[13] For this reason Jesus' death discloses nothing of his person and work not already manifested in the incarnation itself. If his death is "the manifestation of divine self-giving love," then so is his incarnation.[14]

Käsemann departs from Bultmann by arguing that the center of the Fourth Gospel is not the incarnation, but the "unity of the Father with the Son."[15] The key term for the articulation of this unity is the word "glory," found in the Prologue of John's Gospel (1:14) and at the beginning of chapter 17. Read with "glory" in mind, John's Gospel does not proclaim the humanity of Jesus but his divinity, as the divine glory is exhibited in Jesus.

7. Ibid., 54–55.

8. Ibid., 54.

9. Ibid., 56.

10. Ibid., 52–53.

11. Ibid.

12. Käsemann, *Testament of Jesus*, 17–18.

13. Ibid., 12 and 20.

14. Ibid., 10 and 59–60.

15. Ibid., 24.

The Gospel elicits faith through the unity of the Son with the Father. The sojourn of Jesus reveals the earthly manifestation of divine glory. The goal of the incarnation is the visible presence of God on earth, and is not proof of a "realistic incarnation."[16]

Käsemann argues that the Johannine Jesus has few human features. The physical countenance is simply a deception. Jesus' divine glory is not paradoxically hidden in his fleshly, earthly body as Bultmann claimed. Instead, Jesus is God striding across the earth. He is God's envoy on earth and only in unity with God is his mission on earth accomplished. This means that Jesus is in complete unity with God even in his death.[17] Because the theme of glory determines the entire presentation of Jesus in the Fourth Gospel from the beginning, the death "takes place on the cross, as tradition demands," but this cross is "no longer the pillory, the tree of shame."[18]

Both Bultmann and Käsemann contend that John presents Jesus as "the heavenly revealer" who has come into the world and returns to the Father. While Bultmann emphasizes the human nature in the incarnation and Käsemann emphasizes the divinity, the basic clue to Jesus' identity and works lies in the incarnate revealer of God on earth.[19] For this reason his death adds nothing not already disclosed or given in his earthly manifestation and work."[20]

Death of Jesus as Non-Atoning Soteriological Event

Terence J. Forestell offered the first significant reaction to Bultmann and Käsemann. Ulrich. B. Müller, Mark L. Appold, Godfrey C. Nicholson, Martinus C. de Boer, William Loader, and Frank J. Matera followed Forestell's work, agreeing with Bultmann's and Käsemann's basic conclusions that in the Fourth Gospel the death of Jesus is not an expiatory event. However, they differed on the degree of salvific significance that could be attributed to the death of Jesus.

Terence Forestell holds that a properly Johannine theology of salvation does not consider the death of Jesus to be a vicarious and expiatory

16. Ibid., 9.
17. Ibid., 10–11.
18. Ibid., 10.
19. Boer, *Johannine Perspectives*, 23.
20. Ibid.

sacrifice for sin.[21] The death of Jesus should not be understood by way of the cross as an atoning event, but in the context of John's theology of revelation. Christ's work is the light of the glory of God through his word which involves his whole ministry including the cross, and effects the salvation of humankind through faith.[22]

Forestell observes that the sacrificial aspect of Jesus' death emerges in John 1:29. Here, Jesus is presented as the Lamb of God who takes away the sins of the world. However, to Forestell, this interpretation is "secondary with reference to the Johannine theology" because this particular text is "not sufficient to overthrow a point of view," which he claims "pervades the whole Gospel, namely an act of love and revelation of the Father."[23] In John, the idea that Jesus died "for" (ὑπέρ) others should be understood primarily as "an act of life-giving love and revelation of the father."[24] The idea that Jesus died "for the people" (ὑπὲρ τοῦ λαοῦ) should "always designate the purpose of Jesus' death but never its cause."[25] In the same way, the preposition "for" (ὑπέρ) designates the salvific meaning of Jesus' death, but it does not in itself indicate the manner of its efficacy.[26] The text does not tell us how Jesus' death benefitted the people of God; the evangelist only tells us that it achieved this effect by drawing together the children of God scattered throughout the world. Forestell concludes that "none of the hyper-texts" (ὑπέρ-texts: John 11:50–52 and others) in the Fourth Gospel "demand a sacrificial evaluation of death."[27]

Unlike Bultmann and Käsemann, Forestell sees the death of Christ on the cross not merely as "the release of his mission" or the "transition back to the Father," but as a revelatory event. It is the "exaltation of the son of man" and "the supreme revelation of the love of God" for humankind because "Jesus effectively lays down his life for his sheep."[28] The cross then becomes a symbol of the gift of eternal life and the means of the bestowal of eternal

---

21. Forestell, *Word of the Cross*, 191.

22. Ibid.

23. Ibid., 148 and 193.

24. Ibid., 194.

25. Ibid., 193.

26. Ibid., 194.

27. Ibid., 82.

28. Ibid., 191–92.

life on humanity.[29] In this way he demonstrates that the cross has salvific significance.

Yet Forestell's argument leaves some issues unattended. Forestell focuses on the importance of the cross but does not explain why this death of Jesus is necessary at all, or how it reveals God's love. He rightly points out that Jesus' death for the people does not clearly indicate how the death saves the nation from perishing (11:50) or how it will gather together the scattered children of God (11:52). Moreover, the idea of "saving the nation" and of the "unity of God's people" is already in itself soteriological, even if the mechanism for achieving them is not explained. Additionally, Forestell's emphasis on the revelation of the Father is extreme when placed in context with the language and assertions made in 11:50–52 and in the other ὑπέρ-text passages.

Ulrich B. Müller continues the objections to Bultmann and Käsemann by attempting to show that, in the Gospel of John, the death of Jesus was an integral part of his mission. Müller emphasized the importance of the topic of the "descent" and "ascent" of the Son of Man. When considering Jesus' death, the Gospel is principally orientated towards Jesus' return to his Father and not towards Jesus' suffering.[30] In Jesus' sovereign passage through death to the Father, the fourth evangelist emphasizes glory as the primary significance of the death of Jesus. It is therefore not Jesus the crucified one but Jesus the glorified one whom the Johannine community proclaimed. According to Müller, the cross is a "necessary step" towards Jesus' glorification and return.[31] While the emphasis on the cross marks a clear difference between Müller's work and the Bultmann-Käsemann view, his failure to address the ὑπέρ-texts undermines his conclusions on the meaning of Jesus' death.

Godfrey C. Nicholson moves forward with Müller's emphasis on the "lifting up" of Jesus (v.32), focusing on John 12:20–36. Nicholson interprets the verb primarily as Jesus' ascent to the Father, and approaches the cross as an embarrassing event to be explained away in the context of descent and ascent. He writes that "for the fourth evangelist, the death of Jesus is only a means to an end, a stage on the way that takes him back to the Father."[32] It is the heavenly ascent of Jesus and not his death that is central; the descent

29. Ibid., 192.

30. Müller, "Bedeutung des Kreutzestodes," 53–54.

31. Ibid., 68–69. See also Nicholson, *Death as Departure*, 163–68.

32. Nicholson, *Death as Departure*, 128.

takes place in the incarnation while the ascent is when Jesus returns to the heavenly father through his death.

The one who descended to this world had to ascend to the world above, a return that was accomplished through his death by crucifixion. The 'lifting up of the Son of Man' texts receive their meaning from the descent-ascent schema.[33] According to Nicholson, Jesus' death should then be understood "not as an ignominious death but a return to glory."[34] The event of salvific revelation is not the cross as an event of suffering, but the cross as an event of glorification.[35]

Unfortunately, these scholars fail to see that the texts which allude to atonement do in fact speak directly to the purpose, and therefore to the significance, of Jesus' death. In John 6:51, Jesus' giving of his flesh effects life "for" (ὑπέρ) the world; in 10:11, Jesus lays down his life for the sheep which results in their "life" (see also 10:15); and in 11:52, Jesus' death for others effects the gathering of the dispersed children of God into one.

Mark Appold, like Käsemann, characterizes the significance of Jesus' death in the Gospel of John as contained within his "glorification and exaltation," and in his "return."[36] Appold understands the death of Jesus primarily as his departure, which in turn "causes judgment (κρίσις): a final κρίσις for the Jews and an on-going κρίσις for the world." With the judgment in mind, Jesus' death has "a causative function" in exposing unbelief and "laying bare the roots of one's origin, whether of God or of the devil" (John 8:44, 47).[37]

The basis for Appold's claim for the soteriological significance of Jesus' death is his identification of a "oneness motif." Appold argues that Jesus' oneness with the Father is the foundation for Jesus' identity in John's Gospel. This essential oneness is manifested even in Jesus' death, as it reveals his glory (his oneness with the Father), and thus "has functional priority" for locating the heavenly oneness of the Father and the Son in the earthly sphere. Consequently, Jesus' death salvifically integrates believers into the oneness of the Father and the Son.[38]

---

33. Ibid., 163.

34. Ibid.

35. Müller, "Bedeutung des Kreutzestodes," 70.

36. Appold, *Oneness Motif,* 274.

37. Ibid., 273.

38. Ibid., 274–75.

However, Appold's work falsely attributes the motif of oneness of Jesus and the Father onto John 11:47–52. Moreover, Appold does not explain how the oneness between the Father and the Son manifested on the cross effects soteriological oneness either in 11:51–52 or elsewhere. Finally, Appold does not address the clear textual theme of "death for others," despite his elimination of the possibility of sacrifice as a theme.

Martinus C. de Boer redirects the significance of the death of Jesus by exploring "composition history of the Gospel."[39] He argues that each edition of John's Gospel is "a recontextualization of the previous edition in order to reinterpret the Gospel for new contexts."[40] The "new contexts" involved three crises experienced by the Johannine community, namely the expulsion from the synagogue, martyrdom because of the community's high Christology, the schism and the subsequent dissolution of the community at the turn of the century. These crises required new, recontextualized editions of the Gospel that did not do away with or reject the emphases and theologies of the earlier editions but rather reinterpreted them so that each edition becomes a "new literary entity."[41]

Boer claims that the language of Jesus' death "for" (ὑπέρ) others (6:51; 10:11, 15; 11:50, 51, 52) emerged after the schism in the surviving Johannine community. This language, however, has nothing to do with a cultic, expiatory, or atoning death but rather points to the "self-giving love for others" which was fully developed in the letters of John (1 John 1:7–8; 2:2; 4:10).[42] The author of the letters of John interpreted Jesus' death in this manner in order "to protect his Johannine audience from the propaganda of Johannine Christians who had left his own community (or communities)."[43] Boer therefore concludes that there is "no single theology of the death of Jesus in the extant Johannine Corpus" and that there is "no evidence that the Johannine writers attempted or achieved a synthesis."[44] While it is reasonable to concur with de Boer that there was no one single theology of the death of Jesus, he contradicts his own assertion by defining that death in a very limited way as self-giving love.

39. Boer, *Johannine Perspectives*, 76.

40. Ibid., 76–79.

41. Ibid., 79.

42. Ibid., 314.

43. Ibid., 313.

44. Ibid., 315.

William G. Loader, like Bultmann, holds that the death of Jesus is simply a return of the Son to the Father. He argues that "the central act" of John's Christology is "the Son's making the Father known, bringing light and life and truth, and completing the works of the Father."[45] For this reason the Son came from the Father. After accomplishing this mission, the Son returns to the Father, completing the cycle. From Loader's perspective therefore, "Jesus' death is his exit."[46]

Loader acknowledges that Jesus' death is more than the exit route of the revealer. It is the "completion of the task of revelation and judgment."[47] The revealer motif, in Loader's view, is predominantly associated not with the Son of Man but with Son—Father Relationship.[48] The "Son of man" designation and its associated imagery of being lifted up and glorified interpret the climax of Jesus' ministry, his death and return to the Father."[49] The Gospel retains "a temporal and spatial distinction between the fullness of divine glory possible on earth (as in 1:14) and the fullness of divine glory possible in heaven (through glorification)." The former is "revelatory glory" while the latter concerns "his return to the Father."[50] As a return to the Father, Jesus' death is the completion of the work of revelation although not a completion of the revelation of the glory of the oneness shared by Father and Son.[51] Loader argues that the passive voice in the glorification sayings indicates that something is being done to the Son by God. Glorification means God's restoration of Jesus to glory in heaven, the glory which belongs to God himself and which he shared with the Son before the world began.[52] For Loader then, the imagery of glorification applies not only to the crucifixion or death alone, but "to the total event of resurrection and return to glory of the Father."[53] Frank J. Matera, like Bultmann and Käsemann, finds no evidence for an expiatory interpretation of Jesus' death

---

45. Loader, *Christology of the Fourth* Gospel, 93.

46. Ibid.

47. Ibid., 102–3.

48. Ibid., 123.

49. Ibid.

50. Ibid., 113.

51. Ibid., 116 and 111.

52. Ibid., 110.

53. Ibid. Loader's view corresponds to Raymond Brown's opinion that the crucifixion-death is the first rung on the ladder of Jesus' return to the Father, a return that constitutes his glorification. See Brown, *Gospel According to John*, 610.

in the Gospel of John. Unlike Bultmann and Käsemann, he argues that the death of Jesus in the Fourth Gospel does have "salvific effects."[54] To him the Gospel of John employs three images in the understanding of Jesus' death: a death on behalf of others (as in the ὑπέρ-texts), a death which cleanses (as seen in the foot washing), and a death by which Jesus is glorified and returns to the Father. Matera emphasizes that these three aspects of Jesus' death demonstrate that the cross plays an essential role in his [the evangelist's] soteriology and that there is a unity to these three approaches.[55]

Matera also proposes that "there is a greater organic unity between the body of the Fourth Gospel and its passion narrative."[56] The ὑπέρ-texts in particular are basic in Matera's claim of a "saving significance" in John's story of the death of Jesus. Jesus dies "for the sake of (ὑπέρ) his sheep" (John 10:11, 15b, 16a) and "for" (ὑπέρ) the other sheep" (10:16) as well, pointing to the fact that he wants to unify the flock. He freely lays down his life for (ὑπέρ) the sheep so that there will be one flock, one shepherd."[57] In 10:16, Jesus' death for others is not an expiatory sacrifice for sins; rather, "the expression 'to lay down one's life for others" suggests that the evangelist views Jesus as sacrificing his life for the sake of others in order to bring them into unity." [58] Thus, without Jesus' sacrifice, the sheep will remain scattered. In the same way, in John 11:51–52, Jesus dies on behalf of the nation and the scattered children of God "to unite them into one flock." Matera therefore agrees with Appold in so far as soteriology is explained in terms of the oneness motif. The salvific effect of Jesus' death comes from its ability to gather together others into unity with him and the Father. The Fourth Gospel may not explain Jesus' death as an expiatory sacrifice for sin, but views Jesus' death as a genuine self-sacrifice on behalf of the others. This sacrifice is unique because only this death draws people to God and to Jesus.

Appold's and Matera's studies are limited as neither of them explain what it is about Jesus' death "for" (ὑπέρ) others that effects the salvific gathering and drawing into a unity (10:16; 11:52; 12:32). Quite apart from the precise meaning of Jesus' death in these passages, these questions remain unaddressed: why does Jesus' death bring about these effects? What does this tell us about John's concerns in these passages?

54. Matera, "On Behalf of Others," 161–78.

55. Ibid., 162.

56. Ibid.

57. Ibid., 166.

58. Ibid.

Death of Jesus as Atonement and Glorification Event

Three major views of Bultmann and his followers have been discussed above: first, the death of Jesus as atonement for sin is foreign to the Fourth Gospel; second, the death of Jesus is merely his return to the Father and his glorification; and third, that salvation is only brought about by way of revelation. In 1961, Thomas Müller strongly opposed the second and third views.

Müller holds that a comprehensive Johannine interpretation of the death of Jesus must embrace a synthesis of revelation theology and traditional Christian theology, which he termed *Gemeindetheologie*.[59] As such, the saving event is both revelation and an objective act of vicarious expiation.[60] Müller bases his argument on John the Baptist's witness: "behold the lamb of God who takes away the sins of the world" (John 1:29) and on the ὑπέρ-texts. Jesus' death "for others" therefore has concrete soteriological effects. The expiatory and vicarious death realizes both the gathering of the sheep and their life (10:16), and the objective salvific gathering together of the children of God.[61] Yet, like his predecessors, Müller does not discuss why Jesus' death as such has this effect.

Müller's position has received much support from many scholars. Loader, for example, recommends not to emphasize the Fourth Gospel's *theologia gloriae* (theology of glory) at the expense of *theologia crucis* (theology of the cross): "Jesus' death as exaltation means no lessening of the place of vicarious atonement."[62] In the same way, J. Frey and Th. Knöppler contend that the *theologia crucifixi* dominates, and that the center of Johannine soteriology is Jesus' death understood as an event of vicarious atonement.[63] Müller and his followers hold that the death of Jesus should be understood as both vicarious (for others) and atoning (in light of 1:29, Jesus' death deals with sin).[64] Jesus' death for others effects objective salva-

---

59. Müller, *Heilsgeschehen im Johannesevangelium*, 76.

60. Ibid., 56–57, 110–14.

61. Ibid., 60.

62. Loader, *Christology*, 22. See also Grigsby, "Cross as an Expiatory Sacrifice," 52; Turner, "Atonement and Death," 122; Knöppler, *Theologia crucis*; Zumstein, "L'interprétation johannique," 2130–38; Nielsen, "John's understanding," 237; Green and Baker, *Recovering the Scandal*; Frey, "Theologia crucifixi," 169–238.

63. Frey, "Theologia crucifixi," 169–238; and Knöppler, *Theologia crucis*.

64. Metzner emphasizes this point in his, *Verständnis der Sünde in Johannesevangelium*. See also Carey who argues that despite the scarcity of the sacrificial terminology,

tion, be it as the "light of the world" (6:51) or in the power to unify the people of God (11:52; 10:16).

Jean Zumstein challenges Käsemann's view that the passion of Jesus in John is simply a "literary appendix" without any theological significance.[65] Using "narrative analysis" (l'analyse narratologique), Zumstein demonstrates that John's narrative of the Passion of Jesus is central to the entire narrative of Jesus' earthly ministry, which is oriented towards the hours of the passion.[66] He characterizes the death of Jesus as his departure, glorification and sovereignty, but further demonstrates, using the narrative technique of *inclusios*, that the death of Jesus has salvific significance.[67] He highlights two major *inclusios*. The first *inclusio* frames the narrative within the theme of the divinity of Christ (John 11: "the word of God") and the confession of Thomas (John 20:28: "my Lord and my God"). This affirms that the Gospel of John is essentially about the person of Jesus Christ. The second *inclusio* is John the Baptist's proclamation of Jesus as "the Lamb of God who takes away the sins of the world" (John 1:29) and the paschal symbol and imagery in the Passion narrative (John 19). Although there is no direct mention of the "Lamb of God" in the Passion narrative, Zumstein argues that an allusion is clear in the immolation of the Passover Lamb (18:28 and 19:14).[68] Consequently, he argues that the death of Jesus should be understood in the context of the exodus, a key event in the history of Israel. It is God's act of "liberation" for his people.[69]

Zumstein's work, however, lacks the consideration of the plot to kill Jesus (11:47–52), in which the purpose of the death is defined as being "for the nation" and "in order to gather into one" the children of God scattered abroad. One cannot discuss the significance of the death of Jesus and neglect this aspect.

Finally, C. Dietzfelbinger also understands the death of Jesus as *Stellvertreter* (vicarious representation) and *Sühne* (atonement).[70] Using the basic ὑπέρ-texts and the "Lamb of God" texts, he interprets the death of

---

the image of Jesus as Lamb of God is of primary importance to John. Carey, "Lamb of God and the Atonement Theories, 97–122.

65. Zumstein, "L'interprétation johannique," 2119.

66. Ibid., 2128.

67. Ibid., 2130.

68. Ibid., 2120.

69. Ibid., 2131.

70. Dietzfelbinger, "Sühnetod im Johannesevangelium," 72.

Jesus as the "lifting up" to the Father and the "glorification of the Son of Man." For him, Jesus' death is "not a tragic event," but rather a step toward the glory of the Father (17:1–5).[71] He discourages prioritizing one aspect of the death of Jesus, opting instead for "a multifaceted understanding" that covers aspects such as the return to the Father, glorification, and the sending of the Holy Spirit. Vicarious atonement functions as the "first stage" in the consideration of the significance of the death of Jesus.[72]

Death of Jesus as a Sacrifice

B. H. Grigsby and M. Turner also emphasize the cross as revelation but add that the cross as expiatory sacrifice is a complementary conception of the fourth Gospel.[73] Grigsby substantiates his claim by pointing to the Christ as a "Paschal victim (John 1:29; 19)," as an "Isaac figure (*Akedah*; 1:29; 3:16; 19:14, 29, 36)," and as a cleansing fountain (13:10; 19:34). For Grigsby, "the traditional concept of an expiatory rationale between sin's removal and Christ's death has exerted its influence on the Fourth evangelist."[74]

Turner views the cross as the supreme revelation of God's love derived from John's belief that God dealt with humankind's sin in the Son's death.[75] His argument is based on the "Lamb of God" text (1:29–34), wherein Jesus as Lamb of God is understood both as "apocalyptic lamb" and the "paschal lamb."[76] Jesus, as the shepherd who "lays down his life for the sheep" (10:11, 15) and dies for the nation (11:50–52), should be read in the light of Jesus as the Lamb of God, a title that is used to define the ministry of Jesus only at its outset.[77]

Craig Koester has also encouraged viewing the death of Jesus as central to the Fourth Gospel, yet does not see atonement in John. He argues that "the imagery is sacrificial, but it is used in a distinctive way to describe

---

71. Ibid., 76.

72. Ibid.

73. Grigsby, "Cross as an Expiatory Sacrifice," 52; Turner, "Atonement and Death," 122. The same views are held by Loader, Knöppler, Nielsen and Frey. See Loader, *Christology*; Knöppler, *Theologia crucis*; Nielsen, "John's understanding"; and Frey, "Theologia crucifixi."

74. Grigsby, "Cross as an Expiatory Sacrifice," 62.

75. Turner, "Atonement and Death," 121.

76. Ibid., 121–22.

77. Ibid., 122.

the effects of the death of Jesus as the supreme manifestation of the love of God, as something that transforms people from antipathy into faith, thereby effecting reconciliation."[78] Koester considers the crucifixion to be "an expression of love in human terms, a sacrifice for sin, as conflict with evil, and as revelation of divine glory."[79] He argues that throughout the history of theology, these perspectives have always followed separate trajectories, but they nevertheless appear together in John's Gospel, "opening up multiple dimensions of the human condition."[80] The greatness of love in human terms comes from laying down one's life for one's enemies (John 15:13). He appeals to ancient Greek philosophers Plato, Aristotle, Seneca and Diogenes, and to Paul who agree that true love and friendship might mean that one person would willingly die for another (Plato, *Symposium* 179b; Aristotle, *Nicomachean Ethics* 9.8 1169a; Seneca, *Moral Epistles* 9.10; Diogenes Laertius, *Lives* 10. 120; and Rom 5:7). Koester contends that the image of Jesus' "death as a sacrifice for sin" is founded on "the lamb of God" text (John 1:29). Rather than relating the crucifixion to the circle of Jesus' friends, the passage relates it to "the world and its sin," in the same way that the "Passover Lamb" is associated with deliverance from death.[81] The "sin of the world" that alienates people from God is "unbelief," and the Lamb of God takes away the sins by removing unbelief. In Johannine theology, the evocation of faith removes sin; while sin alienates one from God, faith restores the relationship with God. If sin is the hatred that separates people from God, then "faith awakens the love that binds people to God and the death of Christ calls forth human love for God by conveying God's love to humankind."[82]

For Koester, however, the sacrifice in John is "atonement" only in the sense that it reconciles parties that have been separated. Such an interpretation contrasts with scholars who assume that if the Gospel uses sacrificial language, it must construe Jesus' death as a vicarious or substitutionary sacrifice. The notion of vicarious or substitutionary sacrifice revolves around the notion of "justice and mercy."[83] When a person transgresses a law, justice requires the person to be punished. However, as an act of

---

78. Koester, *Symbolism*, 200.

79. Koester, "Death of Jesus," 143.

80. Ibid.

81. Ibid., 145.

82. Ibid., 146.

83. Ibid., 147.

mercy, a transgressor might be allowed to offer something in exchange for his or her life: a vicarious sacrifice. Theologically, human beings regarded as sinners are justly condemned by God, but because God is merciful, God has allowed Jesus to pay the sinners' debt through his own death. Jesus' self-sacrifice honors the need for divine justice while making room for divine mercy. However, in Johannine theology, the framework is different. John does not relate Jesus' death to the need for justice but to the need for human faith. According to Koester, only in this way can one consider Jesus' death as "atonement."[84]

Death of Jesus as Atoning Event

In opposition to Bultmann and Käsemann, scholars such as R. Metzner, T. Knöppler, and J. Frey argue that not only does John's Gospel understand the death of Jesus as a vicarious atonement, but also that the motif of atonement is central to the theology of the Fourth Gospel.

Metzner's work is a reaction to Haenchen's claim that sin is not a fundamental concept in the Fourth Gospel.[85] Metzner argues that the concept of sin is not casual but basic and central to John's concerns: John presents God in confrontation with the world, a confrontation which takes the form of a lawsuit between the Son and the world, and the Son and the Jews.[86] This confrontation begins at the Prologue and runs through the entire Gospel. The idea of taking away "sin" (ἁμαρτία) appears at the beginning of the Gospel (1:29) and at the end (20:23), indicating its centrality for the evangelist. Metzner argues that the first appearance of "sin" provides the "hermeneutical key" to understanding John's approach to sin and therefore the Gospel's "Lamb of God who takes away the sin of the world" (1:29) functions as the *programmatische Leitthese* (leading thesis) of the Christology of the Fourth Gospel.[87] The Fourth evangelist presents Jesus as the Passover lamb who takes away the sin of the world by means of his vicarious atoning death (*stellvertretende Sühnetod*).[88] In this perspective, the "sin of the world" is the

---

84. Ibid.

85. Haenchen, *Johannesevangelium*, 167.

86. Metzner, *Verständnis der Sünde*, 23, 30–113.

87. Ibid., 9 and 137. See also Knöppler, *Theologia crucis*, 67 and Frey, "Theologia crucifixi' in des Johannesevangeliums," 201–3.

88. Metzner, *Verständnis der Sünde*, 22–23, 132–37. Against scholars who claim that the Passover lamb in the Old Testament was not considered as an atonement sacrifice,

"totality of sin which power is broken once and for all on the cross."[89] God therefore confronts the world through the Lamb, and defeats sin through the Lamb's atoning death.

According to Metzner, all other texts about the death of Jesus in John should be read with the *programmatische Leitthese* in view, including the ὑπέρ-texts (6:51; 10:11, 15; 11:51–52; 15:13; 17:19; 18:14). He argues that Jesus' death "for" others connotes the idea of "benefit," insofar as the death benefits the nation as the Lamb of God who takes away the sin of the world. It is a death that breaks the power of sin in humanity.[90]

Metzner furthers argues that the idea of atonement for sins on the cross contains within it a criticism of the temple cult, an idea earlier noted by Raymond Brown.[91] If the Fourth Gospel portrays Jesus as the eschatological sanctuary (1:14), Jesus' death and resurrection reveal him as the new temple (2:19–52), and the new and true place of worship (4:20–24). The temple, which was regarded as the place of the presence of God and of atonement for sins, is now replaced by Jesus, in whom God dwells and who brings about the atonement for sins, independent of the cultic ritual of institutional Judaism.[92]

Like Metzner, Thomas Knöppler argues that vicarious atonement is central to Johannine Christology, and that John the Baptist's confession of Jesus as the "Lamb of God who takes away the sin of the world" (1:29) undergirds atonement interpretation.[93] Later statements about the "Passover Lamb whose death atones for sin" (19:14, 29, 33 and 36), blood and water flowing from Jesus' side (19:34) and the ὑπέρ-texts, indicate that Jesus' death purifies and atones for sins.[94] While atonement is only possible with some kind of vicarious event, not all vicarious passages in John convey the idea of atonement. For Metzner, atonement is defined by two elements:

Metzner argues that the atonement character of the Lamb of God is consistent with the OT, post-biblical Judaism and the New Testament, citing Deut 16; 2 Chr 30; Jub 49; Philo, *Spec. Laws* 2:145, and Josephus, *Antiquities* 2:312. In the NT there is much agreement about the Passover Lamb as "atoning sacrifice." See Metzner, *Verständnis der Sünde*, 129–30; Lohse, *Märtyrer und Gottesknecht*, 142.

89. Metzner, *Verständnis der Sünde*, 129.

90. Ibid., 131.

91. Ibid, 135. See also Brown, *Gospel According to John*, 34.

92. Metzner, *Verständnis der Sünde*, 135.

93. Knöppler, *Theologia crucis*, 88 and 67; Knöppler, *Sühne im Neuen Testament*, 49 and 233.

94. Ibid., 97; see also Knöppler, *Sühne im Neuen Testament*, 294.

God's act of salvation which rescues humanity lost in death because of sin, and the granting of life.[95] A genuine atonement passage (*Sühneaussage*) should have both elements.[96]

Against the above background, Knöppler acknowledges the "bread of life discourse" (John 6:51) as the only unambiguous instance of Johannine atonement passages. The rest of the ὑπέρ-texts do not have salvific significance. In John 6:51, Jesus gives his flesh as a vicarious offering that mediates eternal life to the world (vv. 27, 33, 51b, 54, 57) and saves it from sin and death (v. 50).[97] In this passage, we find the two elements that define atonement. According to Knöppler, the other ὑπέρ-texts reference Jesus' vicarious death for others, yet their redemptive deliverance is not from sin, but rather from *Unheil*, a kind of trouble or disaster. Hence, in the shepherd discourse, Jesus gives his life to protect the sheep from the wolf, and in John 11:50–52, the decision to kill Jesus is taken to prevent Rome from destroying the people and the nation. Here, Knöppler differs from Metzner, narrowly limiting the atonement boundary to include only one ὑπέρ-text.

Frey addresses the question of whether the salvific significance of the death of Jesus is linked to a theology of the cross or a theology of glorification.[98] He holds that the death of Jesus has soteriological significance based on the atoning event which is central to John's Gospel.[99] In his analysis, the proleptic statements leading up to the cross indicate the centrality of the cross in John's narrative of Jesus' death.[100] The primary proleptic statement is the "Lamb of God" confession in John 1:29, while others texts include the "lifting up" (John 3:14–15; 8:28; 12:32–34) and the glorification (7:39; 11:4; 12:16, 23; 13:31; 17:1, 5) of the Son of man, the "hour" of the Son of Man (2:4; 7:30; 8:20; 12:23, 27, 38; 13:31; 17:11), the cleansing of the temple (2:14–22), and the death threats and attempts to stone Jesus (5:8; 7:1, 19, 25; 8:37, 40; 11:53; 12:10; 10:31–33; 11:8). All of these statements point to the execution of Jesus on the cross.[101] These passages, the ὑπέρ-texts, and the entire Fourth Gospel should be read in the light of the "Lamb of God

---

95. Ibid., 91; See also Knöppler, *Sühne im Neuen Testament*, 250.

96. Knöppler, *Sühne im Neuen Testament*, 252.

97. Ibid., 245–46.

98. Frey, "Theologia crucifixi," 169–76.

99. Ibid., 191.

100. Ibid., 197. Here he concurs with Knöppler; see "Theologia crucis," 67; and *Sühne im Neuen Testament*, 49.

101. Ibid., 198–99.

who takes away the sin of the world" (1:29), recalling Metzner's *programmatische Leitthese*.[102]

Interpretations contextualized by John 1:29 must incorporate the ὑπέρ-texts into an "overall picture" (*Gesamtbild*) of John's understanding of the death of Jesus as vicarious and atoning.[103] This challenges the view of Knöppler that limits vicarious and atoning death only to John 6:51. In Knöppler's opinion, the decision to kill Jesus was made in order to avert some possible danger unrelated to sin. Interpreted synchronically in the context of the Johannine narrative and in the light of John 1:29, the ὑπέρ-texts would have soteriological significance. Frey observes, for example, that the decision to kill Jesus is only "superficially" justified as averting the danger of destruction by the Romans. Interpreting this passage must not neglect the preceding Lazarus narrative (John 11:1–44), which is framed by the notice that Jesus "went across the Jordan to the place where John at first baptized . . . and many came to him and they said, 'John performed no sign, but everything that John said about this man was true'" (John 10:40–42). This allusion to the Baptist's confession of the "Lamb of God" provides a common denominator for interpreting not only the Lazarus narrative but also the decision to kill Jesus, framing the Lazarus narrative from the beginning. The confession that Jesus is the one who "takes away sins" is confirmed (10:41) in Jesus' death for the nation and the people (11:50–52). Jesus' death is therefore an atoning sacrifice so that the people may not perish. It rescues the people from death and produces a new community by gathering together the children of God spread abroad.[104]

Frey reads the shepherd discourse (John 10:11–15) in a similar manner, as saving the sheep from the destruction of the wolves (the leaders of Israel), yet bringing about the salvific significance of the restoration of the true people of God in the light of Ezekiel 34–37 and Jeremiah 23.[105] He urges that the Gospel be read in line with the community tradition evident in the first letter of John, where Jesus' death is understood as an atoning event (1 John 2:2; 4:10) and as a vicarious "laying down" of his life for (ὑπέρ) others (1 John 3:16).[106] Frey exposes the weakness of Knöppler's argument and demonstrates that if the ὑπέρ-texts are read against the background of

102. Ibid., 198.

103. Ibid., 215.

104. Ibid., 217–18.

105. Ibid., 214.

106. Ibid.

the entire Gospel, they reveal the salvific significance of the death of Jesus for others in the Gospel of John.

Death of Jesus as a "Sign"

C. H. Dodd referred to the story of the arrest, trial and crucifixion of Jesus as "a σημεῖον (sign) on a grand scale," the significance of which gave coherence and full expression to the preceding "signs" of Jesus' ministry. The details of the passion of Jesus are therefore expounded throughout the Gospel:

> [T]he sign of the wine of Cana, which we now perceive to be the blood of the true vine; the sign of the temple (which is the Body of Christ) destroyed to be raised again; the signs of the life-giving word (at Cana and Bethesda), since the Word Himself is life and dies that men may be saved from death; the sign of the bread, which is the flesh of Christ given for the life of the world; the sign of Siloam—the light of truth which both saves and judges; the sign of Lazarus—life victorious over death through the raising down of life; the sign of the anointing for burial; and the sign of the "King of Israel" acclaimed on His entry to Jerusalem to die. Along with these, other symbols, which although they have not been embodied in dramatic incidents have been woven into the discourses, have the significance clarified and enhanced in the supreme σημεῖον: Moses' serpent . . . , living water, the good shepherd, the grain of wheat, the woman in travail. As everywhere, so most emphatically in the story of Christ's arrest, trial and crucifixion, what happens and is observed in the temporal and sensible sphere signifies eternal reality: the life eternal given to men through the eternal word. In this sense the Passion of the Lord is the final and all-inclusive σημεῖον.[107]

In Dodd's view, the revelatory significance of the death of Jesus is found in the commonly occurring language of glorification. Jesus is primarily glorified, honored by his true identity being shown forth in his death.[108] Jesus' death not only atones for the sins of humanity but this very work of atonement reveals his true identity. The death of Jesus is hence the "final and all-inclusive σημεῖον" in the Fourth Gospel because it reveals

---

107. Dodd, *Interpretation of the Fourth Gospel*, 438–39.

108. Ibid., 441.

Jesus' true identity in the ultimate manner.[109] As D. Senior also argues, "the entire Gospel of John is oriented toward the death of Jesus and the meaning of the death of Jesus . . . is the foundation of its theological perspective which gives coherence to all the other parts of the Gospel."[110]

Death of Jesus as a Revelatory Act

Discussing death as a revelatory act returns us to Forestell, who observed that the vocabulary of redemption and expiation is absent from John's Gospel. The "remission of sin" is mentioned only once (John 20:23) as is the action of Christ against sin (1:29).[111] In his view, incarnation is basic to the life of Jesus, yet incarnation is not a saving event to which the cross is entirely subordinate. The incarnation of the Logos is rather the beginning of the revelatory process that culminates in the supreme revelation of Jesus' death as his glorification.[112] A similar argument is made by Lindars for whom "the glorification theme makes of the passion a revelatory act."[113] The death of Jesus is a "decisive factor in the whole argument, just as it is the climax of the narrative structure of the Gospel as a whole. It is also the proof that he is the pre-existent Son of God."[114] Likewise, in D. M. Smith's understanding, "the description of Jesus' exaltation and glory is a way of underscoring its revelatory character."[115]

Ashton remarks that the painful and shameful elements in John's account of the death of Jesus are so suppressed that it is a "misnomer" to refer to the story as "passion" – meaning "suffering," since "Jesus controls and orchestrates the whole phenomenon."[116] "From this perspective what is disturbing is not the crucifixion with its horror and shame but John's treatment of the crucifixion, a treatment that replaces suffering with glory and humiliation with triumph."[117] Death becomes characterized as a mere

---

109. Ibid., 439.

110. Senior, "Death of Jesus," 273.

111. Forestell, *Word of the Cross*, 60–61.

112. Ibid., 18–19.

113. Lindars, *John*, 81. See also Lindars, "Passion," 79; Lindars, *Jesus Son of Man*, 155.

114. Ibid.

115. Smith, *Theology of the Fourth Gospel*, 121.

116. Ashton, *Understanding the Fourth Gospel*, 2: 464.

117. Koester, "Death of Jesus and Human condition," 142.

termination of Jesus' earthly career, and as the end of his earthly sojourn as the Word and the heavenly Son of God. Ashton writes thus:

> Jesus enters the world with a mission from the Father and leaves it when his mission is completed. By an extraordinary involution his mission is simply to reveal to mankind his origin and his destiny, his entry and his departure. From this perspective the true significance of his death has nothing to do with the manner of it. No doubt one could say of him that 'nothing in his life became him like the leaving of it', but this is only because it satisfactorily rounds off his mission, allowing him to say, for the first and only time: "it is accomplished."[118]

Ashton finds the suggestion that the death of Jesus is merely a departure inadequate. While he accepts that departure is an aspect of Jesus' death, he argues that "the theology of glory" in John "is first and foremost a theology of revelation."[119] He agrees with Brown's remark that glory in the Fourth Gospel involves a visible manifestation of God's majesty in acts of power but observes that the English word that springs most insistently to mind in connection with John's theology of glory is revelation.[120] The language of glory-glorification-exaltation should not be interpreted as a synonym of departure. Critics of the "departure theory" rightly suggest that the language of exaltation-glory-glorification proposes that the death of Jesus is a means for revealing God the Father, as evidenced by the term δόξα (when understood in the sense of the visible display of the divine presence or power).[121]

However, I argue that viewing the death of Jesus as revelation conflates the language of glory with the theme of revelation. Glory is certainly not synonymous with revelation. Without refuting the possibility that the language of exaltation-glory-glorification should be understood in the light of the theme of revelation, interpreters must remain open to other possibilities.

---

118. Ashton, *Understanding the Fourth Gospel*, 467–68.

119. Ibid., 472.

120. Ibid.

121. Ibid. See also Lindars, "Passion," 79.

Death of Jesus as a Cosmic Battle

J. Kovacs, relying primarily on John 12:20–36 and the two "ruler of this world" texts (14:30–31 and 16:8–11), along with the "cosmic conflict and dualism in the Fourth Gospel," interprets the death of Jesus as a "cosmic battle" between Jesus and Satan.[122] In her view, the introduction of the duality between "light and darkness" in John's prologue (1:5) establishes "a prominent theme in the Fourth Gospel," i.e., "the conflict between the forces of light and darkness, between God and Satan."[123] Jesus, "the true light in the world," came to the world and the world responded both positively and negatively to him, creating "two camps" of human beings, namely "the children of God" ("children of light" in 12:36) and the children of darkness (3:14–16, 19–21).[124] These divisions and conflicts are illustrated in the encounters between Jesus and the "Jews," which follow in John 5–8.

Jesus' confrontations and "legal debates" with the Jewish leaders intensify, as demonstrated by the repeated desires to kill him (7:1, 19, 20, 25; 8:37, 40, 59) and by the attempts to arrest him (7:30, 32, 44, 45). The conflicts reach their climax on Golgotha.[125]

Kovacs' interpretation of the conversation in John 8 is intriguing. The harsh words, "your father the devil" (8:44), illustrate the concern of the Gospel, i.e., "the battle between God and Satan—a battle acted out in the sphere of human history."[126] The announcement of the casting out of the ruler of this world (12:31) is crucially important in the fourth Gospel. The introduction in John 12 of the revelation that the turning point in the cosmic conflict has arrived, "the hour has come" (12:23) and "now is the judgment of this world" (12:31) is new. The crucifixion of Jesus thus reveals that "the critical moment towards which the author has been pointing ever since 3:14 (or ever since 1:5), is about to occur. On the cosmic level, this moment brings the decisive victory over the evil ruler of this world. On a human level it involves the division of the children of light from those who follow darkness (12:35–36, 46)."[127]

---

122. Kovacs, "Now Shall the Ruler," 227–47.

123. Ibid., 231.

124. Ibid.

125. Ibid., 232. See also Harvey, *Jesus on Trial*; Neyrey, *An Ideology of Revolt*, 11–15; Martyn, *History and Theology*, 64–89.

126. Ibid., 233.

127. Ibid.

In the second "ruler of this world" text (14:30–31), Jesus says that he will not talk much to his disciples because the ruler of the world is coming. The ruler has no power over him; he does what the Father has commanded him. Jesus concludes by asking the disciples to rise so that they can be on their way. Here, Kovacs notices a connection between the ruler (ἄρχων) and the death of Jesus (14:2–3). Jesus' decision to take up the cross affects the leader of this world, for through it the leader will be "cast out" and (t)his world is judged.

In the discourses that follow (13:31—17:26), the central theme of conflict continues. Hence, in 17:15, Jesus prays, "I do not ask that you take them out of the world, but that you keep them from the evil one," demonstrating that the death of Jesus will not bring to an end the struggle with the evil one. Although the death and glorification are "turning points in the conflict" (12:31), "Satan, refusing to concede defeat, will focus his attack on the human allies of Jesus" left behind (15:18–29; 16:33b).[128]

However, the Holy Spirit as the Paraclete will fight with his allies, as seen in the third "ruler of this world" text (16:8–11). In this text, the "ruler" ἄρχων and the "world" κόσμος are closely associated and conflict continues to be emphasized in the death of Jesus. The Paraclete will combat the forces of evil (sin) and prepare the disciples of Jesus for Jesus' death and the persecution they will experience. The Paraclete will "prove the world wrong" and reveal how sin, righteousness, judgment are brought to light in Jesus' death and exaltation: "here the struggle between Jesus and the ruler of the world is described in forensic imagery."[129]

Despite Kovacs's assertion that the ruler of this world is Satan, the references cited above point strongly to the idea that "the ruler of this world" sayings refer specifically to the forthcoming trials and crucifixion of Jesus. I contend that when Jesus says that "the ruler of this world will be cast out" when he is "lifted up" (12:31–32), he is referring to what the Roman soldiers will do to his body. Similarly, when Jesus says that "the ruler of this world is coming" to silence him (14:30), it is most probable that he is referring to the fact that the Romans are about to arrest him (18:3, 12) and that Pontius Pilate will soon put an end to his preaching. When Jesus says in 16:8–11 that "the ruler of this world" has been "judged about judgment," he is referring to Rome's responsibility for his own violent death (19:11).

128. Ibid., 234.

129. Ibid., 231, quoting Schnackenburg, *Gospel According to St. John*, 3: 128. See also Brown, *Gospel According to John*, 2:705.

The events of Golgotha therefore point to the reigning Roman emperor as the ruler of this world. Perhaps Thatcher is right to propose that the ruler of this world is Caesar.[130] Spiritualizing Jesus' conflict raises the question of whether Jesus could have been the only one unaffected by his socio-political context.

Death of Jesus as a "Noble Death"

Using ancient literary tradition of the "noble death" to interpret the "noble"[131] shepherd discourse in John 10:11–18 and the decision to kill Jesus in John 11:46–53, Neyrey demonstrated that the death of Jesus falls within the category of a noble death. This literary tradition extends from Thucydides' records of Pericles' funeral rhetoric, through Greek funeral orators, Aristotle, and to the school exercises called the *progymnasmata* (taught in the first century, a criteria for praise in epideictic rhetoric), which all rely on the concept of a noble death.[132] In a similar way, the Greek Maccabean literature of Israel also exemplifies ancient articulations of the concept of "noble death." A noble death is characterized as beneficial to others (particularly fellow citizens), at the service of justice, voluntary, and displaying courage. An "unvanquished death" preserves the nobility of the warriors because according to the logic of honor they are judged undefeated, and is marked by "posthumous honors" in speeches, annual remembrance at tombs and with games.[133]

Neyrey demonstrates how the narratives of the shepherd and the plot to kill Jesus fit into the cultural milieu of the time. Like the noble deaths of old, Jesus lays down his life for the sheep (10:11–12), he fights on behalf of the sheep with courage, he knows them by their names—which speaks to his "just duty" towards the sheep that are his own (10:14), his justice and obedience point to God his Father (10:15), and he is not a victim but

130. Thatcher, *Greater Than Caesar*, 121.

131. Neyrey prefers the adjective "noble" qualifying "shepherd" instead of the commonly used "good" for the Greek word καλός in John 10:11. To him, the Greek καλός ("noble") belongs in the cultural world of honor and shame but ἀγαθός ("good") belongs in the realm of virtue, where "good" is contrasted with "evil." Because the "nobleness" of the shepherd is linked with his death (10:11), he turns to Greek rhetoric on "noble death" to discover what constituted a noble death. See Neyrey, "Noble Shepherd," 267–80; Neyrey, *Gospel of John*, 180.

132. Neyrey, "Noble Shepherd," 268.

133. Neyrey, *Gospel of John*, 181.

dies voluntarily (10:17–18). Whereas Greek political life conveyed a kind of immortality through annual remembrance and enduring monuments, Jesus enjoys a genuine imperishability in the future.[134] Neyrey shows that the noble shepherd discourse manifests several of the classical criteria for a noble death. While Neyrey's study is convincing, he limits the importance of the death to a selfish fulfillment of Jesus' ego, a realization of his desire for heroism. The relationship between Jesus' death and its significance for his followers remains unexplained.

Death of Jesus as Eschatological Gathering

The preoccupation with the significance of Jesus' death shifted focus as scholars began to consider the theme of "gathering together into one the scattered children of God" (John 11:52). A common observation is that this statement echoes the Old Testament (Jewish) hopes for the return of the exiles. Thus, O. Hofius writes that John has reinterpreted this hope to mean that the eschatological blessing of salvation, in Christ, now extends to both Jews and Gentiles, and that the designation "children of God" for John would have indicated this kind of expansion.[135]

Hofius argues that Isa 56:8 forms the closest parallel to John 10:16 and 11:52. The contrasts between "the sheep of this fold" and "the other sheep not of this fold" in 10:15–16 and the "nation" and the "children of God" in 11:51–52 are meant to indicate an expansion of the eschatological hope for the gathering of the dispersed flock in Judaism to include Gentiles.[136] The new eschatological people of God are now Jews and Gentiles, unified as one people. Hofius' "eschatological expansion" aligns with many scholarly positions that argue that the bringing in of the other sheep and the gathering of the scattered children of God makes use of the traditional Jewish hope for the restoration of Israel to communicate the idea that the true people of God, or the children of God, are now to be identified with both the Jews and the Gentiles who believe in Jesus, the Messiah of Israel.[137]

---

134. Ibid., 182–84.

135. O. Hofius, "Sammlung der Heiden, " 289–91.

136. Ibid.

137. Frey, "Theologia crucifixi," 213; See also Metzner, *Verständnis der Sünde*, 343–44; Borgen, "Gospel of John and Hellenism," 112; Koester, *Symbolism*, 225–26; Carson, *Gospel According to John*, 388.

S. Pancaro proposed that the gathering concerns the creation of a new people of God, the new Israel, which is no longer limited to the Jews but includes Gentiles. He relies on Caiaphas' comments that Jesus should die for the λαός (people) and that the ἔθνος (nation) would not perish (v. 50). Caiaphas' uses λαός and ἔθνος to refer to the Jewish people and nation respectively. When John reinstates Caiaphas' statement in 11:51–52, he does not repeat Caiaphas' λαός but replaces it with τὰ τέκνα τοῦ θεοῦ (the children of God). John's replacement of λαός with τὰ τέκνα τοῦ θεοῦ therefore betrays his theological views that the true people of God are now redefined as believers, made up of both Jew and Gentile.[138] Pancaro examines the use of λαός and ἔθνος in the LXX and the NT to demonstrate that λαός in the LXX is primarily used to refer to Israel, the covenant people, while ἔθνος (especially ἔθνη) is reserved primarily for the Gentiles.[139] In the NT, λαός refers to the new Christian community as the λαός of God, the Church taken out of this world.[140] Thus, according to John's interpretation, Caiaphas was correct to prophesy that Jesus was about to die for the λαός, a new people of God which has now been expanded, in Christ, to include all believers (1:12). "Children of God," a term that traditionally referred to the Jews of the diaspora, now acquires a wider meaning as a "new people of God," both Jews and Gentiles.[141] While Hofius argues that the designation "children of God" describes the Gentiles who are united to Israel, Pancaro understands the eschatological children of God as a "new Israel" made of both Jews and Gentiles. Thus, Pancaro denies that "children of God" is another way of saying "Gentiles."[142]

J. Dennis observed that the focus on ὑπέρ-texts "overlooks other important aspects," including "John's appropriation of restoration theology."[143] He emphasizes the importance of the statement that Jesus' death will bring about the gathering of the dispersed children of God, as well as the implied saving of the "place" from destruction. He argues that these motifs point to the death of Jesus echoing the OT/Jewish hope for the return of the exiles.

138. Pancaro, "People of God," 121–22, 127.

139. Ibid., 118.

140. Ibid., 119–20.

141. Ibid., 127.

142. Raymond Brown identifies "the children of God" with the Gentiles (and not the Jews) and speaks about their "union to Israel," the nation of 11:48, 50, 51. Brown, *Gospel According to John*, 1:440–43. See also Okure, *Johannine Approach to Mission*, 203–4.

143. Dennis, *Jesus' Death*, 24.

Dennis' position is also argued by H. Van de Sandt, who traces the biblical roots and Jewish context of the verb "to scatter" (διασκορπίζω). He contends that "gathering the scattered children of God" implies a reunion of those who have been separated and a future hope for a restored Jerusalem, commonly recited in Jewish prayers.[144] Van de Sandt remarks that in light of Didache 9:4, the gathering is a final assembly into the kingdom of God in the end time.[145] While these arguments are convincing, they insufficiently defend against the claim that their interpretation of the Gospel of John is nothing but a realized eschatology.

The Death of Jesus and Politics

Scholars eventually began to shift focus from reading an abstract theology of atonement in John to exploring the more concrete social and political contexts of the death of Jesus. C. H. Dodd, who applied the form-critical method developed for the synoptic tradition to the Fourth Gospel, was instrumental in adopting this approach, arguing that there is "historical tradition in the Fourth Gospel."[146] R. E. Brown, J. L. Martyn, W. A. Meeks and others further developed this work by emphasizing that a particular social milieu maintained and formed these traditions.[147] This milieu was a Christian community of the late first century CE, locked in conflict with Jewish authorities who were moving to expel its members from the synagogue.[148] This "polemic context," remarked Rensberger, "furnishes us with

144. Van de Sandt, "Purpose of Jesus' death," 637–38.

145. Ibid., 644.

146. Dodd, *Historical Tradition*.

147. Brown, *Gospel According to John*, esp. ixx–ixxv; Brown, "Other Sheep not of this Fold," 5– 22, Martyn, *History and Theology*, 15–18; Meeks, "Man from Heaven," 44–72 (see esp. 46–47, 49–50, 68 on the need to understand John's language and Christology not only in terms of the history of ideas but also as having social functions within the Johannine community. Smith, Jr., "Johannine Christianity," 222–48; Kysar, *Fourth Evangelist*, 149–56.

148. Whether believers in Jesus were thrown out of the synagogue (Louis Martyn, Raymond Brown, and Wayne Meeks) is disputed (Reuven Kimelman and Adele Reinhartz). After a detailed consideration of the New Testament, patristic and rabbinic references to *Birkat ha-minim*, Kimelman concludes that this blessing "does not reflect a watershed in the history of the relationship between Jews and Christians in the first centuries of our era," and that "there was never a single edict which caused the so-called irreparable separation between Judaism and Christianity." Kimelman, "*Birkat ha-minim* and the Lack of Evidence," 2:226–44, 2:391–403. On separation, especially 2:244. Also,

a framework within which John's highly developed theology could have taken shape, and it permits us to ask further questions about the social, as well as the theological, implications of Johannine thought."[149] Dodd argued that the crowd's attempt to make Jesus king (6:14–15) and the fear of a Roman invasion (11:48) fit better with the tumultuous situation of pre-70 Palestine than with any subsequent period.[150] Therefore, John's Christology portrayed not only Jesus and the world that rejected him, but also hints at a relationship between Christology and politics. Perhaps this is why John's Gospel emphasizes the political nature of the accusations against Jesus more than elsewhere in the NT.[151]

The first major work on the political aspect of the death of Jesus was Heinrich Schlier's "Jesus und Pilatus nach dem Johannesevangelium," in which he examined the political implications of the course of the trial of Jesus before Pilate in John's Gospel. Schlier concluded that the focus on the political aspect demonstrates that Jesus' life was connected to the politics of his time.[152] This idea was later developed in his *The Relevance of the New Testament*, where Schlier discussed "the state" in the New Testament world. He argued that all NT authors were convinced that Jesus "was not merely a private individual" and that "the Church was not merely a voluntary association."[153] These authors all narrate the encounter of Jesus with "the political world of the state and its authorities," with John presenting the most challenging interpretation of this relationship. He distinguished the political world of "the state and its authorities," represented by Pilate, from

---

see Reinhartz, "Johannine Community and its Jewish Neighbors," 111–38. Eugene Boring instead opts for a separation from the synagogue. To him, the Johannine community began as Jews within the synagogue who came to believe that Jesus is the messiah (John 1:35–39). The Johannine Christians increasingly seemed to the Jewish leaders to be in danger of making Jesus into a second God. Such claims were considered blasphemy, punishable by death penalty. Disputes intensified; there may have been trials and executions, or delivering of Christians to the Romans for punishment. Those followers of Jesus who found themselves outside the synagogue believed they had been involuntarily expelled. They continued their evangelizing, within and outside the synagogues, and appealed to their fellow believers in Jesus who had kept a low profile and remained within Judaism to stand up and be counted. See Boring, *Introduction to the New Testament*, 635–36.

149. Rensberger, "Politics of John," 395–411.

150. Dodd, *Historical Tradition*, 213–15.

151. Ibid., 112; Haenchen, "Jesus von Pilatus," 149, 152; Meeks, *Prophet-King*, 64, 76, 81.

152. Schlier, "Jesus und Pilatus," 56–74, esp. 56–57, 61–64.

153. Schlier, *Relevance of the New Testament*, 215.

"the world," represented by the Jews, with the latter seeking its salvation from "Caesar."[154] By telling the story of the trial of Jesus, he claims that "the evangelist was thinking of the problem of the state,"[155] and intended to "attain fundamental insight into the nature of the state as it appeared to the New Testament."[156] In the trial, "the world" (the Jews) makes accusations against the "sacred power" (Jesus) to a secular and pagan Roman political power, represented by Pilate. During the trial, both the political power and the world are unmasked by the accused.[157]

The weakness in Schlier's argument is the abstract nature of his analysis of the philosophical concepts of "the state" and "the world." He does not attend to the experiences of the parties involved. The Roman state was real and present, a hostile power that oppressed and sought submission from the subjects. Such oppression provoked resistance from real, suffering people. In the same way, Pilate and the Jews are not merely representations, but flesh and blood individuals who experienced the political realities of their time. The statement that the basic intention of the author is to describe the nature of the state is narrow and unconvincing.

The centrality of politics in John's narrative of the death of Jesus has always been apparent. The tendency has been to interpret John's interest as "apologetic, seeking to relieve the Romans of responsibility for the death of Jesus and to show that neither Jesus nor the Church were a threat to the Empire."[158] This is slippery, given that some of the features of John's Gospel demonstrate that the attitude toward the Roman government was not always very amicable.

David Rensberger discusses the political subjects—Pilate, the "Jews," and Jesus in the Fourth Gospel's narrative in light of John's social setting and in the context of first century Jewish attitudes toward Rome. He explores the emergence of the Pharisees during prerevolutionary times, exploring their ambition and claim to leadership within the Jewish community, a claim which had broader political implications.[159] They did so by accommodating

154. Ibid., 224–25.

155. Ibid., 224.

156. Ibid., 216.

157. Ibid., 216–17.

158. Dodd, *Historical Tradition*, 115. See also Haenchen, "Jesus von Pilatus," 149–52; Lindars, *John*, 536; Hoskyns and Davey, *Fourth Gospel*, 2:521; Dauer, *Passionsgeschichte*, 307–11.

159. Rensberger's argument is based on Morton Smith who has demonstrated that Josephus' account of the Pharisees in the *Antiquities* was designed to commend them

themselves to Roman rule as they gained influence in Judaism, which they steered toward a concentration on religious faithfulness.

Together with Meeks, Rensberger contends that John's narrative does not provide a model for Christians trying to ward off a charge of sedition, since "it calls for a choice between the choice of the kingship of Christ and that of Caesar."[160] With this in mind, the attitude does not seem to be as conciliatory as the holders of the apologetic view may hope. Against the backdrop of the late first century, one cannot but interpret the death of Jesus (the Johannine story) in relation to the political realities facing the Jews and Jewish Christians of the time, yet it does not require indisputable conciliation. Attempts at pacification did not eliminate the hope for deliverance from Romans.

Rensberger explores this by referring to Yohanan ben Zakkai, who is said to have died with hope for the Messiah on his lips (*Abot R. Nat.* 25a). Moreover, apocalyptic writings continued to express vivid anticipations of the messianic destruction of Roman power (2 Esdras 11–13; 2 Baruch 82). Such works indicate that the very movement towards a penitent obedience to God was also "oriented towards deliverance."[161] E. Schürer thus accurately writes: "the messianic hope was a remarkable mixture of religious and political ideals . . . the political freedom of the nation which they longed for was viewed as the goal of God's ways."[162] In the diaspora, the situation was the same. Josephus' *Jewish Wars* had been written with the aim of convincing Diasporic Jews that it was wrong for Judah and Galilee to rebel.[163] The *Sibylline Oracles* mourned the destruction of the Temple and looked for the coming of the Messiah and God's judgment on the Gentiles and the restoration of Jerusalem (4.2.5–4.3.1 par.115–26; 4.3.10 par.171–192; 5.9.4–5.10.3 par. 403–433). In the decades immediately following the writing of the Fourth Gospel, a violent messianic rebellion broke out among

---

to the Romans as the one party commanding popular allegiance to maintain stability in Palestine. See Smith, "Palestinian Judaism in the First Century," 74–77. Likewise, J. Neusner writes about the roles of R. Yohanan ben Zakkai and others of his kind who worked tooth and nail creating a post-war structure for Judaism, dedicated to the cultivation of piety that would be acceptable to the Romans and would ensure the survival of the Jewish people. See Neusner, *From Politics to Piety*, 143–54. See also his *A Life of Yohanan ben Zakkai*, 166–73.

160. Meeks, *Prophet-King*, 64.

161. Rensberger, "Politics of John," 397–98.

162. Schürer, *History of the Jewish People*, 1:527.

163. Rensberger, "Politics of John," 398.

the Jews of Egypt and Cyrene, and spread to Cyprus and Mesopotamia (115–117 CE).[164] This was the political setting of the writing of the Fourth Gospel, a period of "accommodating Rome in some quarters," while in others, a rebellious spirit striving for political and religious aims inspired the Maccabees and the Zealots.[165] Such history makes it reasonable to read the Fourth Gospel politically. This context is the rationale for a political reading of the death of Jesus.

Rensberger arrives at two basic conclusions. First, the trial suggests that the disciple will always have to decide vis à vis the Empire whether Jesus is the king or whether Caesar is.[166] Pilate is contemptuous of Jesus and of Israel's political hopes that Jesus both fulfills and transcends.[167] Jesus restores the sovereignty of Israel by asserting the sovereignty of Israel's God over and against the sovereignty of this world.[168] Secondly, it is because the kingship of Jesus is not of this world that the confrontation between the two sides does not take place according to the standards of the world or according to its means.[169] Jesus is contrasted with both Barabbas (a freedom fighter) and Caesar, and by preferring Barabbas and declaring allegiance to Caesar, the Jews betrayed their true king. By having Caesar bully the Jews into accepting the kingship of Caesar, the fourth evangelist shows that he is critical of Caesar's kingship. Unlike the zealots, Jesus asserts the true sovereignty of God and of Israel against Caesar, in a kingship "not of this world." John's Gospel therefore confronts the issue of Israel's freedom "with an alternative to both zealotry and collaboration," by calling for adherence to Jesus, whose kingship is not of this world and "whose servants do not fight but remain in the world, bearing witness to the truth before the rulers of both the synagogue and Empire."[170]

J. Beutler, analyzing the plot to kill Jesus, states that the "advantage" that the council intended to realize is political. He argues that the correspondence and contrast between the two gathering-words form an "inclusio," one at the beginning of the pericope (συνήγαγον οὖν; John 11:47), the other at the end (συναγάγῃ εἰς ἕν; John 11:52). The *inclusio* functions

---

164. Schürer, *History of the Jewish People*, 529–33.

165. Rensberger, *Johannine Faith*, 88.

166. Ibid., 98.

167. Ibid., 95.

168. Ibid., 99.

169. Ibid.

170. Rensberger, *Johannine Faith*, 100.

as narrative frame for the story.[171] The Sanhedrin gathers together (11:47) in order to maintain their own power, which is connected to the people, nation and temple as "objects of possession." Jesus' activities threaten these "objects" and Caiaphas' realpolitik is therefore meant to protect the leaders' power.[172]

Conclusion

Studies on the death of Jesus in the Fourth Gospel have concentrated on its salvific importance. The results of these studies are incohesive, as demonstrated in the various themes discussed above, and the lack of agreement has contributed to a continuation of the conversation. The late twentieth century saw a move from a common inquiry into soteriological significance to the centrality of politics. The political aspect of the death of Jesus mainly centered on the fact that the trial utilizes political accusations, and scholarly inquiry expanded to consider the Roman Imperial context of the death of Jesus, in order to apportion blame either to the "Jews" or to the Romans. While the tendency has been to interpret John's interest as apologetic, seeking to relieve the Romans of responsibility for the death of Jesus and to show that neither Jesus nor the Church were a threat to the Empire, some scholars have demonstrated that Christians had to make a choice between Caesar and Jesus. According to these scholars, the Church did not have to be apologetic at all times.

Studies focused in politics began to employ a postcolonial hermeneutic, arguing that the text was a product of the imperial Roman context. Not only do these texts carry the political ideologies of the oppressor, but also of the oppressed Jewish community and the minority Johannine community.

171. Beutler, "Two Ways of Gathering," 400.

172. Beutler also observes the soteriological importance of the plot to kill Jesus. By his death Jesus will "gather the scattered children of God," a death "no longer considered politically but soteriologically" (ibid., 402). He considers diachronic issues such as the traditions of Jesus' death "for others" and the gathering of the scattered children of God, which he observes, originates from the song of the servant (Isa 52:13—53:12) and numerous other texts which show that the tradition of the "gathering of the scattered children of God" was common in Judaism. It included the gathering of God's "sons and daughters from their dispersion" and bringing them home to Zion (ibid., 403–4). Like Hofius, he suggests Isa 56:8; 66:18 and Jer 3:17 as tradition behind the concept of gathering and proposed that these texts speak about the gathering of the non-Israelites to Zion. This is indicative of a universal gathering of the children of God in John 11:52. See ibid., 404.

According to postcolonial criticism, the Roman imperial ideologies in the text must be exposed and resisted, while those of the Jewish leaders should be considered either as survival techniques or strategic responses to the Empire.

This book will carry forward the postcolonial conversation, discussing the political aspects of the death of Jesus in its imperial context. It will focus on the context of the social and political geography, an aspect insufficiently considered. Chapter 1 has demonstrated the gap left by a focus on soteriological significance and provided a rationale for a political reading of the death of Jesus. Chapter Two will look at Johannine studies that have considered the importance of the notion of "place," and define the methodology in this study.

CHAPTER 2

Methodology

Introduction

In chapter one, I discussed studies centered on soteriology and politics, and expressed the need to consider a political interpretation of the death of Jesus. I opted for a postcolonial reading that addresses the impact of Empire and the dominated people's response to imperial ideology in the text. Chapter two explores the Johannine studies that have considered the importance of the notion of place, and establishes a theoretical framework for a postcolonial geographical reading of the death of Jesus that is based on John's construction of diverse "places" in the narrative of the death of Jesus.

Place Scholarship in John's Gospel

Scholarship on *place* in the Fourth Gospel was initiated by Helmut Koester. He studied the use of the Greek word τόπος (place) in Greek literature, the Old Testament, the later Jewish usage, and the New Testament, citing only a few examples from the Gospel of John.[1] The New Testament usage includes τόπος as a general term for place, specific place, the name of a place in question, temple, the right place for opportunity, and as the place of Scripture. John uses τόπος as a general term for place in 6:23, 11:30, and 19:20. In 10:40; 11:16 cf. v. 30; 19:41, *Place* is translated in such a way that it is substituted by an adverb of place and a relative pronoun: "there were."

1. Koester, "τόπος," 187–92.

In 4:20 and 11:48 place refers to the temple.[2] He also cites *place* as "the right place for opportunity," referring to the father's house, the heavenly place of the community or the individual in 14:2–3.[3] To Koester, John rarely uses the word τόπος with the name of the place in question. In 19:17, κρανίου τόπον (place of the skull) is described by its Hebrew original, Golgotha.[4]

Koester's analysis of the use of *place* in John is limited to the cited examples, with *place* referring to a physical location. His study falls short of the possibility of *place* as a mental space. G. Haufe, like Koester, explores the use of τόπος in the New Testament with several references to John's Gospel. He notes that τόπος occurs 95 times in the New Testament, 17 of which are in the Fourth Gospel.[5] John uses the word to refer to place or locale, a specific locale, a specific building, specific place of persons or things, and "figuratively"[6] to refer to a specific position in the Church.[7]

As a specific locale, one reads of the place of Jesus' crucifixion (19:17). There are formulations of *place* with relative clauses, e.g., τόπου ὅπου, that follow the pattern of Hebraisms. John uses this construction very often when referring to an important place connected with the story of Jesus or with John the Baptist. The reader is explicitly reminded of such places by references to "the place where" the people ate the bread (6:23), "the place where" John was first baptizing (10:40), "the place where" Martha met with Jesus before Jesus came into the village (11:30), "the place where" Jesus was crucified (19:20), and that there was a garden in "the place where" Jesus was crucified (19:41).[8]

John also uses τόπος as "the setting of the current action," in which case it serves to connect locales within a narrative and can be translated simply as "there."[9] We therefore read of Jesus slipping away after healing on a Sabbath, when the crowd was still "there"—in that place (5:13). At the multiplication of the loaves, Jesus had the crowd sit down for there

---

2. See Koester, "τόπος," 204. Later studies reveal that *place* in this case could mean something other than temple. This will be discussed later in the chapter.

3. Ibid., 205–7.

4. Ibid., 203.

5. Haufe, "τόπος," 366. The concordance confirms the statistics on the occurrence of τόπος in John. See Moulton and Geden, *Concordance*, 104.

6. Haufe writes about the figurative usage of τόπος as a "specific position in the Church," citing examples from other New Testament texts but none from John.

7. Haufe, "τόπος," 367.

8. Ibid., 366.

9. Ibid.

was much grass "there"—in that place (6:10). Τόπος also refers to a specific building such as a temple or to a city such as Jerusalem (4:20) and the heavenly house of Jesus' Father (14:2–3).[10] Lastly, John uses τόπος as a "specific position of something." In John 20:25, we read of the position of the nails in the crucified Jesus.[11]

Koester and Haufe carry out a philological study of τόπος. Haufe's treatment adds the element of *place* as a position of responsibility, though it falls short of indicating any possibility of such occurrence in John. Both Koester and Haufe do not take into consideration places that are indicated by the use of proper names. Haufe also mentions that scholars do not agree on the meaning of *place* in 11:48 but does not address the issue. Although these works were rather general, they paved the way for a further study of the significance of space in John.

The Ambiguous Place in John 11:48

In the plot to kill Jesus, the chief priests, the Pharisees and Caiaphas fear that if Jesus is not stopped from performing signs, all will believe in him, and the Romans will come to take away their place (τόπος) and nation (ἔθνος) (John 11:48). While A. Schlatter and W. Bauer hold that the *place* is the Temple, B. Lindars contends that *place* refers to Jerusalem. C. Umoh instead argues to the point that *place* in this passage refers to a position of responsibility of the Jewish leaders during Jesus' time.

Schlatter quotes Jer 7:14; *Mi. Bikkurim* 2:2; *Tos. Sanh* 3:5 to argue that τόπος means the Temple.[12] To Schlatter, τὸν τόπον is "die befestigte Formel"[13] (the fixed formula) for the gathering of the first fruits in the

10. The meaning of place in John 11:48 as Temple or Jerusalem is disputed; the ambiguity of place in this passage will be discussed in the following section.

11. Haufe acknowledges that the text ὁ τύπος τῶν ἥλων is uncertain (Haufe, "τόπος," 367), yet does not discuss the variants. The manuscripts' textual variations offer differing implications between whether Thomas talks of putting his finger into the *print* [*mark, impression*], indicated by τύπον, or into the *place* (τόπον) of the nails. For the first word, τύπον is well supported by older manuscripts ℵ D L W and should be retained. For the second, it is better to read τόπος with the stronger evidence of A Θ Latin and Syriac manuscripts. While in the first instance, τύπον has a stronger attestation, it would be easy and reasonable to corrupt an original τόπον into τύπον.

12. Schlatter, *Der Evangelist Johannes*, 257. In line with Schlatter, Bauer also contends that the place is the Temple, based on II Macc. 5:17–20, in which Antiochus is portrayed as unconcerned about "the holy place." See Bauer, *Johannesevangelium*, 156.

13. Schlatter, *Der Evangelist Johannes*, 257.

Temple. Schlatter's citing of Jer 7:14 is not without problems. He does not explain why Codex Alexandrinus has τόπῳ τούτῳ, if τὸν τόπον (the place) and not τόπον τοῦτον (this place) was the fixed formula reflecting the gathering of the first fruits in later documents, such as *Mi. Bikkurim* 2:2; *Tos. Sanh* 3:5. It would seem reasonable that the latter, not the former, has been the fixed formula. The reading of Codex Alexandrinus seems to be an attempt to correct a seemingly abnormal reading of "the place" to the usual "this place" for the Temple.

Lindars calls our attention to the absence of the adjective "holy" (ἅγιος) that qualifies place, which could suggest that Jerusalem itself is meant rather than the Temple (so Sinaitic Syriac and Chrysostom).[14] Despite noting the possibility of reading place to mean Jerusalem, Lindars still thinks that its use in the "specialized sense of temple" is well-attested "as evidenced in John 4:20." The fear would then be that "the destruction or desecration of the Temple would put an end to the Jewish religion," for which the Temple was central, "and that the national identity of Judea would be brought to an end, to prevent any other nationalist uprising."[15] Lindars makes this important observation of the absence of the adjective "holy," yet fails to draw the conclusion that place in this passage could mean something other than a location. Moreover, Lindars' use of John 4:20 as evidence presents a weak argument: in the case of the Samaritan woman, Jesus corrects the notion that identifies Jerusalem as the only place, ὁ τόπος, in which one can worship, something that is clearly identifiable from the context. Furthermore, evidence shows that where the Temple is meant, it is very specific: it is either the "holy place" or "this place." Jesus tells the Jews, destroy "this sanctuary" (ναὸν τοῦτον), and the Jews tell Jesus that it has taken forty days to build "this sanctuary" (ναὸν τοῦτον).[16] Despite Lindars' failure to advance another interpretation of the place, his observation becomes the basis of Umoh's further investigation into the matter.

---

14. Lindars, *Gospel of John*, 405.

15. Ibid.

16. Other NT evidence seems to confirm that where Temple is meant, the text is very specific. In Acts 6:14, Stephen is accused of claiming that Jesus would destroy "this place" (τὸν τόπον τοῦτον). Paul is arrested in the Temple because he teaches everywhere against the people, the law and "this place" (τοῦ τόπου τούτου) and brings Greeks into the Temple and consequently has defiled "this holy place" (τὸν ἅγιον τόπον τοῦτον) (Acts 21:28).

Umoh undertakes a textual and historical critical study to propose that place in this verse means a "position of responsibility."[17] Basic to Umoh's argument is the use of αἴρω (John 11:48) in relation to τόπος. He translates αἴρω as "take away," contrary to the common translation of "destroy." To him, the Greek equivalent of "destroy" is ἀπόλλυμι (11:50) in the sense of "ruining." Αἴρω, on the other hand, basically means "to withdraw something" (like money from the bank) or to "take away."[18] In the shepherd discourse (10:10), the thief comes to steal, kill and destroy (ἀπολέσῃ). Withdrawing or taking away has a different sense than destroying.

In the Fourth Gospel, argues Umoh, αἴρω is hardly used to mean "destroy." All the 19 occurrences of αἴρω in the Fourth Gospel have to do with "taking away" or "removing."[19] It is thus more likely that the Sanhedrin fears that the Romans will come, not to ruin (destroy) the place, but to take away the place/position from the leaders. This is their greatest fear: losing their "place" in society.

Umoh corroborates his argument with the use of the personal pronoun ἡμῶν, which does not refer to the whole of Jewish people, but to the Sanhedrin members themselves. The subject of ἡμῶν from whom the place is withdrawn is the same as the subject of ἀφῶμεν in v. 48.[20] The τόπος in v. 48 is not exactly to be ruined or destroyed when the Romans come, but it is to be "taken away from us,"[21] ἡμῶν referring to the leaders, or, better still, it is withdrawn from them. This means that place is what the leaders possess or what has been loaned them through trust, (i.e., their position of responsibility) as political leaders. It is their possession of place that guarantees their claims to the ἔθνος (nation) which they are also afraid to lose. The combination of place with ἔθνος[22] (nation), which is also a

17. Umoh, Plot to Kill Jesus, 88–95.

18. Ibid., 88. For the meanings of αἴρω, see also Louw and Nida, Greek-English Lexicon of the New Testament, 582.

19. Umoh, Plot to Kill Jesus, 88–89, quoting Perschbacher, ed., The New Analytic Greek Lexicon, 8. See the Lamb of God who takes away the sins of the world (John 1:29), nobody takes away life from Jesus (John 10:18), the stone from Lazarus' tomb was taken away (John 11:41), Mary tells Simon and the beloved disciple that some people have taken away the body of the Lord from the tomb (John 20:2).

20. Umoh, Plot to Kill Jesus, 89.

21. For the translation of ἡμῶν see Haenchen, Johannesevangelium, 421.

22. The use of ἔθνος here must be distinguished from the use of its plural τὰ ἔθνη outside the Johannine Corpus to designate non-Jews or the so-called pagan nations as against Jewish or chosen people of Israel. The differentiation of peoples on the basis of religious affinity as "pagan" or "chosen people" which is carried over from the LXX in the

politically-charged term, further strengthens Umoh's argument that the *place* in question is the *position of responsibility* of the Sanhedrin members. The importance attached to *the place* by the Sanhedrin members is decisive for their determination to put Jesus to death. Therefore, it is not accidental that *place* is taken together with the purely political entity—the nation (11:48). Seconds later, the word "place" drops from their discourse (11:51)—for Jesus will not die for their will to political power, their "place," of course—rather, Jesus will die for the *nation*, and better, for the gathering of all of God's children.

Historical evidence supports the fear of losing a political position of responsibility. Traditionally, the office of the high priest was held for life, but during Roman occupation one could lose this office depending on one's relationship with the imperial power in Rome. Strathmann observes that from the time before Caiaphas became high priest, even in the Maccabean times, to hold the office of high priest for life was already a thing of the past.[23] Hengel records that in the years between 37 BCE and 70 CE, twenty-eight known high priests held the office of high priest and in reality there may have been more.[24] The Roman authorities could remove one high priest and appoint another at any time. Annas, the father-in-law of Caiaphas, was appointed by Quirinus to succeed Joazar in 6 CE.[25] The place that Caiaphas, the chief priests, and the Pharisees feared to lose could reasonably be their position of authority. Umoh thus concludes that if there is any thought about the Temple or the city of Jerusalem at all, "such thought is not primary in the present argumentation."[26]

Umoh's position on place is more convincing. Proponents of the view that place in John 11:48 denotes the "Temple" and/or "Jerusalem" are based on II Mac 5:17–20 and Jer 7:14. Bauer does not notice that in II Mac 5:17–20 the place is described as "the holy place." In the same way, Jeremiah

---

NT is lacking in the Johannine vocabulary. This however does not mean that nationality plays no role in the Gospel; in fact, it does. There are evidences of identification of peoples according to their villages of origin (John 1:44; 1:45–46; 4:7). See Schmidt, "ἔθνος," 366–70; H. Strathmann, "λαός," 29–30. It is surprising that John uses λαός and ἔθνος as if they were synonymous, substituting ἔθνος (John 11:51) for λαός (John 11:52), yet as Pancaro observes, the two terms are not equivalent. For details, see Pancaro, "People of God," 120.

23. Strathmann, *Evangelium nach Johannes*, 172.

24. Hengel, *Johannine Question*, 215.

25. Umoh, *Plot to Kill Jesus*, 93.

26. Ibid., 91.

clearly mentions the "temple" as the place that "bears God's name" and the place that God gave to the people and to their ancestors. The meaning of place is not as transparent in John 11:48. Since the temple belonged to the whole nation; its destruction would not be a direct personal loss only to the leaders (ἡμῶν), as indicated in the context of 11:48. It is reasonable to hold that *place* is an office, a meaning that is demonstrated by the first century Greek usage as well. With place as office, we observe that the Sanhedrin have a selfish interest in maintaining their political position and that the concern for the nation is secondary, merely a means for maintaining the leaders' place. Jesus' death would save the nation from destruction, and the nation's existence guarantees the leaders' continuous exercise of power.

Attempts to define *place* in John 11:48, through philological and historical criticism has not yielded definitive results. The significance of *place* in John 11:48 remains ambiguous. Whether *place* refers to Jerusalem, the Temple, or the place of responsibility of the leaders, the common denominator is that decisions are taken with the selfish aim of maintaining and protecting that through which the council members influence society.

The historical and philological studies on the use of τόπος in various Johannine passages were then followed by interest in the hierarchical constructions of geographical locations in John, focusing mainly on two locales, Jerusalem and Galilee.

Jerusalem and Galilee

Sean Freyne noticed the surprising amount of detail on places mentioned in the Gospel of John.[27] This prompted him to examine the meanings John invests in various locations. He focused on how Galilee and Judea are classified into the symbolic world of the author, concluding that John presents Galilee in a positive light as opposed to Jerusalem. Freyne argues that John presents Galilee usually as the point of arrival or departure in the journeys of Jesus.[28] Most of Jesus' journeys are centered on going to Jerusalem for the great feasts (John 2:13; 5:1; 7:1–10; 12:12), and it is there that most of

27. He refers to Barrett's, "St. John: Social Historian," 26–29, in which John's strikingly detailed description of places is delineated. Barrett mentions places like Cana in Galilee, Aenom near Salim with its plentiful supply of water, Sichar and it's well, the pool of Bethesda having five porticoes, the *Lithostratos* or *Gabbatha*, etc.

28. Freyne, *Galilee*, 117.

the dialogue occurs. On each of these occasions there is a confrontation between Jesus and his opponents, usually designated as the "Jews"[29] or the Pharisees.

The first journey of Jesus to Jerusalem is for the feast of Passover. At this feast he casts out of the temple those who bought and sold there, claiming it was his father's house. The "Jews" challenged him to validate such claims, to which Jesus said "destroy this temple and in three days I will raise it up again" (2:15). While it is reported that many believed in him seeing the signs which he did (2:23), it is also clear that tension is established between Jesus and the inhabitants of Jerusalem. As such Nicodemus, one of the Pharisees, would go to Jesus by night, confirming the experience of opposition and hostility to Jesus (3:2). Jesus then left Judea and withdrew to Galilee (4:3).

The second journey of Jesus to Jerusalem is for an unspecified feast (5:1). At this feast he performs a miracle on a Sabbath, leading to a theological controversy of a very serious kind. He is accused of violating the Sabbath and of blasphemy as he claims equality with God. While there is no explicit mention of Galilee, all of a sudden we are told that Jesus is across the Sea of Galilee, which is Tiberius (6:1–4). The same pattern applies to the third and the fourth journeys of Jesus to Jerusalem (7:1–10; 12:12). Freyne also observes an increasing hostility with each visit as Jesus' challenge to the claims of Jerusalem becomes more explicit, climaxing in the final

29. The term Ἰουδαῖοι can be translated as "Jews" or "Judeans." The prolific scholarship on this expression shows that there is no consensus on the issue. Bultmann maintains that the expression is symbolic of those who represent unbelief. Bultmann, *Gospel of John*, 86. Von Wahlde claims that when the term is used in a hostile fashion, John has in mind the opponents of Jesus, the political-religious authorities. Von Wahlde, "Johannine Jews," 33–60; See also Schneiders, *Written That You May Believe*, 75–76, 81–82. Motyer argues that it is difficult to understand what Ἰουδαῖοι signals in the Fourth Gospel, partly because it is very difficult for modern readers to hear John's language with the first-century ears but also because it is used both in a positive and negative sense. He discusses a number of possible meanings such as: the "Jews" as "Judeans," as "representatives of unbelief," "as "opponents of Jesus," "the Jerusalem elite," as "religious of Judea," as "ambivalent divided figures." See Motyer, *Your Father the Devil*, 46–56. Beutler proposes that at the very least, the expression "the Jews" should be enclosed in quotation marks "so that the reader is admonished not to read into the text the general meaning of 'the Jews' in everyday language and to come to conclusion which makes the Jewish people or religious community responsible for the death of Jesus." Johannes Beutler, "Identity of the Jews," 237. With all the above possibilities in mind, Charlesworth suggests that translating every occurrence of Ἰουδαῖοι as "Jews" is "poor lexicography, historiography, narrative or rhetorical exegesis, and theology." James H. Charlesworth, "The Priority of John," 87. See also Wróbel, *Who are the Father and His Children*, 65.

movement towards his death. In each of the cases of hostility, Jesus retreats to Galilee where he is accepted and finds rest. Freyne concludes that it is hostility that forms the backdrop to the various retreats of Jesus to Galilee.[30] The actual Galilean ministry of Jesus is reported minimally in contrast to the Judean ministry, in fact, the Judean ministry with its suspect and hostile reactions get more coverage. The two Cana miracles of Jesus take place in Galilee (2:1, 11; 4:46, 54). No mention is made of any tension that these miracles cause and they receive no negative comments. The Galileans were the first to be reported as believing in Jesus (4:44); they respond positively to Jesus' signs. Freyne concludes that Galilee is presented in a positive light while Jerusalem is presented negatively.

Jerome Neyrey follows Freyne but widens the spaces of study beyond Galilee and Jerusalem. He discusses how the Fourth Gospel is involved with various spaces and places, valuing some but devaluing others. His interpretation is based on the anthropological models of territoriality which shows how all peoples classify space, communicate the classification and control access to or exit from this territory.[31] His understanding of *territoriality* is based on the definition of Robert Sack: "the attempt by an individual or group to affect, influence or control people, phenomena, and relationships, by delimiting and asserting control over a geographic area."[32] The classification of places, a major element in the model, refers to the way "humans invest space with meaning or label it for some purpose."[33] Anthropologists hence classify places as "public and private, sacred and profane, honorable and shameful, unclean and clean, fixed and fluid sacred space, center and periphery, civilization and nature."[34]

Concerning public and private space, he describes them as the "gender-divided space" in the Greco-Roman world of the first century CE "with males in public, in open space and out of doors," and "females in covered space and indoors." He observes that the distinction may be made among males "when they attend to civic affairs in the *boule* or *agora* as public, from occasions when males attend symposia, etc. as private. Honorable men are expected to speak boldly in public, while others spread rumor and sedition

---

30. Freyne, *Galilee*, 118.

31. Neyrey, "Spaces and Places," 60.

32. Sack, *Human Territoriality*, 19.

33. Neyrey, "Spaces and Places," 61.

34. Ibid.

in private."[35] In this case, when in 18:20, Jesus answers to Annas that he has spoken publicly (παρρησίᾳ) in synagogue and temple and has not spoken in private (ἐν κρυπτῷ), he is basically saying that he has acted honorably as is expected of a male in this particular cultural space.

On honor and shame, Neyrey cites John 1:46. To him, the rhetorical question "can anything good come from Nazareth?" is an example of "a classification which denies honor to someone based on an honor-less home-of-origin."[36] He exemplifies the pure and polluted in the behavior of the high priests and the cohort as they handed over Jesus over to the Roman authority. The accusers of Jesus did not enter the *praetorium* so that they might not be defiled and so could eat the Passover (18:28). Pilate's place, the *praetorium*, is classified as unclean by the Jewish leadership. By remaining outside, these leaders both "communicate that the place is unclean and claim respect for observing the purity code."[37]

About fixed sacred place Malina writes:

> Just as persons have their statuses by ascription and perdure in that status indefinitely, the same holds true for places. The topography of the main places where people in this script live out their lives is rather permanent. A palace location, a temple location and a homestead stay in the same place and with the same lineage through generations.[38]

Thus fixed sacred space correlates with fixed roles and statuses. All of these are characterized by redundant aspects of stability, permanence and continuity. The temple city of Jerusalem exemplifies this well.

Concerning fluid spaces Malina writes:

> The situation of the porous boundaries and competing groups stand in great contrast to the solid, hierarchical, pyramidal shape of strong group/high grid [fixed space] ... as groups form and re-form anew, permanence is no longer to be found outside the group; and where the group is, there is stability. Sacred space is located in the group, not in some impersonal place like a temple. The group is central location of importance, where the body of Christ, the Church, for Christians or the synagogue gathering for the Jews, or the philosophical "schools" ... Discourses within

---

35. Ibid., 62.
36. Ibid.
37. Ibid. See also Malina, *New Testament World*, 164–80.
38. Malina, *Christian Origins*, 31.

these groups, whether the words of a portable Torah, the story of Jesus, or the exhortations of the philosopher-teacher, becomes the mobile, portable, exportable focus of sacred place, in fact more important than the fixed and eternal sacred place.[39]

Four comments should be made. First, the group becomes the equivalent of fixed space, and so the social dynamics of a group such as loyalty, love and service rise in importance. Second, since stability and permanence are not found outside the group, we are clued to consider the "spatial" quality of "remain" in the Gospel. Third, the group might be a scholastic enterprise, either a philosophical school or a midrashic one. If worship entails the reading and hearing of sacred writings, then it can occur anywhere; thus, sacred space is mobile and portable. Fourth, the group then is the central location of importance; and so it is not accidental that the New Testament often calls the Christian group "temple" and "household of God."[40]

Communication of these classifications is done by building walls and gates that are guarded (in case of a city) and by having a barred door manned by a guard in the case of a house or residence (John 18:15–17; 20:19, 26). The building of walls around cities and the construction of buildings with barred doors patrolled by guards, a fence and a gate to protect animals or property communicate the idea that the space within is "ours", "sacred," "pure," etc.

On places in the Fourth Gospel, Neyrey comments that Galilee and Judea are not geographical locations but symbolic places.[41] The meaning that the author has invested in these places is mainly based on Jesus "remaining" in one place and not in another. In Galilee "Jesus is accepted, gains disciples and remains," while "in Judea he is harassed, put on trial, and killed. Jesus does not remain in Judea."[42] Territoriality contributes to this conversation by looking at the way the author classifies these two places. The author labels these places in terms of some dualism or binary opposites like "love/hate" or "friendly/unfriendly" or "remain/not remain." The communication is done through the narrative in which we see that Galilee is always welcoming, friendly and safe for Jesus and his disciples while Judea is hostile and unfriendly. To Neyrey, what is communicated by "Galilee" and "Judea," is not classification of real or topological places, but

39. Ibid., 38.
40. Neyrey, "Spaces and Places," 63.
41. Ibid.
42. Ibid., 63–64. See also Bassler, "Galileans," 243–57.

rather social space, in which some control is exercised because the classifi-cation creates a sharp boundary between disciples and foes. This boundary functions as a dividing wall or a fence or a gate which make up a sheepfold (John 10:1–11).[43]

Neyrey makes a good point about the symbolic use of Galilee and Je-rusalem as locations. However, his comment that Galilee and Jerusalem are not geographical locations is arguable. He does not define geography, but his remark falls short of the fact that geographical places can be real as well as imagined. In fact, social place is a geographical location too; it is what Henri Lefebvre calls a "lived experience" and "Soja's thirdspace."[44] This is the case in John's presentation of these landscapes.

Point of View through Setting

James Resseguie studied how point of view in John's Gospel is expressed in the *type* of setting (spaces) and the *arrangement* or configuration of char-acters and objects in a setting. Examining different types of spaces, both architectural (human-made structures such as wells, temples, synagogues, etc.) and topographical (demarcations on physical maps such as sea, moun-tains, cities, etc.), Resseguie shows that diverse spatial points of view illus-trate the narrative's and the Gospel's ideology.[45]

For Resseguie, point of view is expressed in both the type of setting and in the arrangement of characters and props within a particular setting. "The way space is filled up communicates a point of view."[46] The point of view is expressed in three ways: by movements from *periphery* to *center*, by distance between characters as *near* and *far*, or by movements *inside* and *outside*.

First, when the setting involves movement to and from a "focal point," the central point underscores the "ideological perspective of the narrative." This kind of arrangement is called the *center* and the *periphery*.[47] Such is seen in movements of characters to and from fixed settings such as the well, tomb or temple. In John 4, characters trek to and from Jesus at Jacob's well just as they would trek to and from an ordinary well, drawing attention to

43. Neyrey, "Spaces and Places," 64.

44. Soja, *Thirdspace: Journeys*, 11–12.

45. Resseguie, *Strange Gospel*, 68.

46. Ibid., 62.

47. Ibid.

Jesus as a new kind of well, dispensing living water. At times Jesus instead travels to a fixed center encountering resistance at the margins, as in the temple and tomb narratives. In John 7:1–52, Jesus "goes up" to Jerusalem and the temple; the expectations of the people "go up" as the "great day" of the festival approaches; Jesus' voice correspondingly "goes up"; and the tensions and divisions among the people "go up" in response to his action.[48] These tensions will keep mounting until Jesus is killed. On the other hand, as Jesus travels to the "center of the nation," he ascends higher, abandons his secretive pilgrimage and goes public, and gains a voice of epic proportions. As Resseguie puts it, the progression on the various planes of the point of view is from "obscurity to clarity, from darkness to light."[49]

The center is the "focus of transformation: the tomb becomes the threshold of life and the temple is remade from an emporium into 'my' [Jesus'] Father's house."[50] The spatial and phraseological points of view reinforce the strangeness of the ideological perspective: an architectural structure is being remade as a person. In other words, "architectural space becomes *personal* space." The temple has become a house of trade and must be reclaimed as "my Father's house," but the reclamation project is not complete until the temple at Jerusalem is replaced by the temple of Jesus' body.[51]

Second, he considers "distance between characters on land and in the sea," a setting known as *near* and *far*. Characters start out *far* from each other—spatially and in other modes—and end up *near* each other, physically and spiritually, or in other ways. The separation—both literal and figurative—is collapsed when one character moves towards another character.[52] "Spatial distances may reflect emotional, spiritual, cognitive, or other forms of distance."[53] Consequently, when Jesus' followers could not accept his difficult teaching, many "turned back and no longer went about with him" (6:6), "an outward expression of inward apostasy" (8:12; 12:35).[54] On another note, the sea and mountains are used in John to create distance—physically and in other ways. In the two sea narratives (6:16–21;

48. Ibid., 81.
49. Ibid., 82. Quoting Lindars, *John*, 285.
50. Ibid., 75.
51. Ibid., 86.
52. Ibid., 62–63.
53. Ibid., 95.
54. Ibid., 95. Quoting Schnackenburg, *John*, 2: 75.

21:1–19), "spatial distancing elaborates and develops an ideological perspective concerning discipleship."[55] In the presence of Jesus, disciples are successful but in his absence they are unsuccessful. In John 6, the disciples struggle to cross the stormy sea until Jesus arrives to achieve a positive resolution. In the same way, after a whole night of unsuccessful fishing, the arrival of Jesus in the morning transforms a fruitless night into a great success (John 21).

In a third setting, characters go in and out of human-made enclosures. Such a setting is called *inside* and *outside*, in which case "if inside space is secure, then outside space may be threatening," and vice versa. Characters go in and out of the sheep-fold, garden, the courtyard, the *praetorium*.[56] The sheep are safe within the enclosure—the sheepfold (10:1, 16). Outside the pen they are threatened by brigands, thieves and wolves (10:12). Although inside space is safe, pasture is found outside the pen, hence the need for a shepherd who leads the sheep to pasture and protects them there. The gatekeeper has the minor task of opening the door for the shepherd. The sheepfold is therefore a symbolic space capturing "the dilemma of discipleship."[57] Both life and danger lay outside the pen, so the sheep must trust a shepherd to lead them in and out of the pen and to protect them once outside. When disciples are locked behind closed doors, "for fear of the Jews" (John 20:19), from their perspective, this is safe space. From another perspective this space could "convey a sense of confinement and bondage" which prevents them from accomplishing their mission.[58]

Resseguie's study considers place not merely as a physical entity but also as a mental space, an embodiment of meaning. He successfully demonstrates that diverse spatial points of view illustrate the narrative's and the Gospel's ideology. Some of his conclusions however are not very consistent. For example, he portrays "inside" as a space of safety for the sheep and "outside" as dangerous for the sheep. Yet this binary of safety is not a secure permanent state for the people: the sheep must venture outside of the pen in order to graze. Even so, "outside" is not always dangerous for the flock. Similarly the disciples will have to get out of the closed rooms if they have to preach the risen Christ.

55. Ibid., 96.
56. Ibid., 63.
57. Ibid., 65.
58. Ibid., 63.

The interest in place then underwent a transformation with the post-colonial critics who "trace the journeys within John's narrative in order to examine the making and distribution of power on earthly spaces," disclosing imperial ideologies within the Gospel and "challenging readers of the Fourth Gospel to take responsibility for the journeys they make and for the powers they claim over earthly spaces."[59] Scholars include Gary Burge, Tod D. Swanson, Musa W. Dube, and Jeffrey L. Staley.

Suppression of Diversity and Promotion of Universal Standards

Gary M. Burge builds on Raymond Brown's argument that the Johannine Jesus replaced Jewish institutions and religious views, citing "the replacement of the water for Jewish purifications" (6:1—7:59), "the replacement of the temple" (10:22–29), and "the replacement of worship at Jerusalem and Gerizim" in the discourse of Jesus with the Samaritan woman at Jacob's well (John 4:4–42).[60] Burge uses this replacement theme to argue that the Christology of the Fourth Gospel is orientated toward displacing the significance of place in the Christian experience. To Burge, in John's Christology, there is "an answer to the Jewish yearning for the place of God's promise," i.e., Christ is the place of God's promise. He focuses on "Judaism's identity with the land of Israel" and shows "how this identity is uprooted by Christology."[61]

Using the "vine metaphor" (John 15), Burge maintains that the vine image in Judaism could refer to the "land of Israel, wisdom and messiah,"[62] but that "primarily it referred to the land of Israel." Such an image reflects "the Gospel of John's theological relocation of Israel's holy space,"[63] given that John presents a Jesus who "changes the place of rootedness for Israel."[64]

---

59. Dube and Staley, "Descending," 2–3.

60. Brown, *Gospel According to John*, 199–202.

61. Burge, "Territorial Religion, Johannine Christology and the Vineyard of John 15," 389. Burge's study is based on the insights of Walter Brueggemann's and W. D. Davies' study of Israel's ideology of the land. See Brueggemann, *Land*; and Davies, *Territorial Dimension of Judaism*.

62. Burge, "Territorial Religion," 392. See also Köster, *Symbolism*, 244–47.

63. Burge, "Territorial Religion," 392.

64. Ibid., 393. Edward Casey instead argues that the Hebrew word *Makom*, the name for God, means precisely "place" and nothing more. Quoting rabbinical commentary on Genesis, Casey writes that God is called place because God is the place of the world, while the world is not his place. Cf. Edward Casey, *Getting Back into Place*, 17; and Smith,

The people of Israel cannot be rooted into the vineyard unless they are "grafted into Jesus" (John 15:6).[65] By "spiritualizing the land," Jesus becomes the place of God's promise, hence dislocating Judaism's identity with the land.[66] Burge understands place (land) as a physical reality. He does not consider that the physical and the spiritual space could converge or produce another place without dislocating identities. To him, the presence of one automatically dislocates the other, which does not give the possibility of a hybrid situation.

Influenced by Burge's work, Tod Swanson questions why Christians so often thought it permissible and even morally imperative to carry their message across all boundaries, invading the homelands of other communities. To Swanson, "unexamined Christian assumptions about space led to this crossing of boundaries and still serve as a lens through which historians of religion interpret the 'exotic' spaces of the post-colonial world." [67] Faced with a "rapture of social harmony as a result of separation from God," seen in the various "attachments of ethnic identities to sacred places," the Gospel of John, in line with the broader Hellenistic thinking regarding ethnic diversity and divine unity, "advances a Jesus, who, as the word of God, points to a spiritual place in the father's house, thereby putting an end to all the sacred topographies of the world and gathering people together under the one God in a community of the end times."[68] Such a radical project, carried out through reverse reenactments of foundational events by local heroes establishing ethnic differentiation and sacred places (John 4 and 6), yields a Christian claim to all territories. To Swanson, among the many texts, the clearest passage to this intent is Jesus' announcement to the Samaritans that true worship would no longer take place 'on this mountain' [Mt. Gerizim, the center of Samaritan identity], nor in Jerusalem [the center of Jewish identity], but in Spirit (John 4:21–23). The statement is "provocative because it posits the space-bound character of ethnic identity as something to be overcome in the newly opened placeless place of Johannine worship."[69] Such a statement has ethical implications, for "why would this particular Christian community want to abolish the privacy and polite distance by

---

To Take Place, 88.

65. Burge, "Territorial Religion," 393.

66. Ibid., 395.

67. Swanson, "To prepare a Place," 11–12.

68. Segovia, "Johannine Studies," 288–89.

69. Swanson, "To Prepare a Place," 14.

ethnic territories, and what were the ethical consequences of doing so?"[70] Such a claim bears enormous consequences such as the "disenfranchisement of natives who convert (the Samaritans) and charges of betrayal and murder against those who reject (the "Jews")."[71]

By abolishing private places, Swanson argues, "room for unity had actually shrunk, relatedness was asphyxiated and divisiveness exacerbated."[72] This legacy from the Fourth Gospel and Christian origins in general, was appropriated by the West in its own collapse of ethnic space within the historical project of colonialism: having no sense of its own distinctive ethnic space, it approached all other places as "mission fields," without a framework for mediating relations of respect, it sought to "over [run] the globe."[73]

It is precisely such a sense of universality and transplantation, rooted in early Christianity and central to the West, that underlies the project of morphological comparison of religions and the vision of a new humanism espoused by Eliade. Here the true meaning of place may be abstracted from local sacred places, which merely serve to shed light on "place" as a universal category of human imagination. The result of such endeavor is, again, a thorough co-opting of indigenous symbols, marked by the impoverishment of unity and a trampling of respect. Consequently, Swanson concludes, "the presence of place should be seen as irreplaceable and its meaning as not transferable—rituals are irreplaceable responses to irreplaceable places."[74]

Swanson's study discusses very elaborately and convincingly the ideology of spatial construction in John, establishing a direct link between John and the West, specifically in terms of the colonialist ideology of spatial construction—the devaluation of the local and the ethnic, and the overriding of all spaces and all peoples. By spiritualizing the land, the Johannine Jesus devalues the ethnic lands and suppresses diversity. There is need to insist that certain geographical spaces like land are irreplaceable. While appreciating the need to respect and promote diversity, the weakness of Swanson's conclusion is that it gives a fixed meaning to place. Rather, we could think of space as open to transformations in the context of the life experiences of diverse communities. Even the ethnic societies in question

70. Ibid.

71. Segovia, "Johannine Studies," 289.

72. Swanson, "To prepare a Place," 28.

73. Ibid., 29.

74. Ibid., 30–31.

continue to produce their space as they adjust to new life experiences. Reducing the spatial aspect of life to one discreet aspect of ontological reality (the physical) represents an incomplete definition of geography.

Place Superseded by Christ

Inspired by the works of Burge and Swanson, Jeffrey L. Staley explores the interconnections between geography and the reading of John. He reads John through the lens of his own autobiography, using his own childhood experience on a Navajo reservation. Central to his study is the concept of "dis-place" which he does not define but uses it in the sense of "displacement." Staley's own experience of displacement on a Navajo reservation within the United States is portrayed as what the Fourth Gospel represents within the Roman Empire. A concept like Burge's "spiritualization of place" makes it disturbing to Staley to hear the Johannine statement of "places superseded by Christ (John 4:21)."[75] He considers such a statement as typical of the rhetoric of an oppressor and exploiter. By "spiritualizing the land of Israel," (Burge) or "laying claim to all lands," (Swanson) the Johannine Jesus dis-places *place* hence "uprooting" the people from what is basic to them. Such agenda classifies as "colonialist" and "hegemonic." Staley instead suggests that John might be read as advancing a "postcolonial geography" that is neither "imperialistic" nor "territorial": a scenario in which all are victims of Rome, where no place is uniquely privileged as the site of divine presence and power, where all are dis-placed, and where God stands at the side of the oppressed."[76] Both Jesus and the Samaritan woman were under Roman domination. Thus, what one victim of oppression says to another is heard as a liberating voice.[77]

75. Referring to the United States politics of Navajo reservations, Staley observes that Burge's description of Johannine Christology with its "spiritualization of place" troubles him, as a person coming from a world in which European conquerors seized territory from Navajo people and renamed it St. John. He questions what it means to those whose territories have been conquered to hear a statement like, "place has been superseded by Christ." To Staley, upon hearing that "the place once called Jerusalem is now 'Aelia Capitolina,' or that the place once called 'Old Age River' or 'One with a Long Body' has now become the 'San Juan River,' how can one say to ancient or modern peoples that "place is unimportant and has been superseded by a spiritual reality that appears to be only tenuously connected to the physical world"? See Staley, "Politics of Place," 273. See also Staley, "Dis Place, Man," 43.

76. Staley, "Politics of Place," 275.

77. Ibid.

What Burge ignores about the "spiritualized place" is what Staley advances. Staley reads the text as a voice that is calling for liberation. Perhaps Staley could have moved further to indicate that communities divided over place are also being reminded that what divides them, i.e., place, does not really matter. This would demonstrate that Christ is the place where all divisions due to space are reconciled. In Staley's view, the Gospel of John can be approached not as a license for the dis-placement of all but as a witness to the liberation of all. It remains a conflicted Gospel, yet can be read politically, on behalf of the alienated and the dispossessed. Staley concludes that the Gospel of John should, however, be read with "resistance to its hard edges." Musa Dube does this in her "Reading for Decolonization (4:1–42)."[78]

Reading for Decolonization (John 4:1–42)

Dube defines "imperialism" and "decolonization," positing both imperial (expansionist) and decolonizing strategies within all imperial-colonial frameworks. She identifies decolonization as the "postcolonial impulse," and calls for analysis of textual productions along such lines, and for a reading of such production "with liberation in mind."[79] In Dube's definition of imperialism, whether ancient or modern, elements common to imperialism include the ideology of expansion, domination and subordination, yielding power struggles, suppression of diversity and promotion of universal standards. The postcolonial constitutes the decolonizing impulse, thus a socio-psychological category; that which "problematizes and resists imperialism." Decolonizing defines awareness of imperialism's exploitative forces and its various strategies of domination. It involves the conscious adoption of strategies of resisting imperial domination as well as the search for the alternative ways of "liberating interdependence" between nations, races, genders, economies and cultures.[80] In Dube's view, the biblical text is worth interpretation from a colonial perspective because, other than the imperial colonial context from which the text emerged, "history attests to the 'use' of biblical texts" as an imperializing text in Western imperial-colonial frameworks.[81] As such Dube recommends a twofold decolonizing

78. Dube, "Reading for Decolonization," 51–75.

79. Ibid., 60.

80. Ibid., 52, 68.

81. Ibid., 59–60.

strategy, namely a criticism attentive to the ideology of the texts themselves (issues of travel, space and power) and also the functions of the text in imperial projects (the issue of compatibility).

Focusing on John 4, Dube analyses the text as a "mission narrative,"[82] involving a native (Samaritan) woman, whereby the movement across geographical spaces is sanctioned and geopolitical power is deployed. She reads the text from the perspective of a "Motswana woman in Southern Africa," dealing "with the text's imperial settings, hidden interests, travelers, geography, lands, expansion, and the construction of the Samaritan woman/people/land."[83] The imperial setting involves occupation yielding "competition" and "power struggle" among local groups.[84] Expansionism is concealed in the Samaritan invitation. The assumed "superiority of Christianity" due to its association with Jesus the superior traveler, authorizes entering any space, teaching and controlling the natives.[85] The hierarchical construction of geographical spaces is very evident, in which some lands are much holier than others. Some lands like Samaria are characterized as negative, allowing Jesus, "characterized as savior to assert his religious superiority."[86] The Samaritan woman is characterized as inferior, and the faith of the people of Samaria is seen as invalid. The local is devalued, replaced, and suppressed by the global, the woman and land are equated as points of entry, and generic adaptation is seen in the inequality of betrothal. The result is a view of John 4 as imperializing, full of "rhetorical and literary strategies of domination" and "subordination" intertwined with patriarchal ideology.[87]

In Dube's view therefore, mission texts advance geopolitical relations of domination rather than of liberation and thus fit well into imperial-colonial projects. The task of a postcolonial critic is to read for decolonization: "read in a way that exposes the ethos of domination and the relations of power at work." Texts like John 4 should then be "resisted." Dube sees

82. In Dube's definition, a mission text is "one that authorizes its reader-believer to 'go forth,' so to speak." Ibid., 60.

83. Ibid., 61.

84. Ibid.

85. Ibid., 66–67.

86. Ibid., 68.

87. Ibid., 71.

"expansionism" at work. Is it possible that as Jesus breaks limiting separations, he also empowers the feminine as the Samaritan woman becomes a super-apostle?

Places Defining the Power of Jesus

Reading the biblical story as a travel narrative, Musa Dube and Jeffrey Staley discuss how the journeys to different places in the Gospel of John demonstrate the presence, role and power of Jesus. Looking at the prologue of John's Gospel (1:1–18), Dube and Staley observe that the protagonist of the Gospel, the Logos (Word/Jesus), is presented as very close to the only creator God: "the Word was God" and "everything was created through him." However, something is amiss because the world came into being through him (the Word), yet the world did not know him. He came to his own, and his own people did not accept him. But to all who received him, who believed in his name, he gave them the power to become the children of God (John 1:10–14).

Three things must be noted: first, the world does not know the Word; second, the Word's people did not receive him; and third, the Word embarks on a campaign of conferring hereditary rights on all those who believe in him.[88] To Dube and Staley, these images point to the fact that the Word is perhaps not as powerful as the narrator first claimed, for the Word descends from heaven into the world as an unknown and rejected traveler, which leaves many questions. There seems to be the intertwining of absolute power and peculiar powerlessness in the characterization of the Word. Could it be that Jesus' powerlessness provides the readers with a hint as to why he was first characterized as one who was "with God" and "as God," and "creator"? Is it merely a rhetorical claim of the power of Jesus? Can the readers completely rule out the possibility that the Word might be of a tragically dispossessed and forgotten creator? Whether powerful or powerless, the prologue's contradictions seem to signify the Word's/Jesus' struggle for power more than they signify his secured position.[89]

John, however, tends to emphasize the power of the Word. No one has ascended into heaven except the one who descended from heaven (3:13). Fernando Segovia remarks that by talking about origins, John explicitly draws the connection between places of origin and power; the one who

88. Dube and Staley, "Descending and Ascending," 6.
89. Ibid.," 6–7.

comes from above is above all, and the one who is of the earth belongs to the earth and speaks earthly things (3:31–32). Jesus' journeys from heaven to the earth and back into heaven highlight his power over earthly creatures, for the one who comes from above is above all.[90] As Dube and Staley observe, different spaces confer different levels of power over the occupants and travelers.[91] Heaven is the place of the highest power as compared to the earthly places and their occupants. Heaven thus confers unparalleled power to Jesus as compared to those who occupy earthly spaces.[92] The followers of Jesus are promised access to heaven (14:1–7), an event that Tat-Siong Benny Liew likens to "upward mobility."[93]

The occupants of the earth are characterized by the narrator as created by the Word, ignorant of their creator, as darkness, overcome by light, etc. (1:1–18). Dube and Staley thus remark that "the journey of the word from heaven to the earth is an assertion of power over space and time, over people, and over the earth. It is a claim of power where power is not granted and where power has been denied or lost."[94] The narrative of John therefore seems to be a "site of struggle for power, with Jesus claiming absolute power in all spaces and over all things through his pre-existent, creator status."[95] The same Jesus laments dispossession and rejection within his own created world.

While there is reason to look at Jesus' claim to power as imperialistic, it is credible to consider the Word's show of power as an attempt to regain power where it has been displaced, assumed or claimed by colonial powers. If the Word's origin manifests superiority, and the claim is that all was created through the Word, then the rejection of the Word by his own and the claim of superiority by the colonizing power could be seen as displacing the Word's identity. The Word's journey and claims of power could then be seen as an attempt to redefine true power. In this sense, titles that John used can be seen as the Word's reaction to the colonial masters, the Romans, whose emperors claim to be "sons of God" and "saviors of the world." In these titles, the Roman emperors claimed power over unlimited space. John

90. For details see Segovia, "Journey(s) of the Word," 23–25.
91. Dube and Staley, "Descending and Ascending," 7.
92. Ibid.
93. Liew, "Ambiguous Admittance," 193–224.
94. Dube and Staley, "Descending and Ascending," 8.
95. Ibid.

therefore presents Jesus as the one who is greater than the Roman emperor, as a Christ who is the real savior.

The above post-colonial survey of scholarly works interpreting John as a travel narrative discloses the making and distribution of power on different earthly places and how different travels of the world affect identity. Power is often unevenly distributed among the powerful and the powerless. Burge, Swanson, Staley and Musa Dube have noted how Johannine texts can empower certain travelers to invade foreign places, how the movements of these travelers can dislocate identities of the inhabitants of the places they travel to, and how these foreign people can read John's Gospel for decolonization.

The historical and postcolonial critics cited above discussed John's use of place, the latter going even further by looking at John's construction of place. However, all these authors, with the exception of Umoh, limit their understanding of place to geographical markers such as cities, regions, territories, homes, houses, rooms, etc. Their understanding of space is limited to physical realities. There is a need to develop a more comprehensive geographical analysis which would be sensitive to more implicit geographical information carried within the texts, and to how such geographical information shapes the text or constructs meaning. The spatial theory of Henri Lefebvre and Edward Soja will provide this critical tool.

Theoretical Framework for a Postcolonial Spatial Reading

Having determined the extent of postcolonial and *place* studies in John, we define the methods of interpretation that will be used in this essay. The study will incorporate social and political theories of space, socio-scientific approaches and postcolonial theories.

Henri Lefebvre's Spatial Theory

In English, the word *place* is commonly used to refer to a building or a location, a site of significance, a landscape, an environment, a home, city, region or territory. In his work, *The Production of Space*,[96] Henri Lefebvre invites us to think differently about place. He proposes an understanding of space that goes beyond the physical locations to include mental and social space.

96. Lefebvre, *Production of Space*.

Lefebvre's theory of space influenced current political and social theories of geography, especially Edward Soja's *Thirdspace*.

Lefebvre began by challenging "the lure of binarism," the compacting of meaning into a closed either/or opposition between two terms, concepts, or elements. Whenever faced with binary opposed categories such as subject–object, mental–material, natural–social, bourgeois–proletariat, local–global, center–periphery, agency–structure, Lefebvre sought to break them open by introducing an-Other term. This third possibility, or "moment," partakes of the original pairing but is not just a simple combination or an "in-between" position; it is "more than the sum of the two parts."[97] This is the first and most important step in transforming the categorical and closed logic of binary oppositions into the dialectically open logic of both and also.

To Lefebvre, the first concern of spatial thinking is the physical, which includes nature and the cosmos; secondly, he considers the mental, which is comprised of logical and formal abstractions; and thirdly, he looks at the social, which is the space of social practice and the space occupied by sensory phenomena, including products of the imagination like projects and projections, symbols and utopias.[98]

He argues that "space is a social product" or a "complex social construction," based on values and the social production of meanings that affect spatial practices and perceptions. Each space is produced and serves a purpose; and each wears out and/or is consumed, sometimes unproductively, sometimes productively."[99] When the social production of space is commanded by a hegemonic class, it is a tool for reproducing its dominance. The space that is produced "serves as a tool of thought and of action; ... in addition to being a means of production it is also a means of control, and hence of domination, of power."[100] Every society—and therefore every mode of production—produces a certain space, its own space. The city of the ancient world cannot be understood as a simple agglomeration of people and things in space: it had its own spatial practice, making its own space (which was suitable for itself—Lefebvre argues that the intellectual climate of the city in the ancient world was very much related to the social production of its spatiality). Since every society produces its own space, any

97. Soja, *Thirdspace: Journeys*, 31.
98. Ibid., 11–12.
99. Lefebvre, *Production of Space*, 403.
100. Ibid., 26.

"social existence aspiring to be or declaring itself to be real, but not producing its own space, would be a strange entity, a very peculiar abstraction
incapable of escaping the ideological or even cultural spheres."[101] In other
words, "new social relations demand new social space and vice-versa."[102]

Lefebvre holds that social space is not an inert, neutral, or pre-existent
given, but rather an on-going production of spatial relations. He writes
thus: "social space is not a thing among other things, nor a product among
other products: rather, it subsumes things produced and encompasses their
interrelationships in their coexistence and simultaneity—their (relative)
order and/or (relative) disorder."[103]

By way of summary, Lefebvre puts forward a three-part schema for
understanding space: the physical space which is the perceived space, the
mental space which is the conceived space and the social space which is the
lived space. The threefold schema is based on his understanding of the need
for an "Other" in a world which accentuates dyads. It is this introduced
third "Other" that has much influenced Soja's thirdspace.

Edward Soja's Thirdspace

Lefebvre's insistence on the need for a third term, the "Other," influenced
what has become Soja's "thirdspace." Soja's trialectic of spatiality presumes
that binary oppositions can be disordered, deconstructed, and tentatively
reconstructed if they are "spatialized," that is, if their position within a production of space is properly recognized. The result will be third ways which
are both similar and strikingly different."[104] To Soja, "thirding" produces
what might be called a cumulative trialectics that is radically open to ad-
ditional Othernesses, to a continuing expansion of spatial knowledge.[105]

101. Ibid., 59.

102. Based on this argument, Lefebvre criticized Soviet urban planners, on the basis
that they failed to produce a socialist space, having just reproduced the modernist model
of urban design (interventions on physical space, which were insufficient to grasp social
space) and applied it onto that context: "Change life! Change Society! These precepts
meant nothing without the production of an appropriate space. A lesson to be learned
from soviet constructivists from the 1920s and 30s, and of their failure, is that new social
relations demand a new space, and vice-versa." Ibid.

103. Ibid., 73.

104. Soja, *Thirdspace: Journeys*, 61.

105. Ibid.

Soja uses three categories for understanding space, namely firstspace, secondspace, and thirdspace. He observes that all excursions into third-space begin with the ontological restructuring, with the presupposition that being-in-the world is essentially definable as being simultaneously historical, social and spatial, (i.e., that human beings are "first and always historical-social-spatial beings, actively participating individually and collectively in the construction/production—the 'becoming'—of histories, geographies, and societies").[106] In the same way, in discussing the epistemology of space, we have to overcome the double illusion that bracketed the accumulation of spatial knowledge into two distinctive modes of producing spatial knowledge, namely, the physical (the firstspace) and the mental (secondspace). Then we can consider the introduction of the "Other," the imagined (thirdspace).

Firstspace focuses attention primarily on the "analytical deciphering" of what Lefebvre called spatial practice or perceived space. It refers to a material and materialized "physical" spatiality that is directly comprehended in empirically measurable configurations. It is experiential, empirical, and refers to external, material spatiality, to the privileging of objectivity and materiality, and to "the concrete and mappable geographies of our life worlds." It is the building that is constructed or a land that is demarcated. Firstspace has well-defined boundaries. This is the "realm of conventional geography and the locus for toponymy," but, in itself, this perceived space provides an incomplete and partial understanding of the world.[107]

Secondspace refers to the theoretical. Soja's secondspace is "mental projections into the empirical world from conceived or imagined geographies," the privileging of a "world of rationally interpretable signification." It goes beyond the building that one sees to what the building represents. It is the interpretative locale of the creative artist and artful architect, visually or literally re-presenting the world in the image of their subjective imaginaries.[108] Secondspace is articulated, for example, in design, written text, or architectural plans. It is space that is conceived by "the order and design" it imposes on us.[109] In secondspace, the imagined geography tends to become

106. Ibid., 73.

107. Ibid., 74–75.

108. Ibid., 79.

109. Soja, *Thirdspace: Journeys*, 67. When one looks at a building or monument in a city, it is always a representation of something. Looking at a church, it is a representation of the religious, social and political life of a people. The image that it imposes on the observer is the secondspace.

the "real" geography as the image or representation comes to define and order the reality.

According to Soja, modernist thoughts exhibit a "persistent tendency . . . to see firstspace and secondspace as together defining the whole of the geographical imagination, as encompassing in their varying admixtures all possible ways of conceptualizing and studying human geography and the spatiality of human life."[110]

Thirdspace refers to imagination—the creative. It arises from the sympathetic deconstruction and heuristic reconstitution of firstspace-secondspace duality, what Soja refers to as "thirding as ordering."[111] In other words, thirdspace perspective opens up renewed ways of thinking about space, seeking to "break out from the constraining big dichotomy by introducing an-Other."[112] Thirdspace generates "an-Other form of spatial awareness," denying dualism by examining spaces as "simultaneously real [Firstspace], imagined [Secondspace] and more [both and also . . .]."[113] It is the space that transcends, yet includes both firstspace and secondspace. In this manner the dialectic of history and sociality is "spatialized," thereby becoming a trialectic. In Soja's understanding, thirdspace is not designed just to critique firstspace and secondspace modes of thought, but also to reinvigorate their approaches to spatial knowledge with new possibilities. Thirdspace hence "becomes what eternity is to time, the limitless space,"[114] what Lefebvre once called "the city, a possible machine; or a recasting Proust, a Madeleine for a *recherche des espace perdus*, a remembrance-rethinking-recovery of spaces lost . . . or never sighted at all."[115]

To Soja, any one location can and should be analyzed for its manifestations of all three kinds of space. The thirdspace, as other, continually

---

110. Soja, "Thirdspace: Expanding," 267.

111. Soja, *Thirdspace: Journeys*, 81.

112. Soja, "Thirdspace: Expanding," 268.

113. Sleeman, *Geography and Ascension*, 44–45; Soja, *Thirdspace: Journeys*, 11.

114. Soja describes the thirdspace thus: "everything comes together in Thirdspace: subjectivity and objectivity, the abstract and the concrete, the real and the imagined, the knowable and the unimaginable, the repetitive and the differential, structure and agency, mind and body, consciousness and the unconscious, the disciplined and the trans-disciplinary, everyday life and unending history . . . each envisions a complex totality of potential knowledge but rejects any 'totalization' that finitely encloses knowledge production in 'permanent structures' or specialized compartments/disciplines." See Soja, *Thirdspace: Journeys*, 56–57.

115. Lefebvre, *Production of Space*, 26–27.

undermines any claim of a settled firstspace-secondspace binary relationship, and opens up new ways of seeing space, being in space, and ordering space, provoking an "Other world(s) . . . space 'beyond' what is presently known and taken for granted."[116] By its nature, thirdspace is a perspective, a means of reading space, of doing "geography." Third place is found in the lived space of "everyday life" which is place filled with meaning, emotion, and struggle.[117] It is politically-charged space that resists the power plays and closures of materialist firstspace and ideational secondspace, being space wherein alternative territorialities and world views are explored. In Soja's thoughts, thirdspace must be guided by "some form of potentially emancipator praxis, the translation of knowledge into action in a conscious—and consciously spatial—effort to improve the world in some significant way."[118] This should not, however, endow thirdspace with a naïve, inherently positive ethic, as "geographical imaginations" can be expanded for good or ill. The geographer Susan Smith comments: "not all borders and margins are radical and open 'thirdspaces.'"[119]

Both Lefebvre and Soja employ a three part schema of understanding space. Soja's firstspace relates to the realm of experience in Lefebvre's perceived space (the physical space). Soja's secondspace concerns the perception of space—the theoretical space which relates to Lefebvre's conceived space (the mental space). Soja's thirdspace refers to the imagination, the creative life realm which relays Lefebvre's lived space (the social space).

Illustrating Social Space and Thirdspace

Lefebvre invites us to a geographical reading in which "an overriding emphasis is given to spatiality of action, objects, laws, semiotic codes, economic

116. Soja, *Thirdspace: Journeys*, 34; See also "Thirding as Othering", 60–70.

117. Soja, *Thirdspace: Journeys*, 40; footnote 18. Soja observes that Lefebvre rarely used the concept of "place" in his writings, largely because its richest meaning is effectively captured in his combined use of "everyday life" and "lived space." Many cultural geographers have persistently attempted to separate the concepts of place and space and to give place greater concreteness, immediacy and cultural effect, while space is deemed to be abstract, distanced, and ethereal. As Lefebvre's work demonstrates, this is an unnecessary separation/distinction that reduces the meaningfulness of both space and place.

118. Soja, *Thirdspace: Journeys*, 22.

119. Smith, "Cultural Politics of Difference," 147.

processes and cultural practices."[120] An example is Shields' analysis of the action of a protest march in terms of:

> Spatial manifestations (matching bodies, direction, masses of people), objects (truncheons, individual bodies versus the crowd, 'lines' of police), laws (restrictions on free assemblies, rules governing highways, codes of behavior, semiotic codes of behavior), economic processes (the dependence of merchants on orderly conduct and access via streets) and cultural practices (the unusual character of pedestrians blocking traffic and even walking).[121]

Such an approach might bring to light neglected opportunities for political advantage, or it might make the marchers themselves aware of the manner in which the march could be regarded as a utopian form of collective unity, highlighting the contrast between armed representatives of the state confronting the citizenry.

Elden criticizes Soja for creating neologisms for their own sake and for focusing too narrowly on Los Angeles,[122] yet illustrating Soja's schema helps clarify its processes and wider analytic and interpretative applicability. Sang-Kyu Park offers the Lincoln memorial building in Washington D.C. as an example.[123] Considering this building as firstspace, one notices the physical structure, the type of materials used in the construction, the interplay of light and shadows. Tourists visit this place because of what it signifies, which is the secondspace. Being at this place gives a sense of America's history of slavery, the great loss of life in civil war, and the later civil rights movement in the 20th century. Thinking trialectically, thirdspace is realized on that great day in 1963 when this location became the destination of thousands of people, both black and white, as they marched to Washington demanding an end to racial discrimination. The place hence became a "symbol of radical openness and unlimited possibilities."[124] As Martin Luther King, Jr. delivered the "I have a dream" speech while black and white people joined hands and sang "We shall overcome," a thirdspace was created.

---

120. Shields, *Lefebvre, Love and Struggle*, 151.

121. Shields, *Lefebvre*, 151.

122. Elden, "What About Huddersfield," 47–48, and Elden, "Politics, Philosophy, Geography," 809–25. For Sharp criticism see Robert Lake, "Postmodern Urbanism," 393–95.

123. Park, *Spatial Eschatology*, 119–20.

124. Ibid., 120.

A biblical example of thirdspace is seen in Victor Matthew's presentation of the threshing floor of ancient Israel as functioning within the OT as more than simply a place of agricultural production. It assumes thirdspatial connotations, becoming 'a place of covenants and provision for the poor, where the old world comes to an end and a new one begins.[125]

Interpreting John's account of Jesus' death and resurrection spatially, I would see the physical body of Jesus (bodily space) as firstspace. Jesus dies and is buried (John 19: 28–40). The resurrection narrative shows that Jesus' body is absent from the tomb. Christ's bodily absence from the tomb creates a second space, the space of absence. The people who appear at the tomb seek to understand the significance of this absence. The absent Jesus is presented as actively guiding his people; hence, he appears to Mary Magdalene and to the disciples. Christ is active and absent, but he cannot be reduced to these poles. Such irreducibility reflects the "and more" which is constitutive of thirdspace. The resurrected body functions "thirdspatially" in that it cannot be limited by physical structures like the shut doors. It is a new bodily space, capable of new possibilities like passing through walls, thereby disrupting the old and dominant ways of thinking about physical bodies.

The question of space and place is as ancient as the world. Just as in first century Greek literature, today we still understand place as indicating geographical markers, bodily space, topics in a book, occasions for someone to do something, and positions of responsibility. The Johannine scholarship on place examined above also looked at geography in terms of physical places and nature. While not underrating the values of the Johannine scholarship discussed above, the scholars' understanding of place is limited in scope, reducing place to physical structures or geographical markers. These studies consider place as the reservoir of resources, the medium in which strategies are applied, and the disinterested stage or setting of action.

Modern geographical theories challenge us to read geographies in new ways. More than physical geographies, social and political geographies invite us to look at the lived experiences in these places, to consider that places in a narrative are not merely geographical facts but are literary elements in which fundamental significance is embodied. In the words of Joel Green, "geographical markers are not neutral or objective, but are social

---

125. Sleeman, *Geography and Ascension*, 48.

products that reflect and configure ways of understanding the world."[126] Geographical locations may constitute profoundly important social products that reflect and configure ways of understanding the world the author is portraying. As Mieke Bal comments, place should be "thematized," whereby rather than functioning simply as a frame or a place of action, space becomes "an object of presentation itself, for its own sake"—an "acting place" rather than the place of action.[127] Reading the Fourth Gospel's account of the death of Jesus through the lenses of Lefebvre and Soja will not simply be a matter of citing geographical theories but rather of developing renewed readings of John made possible by their insights. The study will also incorporate postcolonial theories discussed below.

Chinua Achebe and his Postcolonial Theories

The struggle for power is a reality in both the contemporary and ancient worlds. It neither started with colonialism nor is it limited to colonial settings. It is evident among individuals and collectively among groups, societies and nations. In a colonial setting there are always contested relationships between the colonized, the collaborators and the colonizers. Power on colonized earthly spaces is always unevenly wielded between the colonizer and the colonized, and even among segments of the colonized people themselves.

The New Testament texts, written mostly in the first century, "originate in a world dominated by the Roman Empire."[128] Reading these texts while rethinking the colonial ambience in which the various books were written includes observing the influence of the imperial domination in the passages. I discuss the political theories of Chinua Achebe's *Things Fall Apart* in order to elaborate a theoretical framework for understanding the struggle for power in John's narrative of the death of Jesus. John tells the story, portraying conflict at various levels and in diverse spaces in its Roman imperial context. Achebe's novel exposes colonial ideology in which honor and power are understood as domination. It also highlights colonial ambivalence and contradictions of life under imperialism as well as the various forms of imperial attitudes such as ideologies of disinterest, superior

---

126. Green, *Gospel of Luke*, 426n99.

127. Bal, *Narratology*, 95–96.

128. Carter, *Roman Empire*, 1.

knowledge, inferior subjects, and hierarchical construction of geographical places.

Imperialism is "an ideology of expansion that takes diverse forms and methods at different times in history, seeking to impose its languages, trades, religions, images, economic systems and political rule on foreign nations and lands."[129] The victims of imperialism are the colonized, i.e., those whose lands, minds, cultures, economies and political institutions have been possessed and rearranged according to the interests and values of the imperializing powers.[130] Imperialism is about controlling certain geographical spaces and their inhabitants. By its practice and goal, imperialism is a relation of subordination and domination between different nations and lands. It actively suppresses diversity and promotes a few universal standards for the benefit of the colonial power. Generally, the colonized react to imperialism in three ways: by fighting back, by collaborating with the colonizer, and through conflict among the different segments of the colonized people. The particulars of such conflicts are discussed here below.

Honor and Power as Domination

In his novel *Things Fall Apart*,[131] Achebe tells two intertwined stories centered on Okonkwo, an Ibo man from Umuofia village in Nigeria. The first is an ancient story of the conflict between the individual and society, tracing Okonkwo's fall from grace in the tribal world. The second concerns the clash of cultures and the destruction of Okonkwo's world with the arrival of the aggressive European colonialists.

Okonkwo is described as a strong man "whose fame rested on solid personal achievements."[132] Unlike his "lazy father" Unoka, Okonkwo has risen to great heights in his society as a champion wrestler and a fierce fighter at battles. He is a wealthy man due to his successful farming of yams, the staple crop of his village. He has a "place among the nine masked spirits who administered justice in the clan."[133] He has three wives and several children. Right from the beginning of the story, we are presented with a society in which honor and shame are pivotal values which everyone up-

129. Maunier, *Sociology of Colonies*, 133.
130. Mudimbe, *Invention of Africa*, 1–2.
131. Achebe, *Things Fall Apart*.
132. Ibid., 3.
133. Ibid., 171.

holds. Okonkwo's honor is by achievement. He rose to great heights despite being born of a father who was a non-achiever (shame). As a result of his success, he won even more honor by attaining much material success and getting public offices.

Because of his fame (honor), the clan had selected him as a guardian of Ikemefuna, a boy taken prisoner by the tribe as a peace settlement between two villages. Ikemefuna would stay with Okonkwo until the oracle decided what was to be done with the boy. For three years, Ikemefuna lived with Okonkwo's family. The family grew fond of him; he also grew fond of them. He considered Okonkwo his father. The oracle then decreed that the boy be killed, but the oldest man in the village warned Okonkwo "to have nothing to do with the murder of Ikemefuna" for the boy was now his own child.[134] Fearful of being considered softhearted and weak, Okonkwo participated in the killing of the boy despite the warning. For Okonkwo and his society, being softhearted is not only a weakness but a shame. His attempt to save his fame, however, marked a turning point in Okonkwo's life.

Shortly after Ikemefuna's death, Okonkwo accidentally killed Ezeudu's sixteen year old son at a funeral ceremony when his gun inadvertently went off. As a punishment, Okonkwo and his family were exiled from his village for seven years. While Okonkwo was in exile, white people began coming to Umuofia introducing Christianity and a new government. When Okonkwo returned to the village, it was no longer the same as the colonialists had control of every aspect of the life of the people of Umuofia.

Together with other tribal leaders, Okonkwo tried to regain control of the village by destroying a local Christian church, but this led them into more trouble. The leader of the white government had Okonkwo and the elders arrested and taken prisoner, tortured and then released only when the village paid the required ransom. Torture of elders was the climax of dishonor shown both to the elders and to the society. The people of Umuofia were finally angered by this humiliation and ridicule of the native leaders. They not only paid the ransom but planned an uprising against the colonial government. This would take place at a village meeting. When messengers of the white government arrived to try to stop the Umuofian meeting, Okonkwo killed one of them, but the other attendants of the meeting let the other messengers escape. To Okonkwo this was a failure on the side of the Umuofians, an indication that they would not fight for their liberation. The

134. Ibid., 57.

days when men were men was gone, all was lost for the Ibo tribe. Okonkwo returned home and hung himself.

What stands out in this novel is the theme of colonial disruption leading to the disintegration and eventual collapse of the traditions and ways of life of Umuofia. However, a more overarching subject is the theme of power and the violence that shape both the traditional life of Okonkwo's Umuofia as well as the colonial regime that seeks to 'civilize' Umuofia. Reading through this lens, Katongole writes that *Things Fall Apart* "serves as an incisive social commentary, with Umuofia and Okonkwo as characters that depict the society formed by a definition of power as domination and invincibility." A society built on this definition of power and strength is "drawn into an ongoing drama of violence in which not only the weak are sacrificed, but the 'strong' themselves get consumed by their own violence."[135]

It is ironic that Okonkwo, who had lived under a dominating vision of strength and power, ends his life by committing suicide. In Umuofia, suicide is considered a sign of weakness, the very reality that Okonkwo hated and feared. But, given the role of the story in creating assumptions, Okonkwo's suicide comes as no surprise. It is clear from the story that Okonkwo's life is shaped by a vision of power. Right from the beginning of the book, Okonkwo is portrayed as a great wrestler, and throughout the story his ambition is to be the greatest warrior. He had no consideration for those whom he considered weak. He despised his father Unoka as a lazy flute player who had won no titles and who was only skillful in the art of conversation.

His upbringing in Umuofia might have shaped Okonkwo's attitude. The stories told in Umuofia are the stories of ancestors when "men were real men." It is a culture that applauds warrior virtues and worries about the show of affection, for affection is a sign of weakness that only women and children display. The ideal in Umuofia is to be a "real man."[136] Stories told in Umuofia are stories of conquest, domination, and invincibility. These stories are "masculine" stories of invasion and conquest, war and bloodshed. In Umuofia, patriarchy and the vision of power as domination go hand in hand, since at its core patriarchy reflects an inability to be at home with virtues such as affection, gentleness, receptivity, and rest, which are considered feminine.[137]

135. Katongole, *Sacrifice of Africa*, 126.
136. Ibid.
137. Ibid., 127.

It is also important to note that Okonkwo's life was dominated by fear. This fear of being considered weak or a failure propelled his drive for success. It was a deep-seated fear of being like his father. Achebe leads the reader to understand how, due to this fear, Okonkwo had become a man with a fiery temper, impatient with less successful people, and unable to tolerate what he saw as weakness in others. Okonkwo ruled his household with a heavy hand. His family lived in perpetual fear of his angry temper.[138]

A number of observations can be made: First, it is ironic that fear dominates the life of a man who is "the greatest warrior." This observation is telling for, like Okonkwo, those who live under pressure to be "the most powerful" or "the strongest" (person, nation, society, church),[139] live in constant fear of failure and of weakness. So in Umuofia, both the weak and strong lived in constant fear. Okonkwo participated in the killing of Ikemefuna because of his fear of being considered weak. Okonkwo's fellow warriors also "lived in constant fear," even though they "mask their fear in a show of manliness" and "find ways to drown their fear through endless entertainments like wrestling, drinking palm wine, and sniffing tobacco."[140]

Second, like any society built on this vision of power, in Umuofia the weak and the innocent are readily sacrificed. Okonkwo kills Ikemefuna. Even though it is an offence to kill a kinsman in Umuofia, women and children are constantly beaten and abused; also twins are abandoned—all following the seemingly high ideals such as "honoring the ancestors" and

138. In the fourth chapter of *Things Fall Apart*, Achebe relates how Okonkwo brusquely cut down an untitled man who interrupted him during a clan meeting, telling the man, "This meeting is for men." It was Okonkwo's temper that caused him to transgress the "Week of Peace" by beating up his youngest wife, Ojiugo, when she spent too long doing her hair and missed setting out dinner for her husband and kids. For that transgression Ezeani, priest of the earth goddess, fined him "one she-goat, one hen, a length of cloth and a hundred cowries." During preparations for the New Yam festival, a restless Okonkwo had found an outlet for his restlessness by beating up his second wife, Ekwefi. And when she made a snide comment about his marksmanship following that beating, he had, in a rage, turned his gun on her and fired. Ekwefi had escaped by scampering over a half wall before Okonkwo's gun discharged. See Achebe, *Things Fall Apart*, 13, 26–35 and 39.

139. Achebe's depiction of Umuofia seems to confirm what we see among modern nations as well. It seems to confirm that modern nation states—not only super powers like the United States, but all nations—are built on a vision of power as dominion and invincibility. The desire of all nations is to be "the greatest, the most powerful, the most successful or the most advanced nation, which means that even small nations like Uganda are born with the soul of an empire." See Katongole, *Sacrifice of Africa*, 129.

140. Ibid., 127.

"the protection of the law of the land." But violence consumes not only the weak; in the end, violence destroys even those who wield it.

The new order established by colonialism sends a message of power in their communication with Umuofia and maintains its power through violence. This is clear from the District Commissioner's constant reference to the queen as "the most powerful ruler in the world,"[141] and the indiscriminate use of violence against the tribal chiefs by the District Commissioner's assistants. The colonial order conceals and justifies its violence using terms such as "civilization," "progress," or "democracy." The irony of its violence is seen in the title of the book the District Commissioner is thinking about writing: "The Pacification of the Primitive Tribes of the lower Niger."[142] In this title the colonial leader's ideology of disinterest is in full play. He conceals imperial interest and presents it as a duty to the natives. It is to their advantage that the colonial power pacify them even through violent means. In the many years in Umuofia, the commissioner "had toiled to bring civilization to different parts of Africa."[143] By calling the tribes "primitive," he also identifies them as preliterate, uncivilized, savage. Such is the rhetoric of superior travelers claiming the natives as ignorant.

Colonial Ambivalence and Contradictions of Life under Imperialism

The fear of Okonkwo as the people prepare for the village meeting is about the divided village and the double life of the colonized people. The life of the people of Umuofia is marked by uncertainties and fluctuations, ambiguities and inconsistencies. This community uses the safety measure of silence or masked talks in the presence of the colonial master and expresses its real feelings on issues in the absence of the imperialist. Okonkwo's hope was that the corporeal torture of the elders would wake up the sleeping Umuofia. Okonkwo knows that the greatest obstacle in Umuofia is the coward Egonwanne, whose "sweet tongue can change fire into cold ash." His speech is said to move men "to impotence," and his wisdom is described as "womanish" because he convinces the people against war, for he says that their fathers "never fought a war of blame."[144]

141. Achebe, *Things Fall Apart*, 194.

142. Ibid., 209.

143. Ibid., 208.

144. Ibid., 200.

A remarkable thing about the dominated people is that their discourse is much shaped by space. Space is defined by the presence or the absence of the dominator. Their discourse in the presence of their master constitutes survival tactics. Their performance in the presence of the powerful is influenced by prudence, fear, and the desire to win favor. Because of this, it is shaped to appeal to the expectations of the powerful. Ideological resistance was disguised, muted and veiled for the safety of the people. This is what James Scott calls "public transcript."[145] Public transcript describes "an open interaction between subordinates and those who dominate," the visible expression of power relations encoded in a particular group's accepted codes of behavior.[146] Crudely put, public transcript is "the self-portrait of dominant elites as they would have themselves seen."[147] By their power they compel performances from others. The discourse of the subordinates is therefore designed to be impressive, to affirm and naturalize the power of the elites, and to conceal or euphemize the dirty linen of their rule. As such, the public life of the dominated people involves acting in a way that supports a social system that is detrimental to one's own well-being, a system that one would like to change immediately. The disparity between what is spoken in the presence of power and unspoken hidden feelings is a rough measure of what has been suppressed.

This worries Okonkwo who realizes that "worthy men are no more," meaning by that men who stood for what is right without fear and fought for their village. The days "when men were men" was over, meaning that public performance has taken the place of sincerity, fortitude and fighting for the truth.[148] Only a few people like Okonkwo are bold enough to say out the truth even when it hurt, but even Okonwo and the elders who many times fought for their village would sometimes prefer silence to save their backs. The people of Umuofia are divided, others have for various reasons supported the intruders. This division is evident in Okika's speech at the village meeting that a good number have "deserted" the community and joined a stranger to soil their fatherland." [149]

In the absence of their colonial masters, the mask of loyalty of the dominated people is lifted, and the real feelings that operate behind the

145. Scott, *Domination*, 2.
146. Ibid.
147. Ibid., 18.
148. Achebe, *Things Fall Apart*, 200.
149. Ibid., 203.

master's back are exposed. Here words of anger are heard, statements indicating revenge are uttered, and the true feelings of the dominated are revealed. This is what Scott characterizes as what takes place "offstage," beyond direct observation by the dominator, referred to as "hidden transcript."[150] It consists of those offstage speeches, gestures, and practices that confirm, contradict, or inflect what appears in public transcript. This is what power dynamics produces in the discourse of the dominated people. By assessing the discrepancies between the public transcript and the hidden transcript, we realize the impact of domination on public discourse.[151]

Things Fall Apart shows this double life of colonized people. Confrontations between the dominated (the powerless) and the dominator (the powerful) are laden with deception; the powerless feign deference and the powerful subtly assert their mastery. The dominated people are not free to speak their minds in the presence of power. These subordinate groups instead create a secret discourse that represents a critique of power spoken behind the backs of the dominant. At the same time, the powerful also develop a private dialogue about practices and goals of their rule that cannot be openly avowed. Achebe describes the ideological resistance of Umuofia village: their silence, which could indicate fear as a survival tactic yet could also be a gesture of defiance. The gossips, folktales, songs, jokes, and use of anonymity and ambiguity by the people of Umuofia are all means of ideological resistance and survival tactics. He also analyzes how ruling elites attempt to convey an impression of hegemony through such devices as parades, threats of annihilation, heavy fines for any sign of rebellion, state ceremony, proclaiming the greatness of the queen, and rituals of subordination and apology.

As seen above, Chinua Achebe analyzes, among many things, the struggle for power in an imperial setting. Aspects of Achebe's postcolonial writing include violence as a tool of the imperial power, language of power and power as invincibility, and the marginality and the double life of the colonized people. Reading John's narrative of the death of Jesus through Achebe's lens will throw more light on the conversations that take place in diverse socio-political spaces in the decision to kill Jesus, his arrest, trial and the crucifixion.

150. Scott, *Domination*, 4.
151. Ibid., 4–5.

Conclusion

Our survey of space-scholarship in John's Gospel has shown that scholars limited their understanding of space to physical locations. We observed the need for a more comprehensive approach to geography which embraces places as physical, mental and social. This is what Lefebvre's and Soja's theories of space will provide. Spatial theories will disclose a wider spatiality in John than has been previously identified. The survey also reveals that the Roman colonial context of John's Gospel has been treated but not in a sustained and systematic fashion. In the words of Fernando Segovia, Rome hovers in the background "as a massive yet unattended presence."[152] By incorporating postcolonial and social-science approaches in this study, I will locate the death of Jesus in the cultural and socio-political world of the first century and carry forward the conversation on how directly or indirectly the Gospel of John addresses the Roman imperial presence. By locating the story within the socio-political space of struggle against domination enlightened by Achebe's postcolonial writing, I will show that John's formulation of the story of the death of Jesus contained responses to the Roman Empire and will identify the cross (crucifixion space) as the Johannine thirdspace of political liberation.

152. Segovia, "Johannine Studies," 284.

CHAPTER 3

Spatializing the Decision to Kill Jesus

(John 11:45–57)

Introduction

John's story of the plot to kill Jesus demonstrates multiple power struggles as the characters journey through diverse political spaces. Jesus journeys from heaven to earth (a spatial journey), claiming absolute power and exceptional status of being above all (3:31). Despite this claim to power, he is not accepted by the inhabitants of the earth, who are described as his own (1:10). The Romans also cross boundaries (another spatial reference) into the indigenous Palestinian land. This leads to contested relationships (a reference to power) between the colonizers, the colonized, and among the colonized themselves. Leaders in Jerusalem, uneasy allies of Rome, live in anxiety as they balance their interests, the interests of their population, and the interests of their colonial master. Seeking to avoid any action that would instigate a larger Roman invasion and clampdown, the authorities perceive Jesus' popularity as a threat to their place and their nation and they decide to kill Jesus to mitigate the impending danger.

This chapter investigates the power dynamics that occur in various political spaces in John's narrative of the decision to kill Jesus (11:45–57). It argues that Jesus' signs construct various political spaces in order to destabilize the power of Rome and its allies. As a result of this destabilization, the political elite executes Jesus, however, even in his death, Jesus transforms the socio-political space by remaking the children of God into a global community.

The Socio-Political Context of Jesus' Signs

Interpreting Jesus' "signs" (σημεῖα) in John through their Roman imperial context of the late-first and early-second century CE provides insight into the political and spatial struggles of that time. It is also an opening into the effects of empire on the daily social and political life of Johannine Christians. This context includes the Roman imperial ideologies vis-à-vis those of the Jerusalem elite, as well as the Galilean peasantry's ideologies and interests, each of which will be considered separately in this section.

Rome's imperial ideological claims rested on the favor of the gods. Rome pronounced that it was "chosen by the gods, especially Jupiter, to manifest gods' rule, will and blessings, to show their presence and favor throughout the world, and rule an empire without end."[1] On this basis, it claimed sovereignty over all spaces. The ideology also implied a right to domination and power, along with a belief in Rome's superiority. Bruce Malina describes the unifying function of such ideology thus: "Religion forms the meaning system of a society and, as such, feeds back and forward into kinship, economic, and political systems, unifying the whole by means of some explicit or implicit ideology."[2] Such ideology meant the control of all spaces: the control of land by expropriation (e.g. through military force),[3] the control of bodies that worked the land by means of the poll tax (tribute capitals) and cheap labor, the control of the social structure through fear, and the control of temples and cults in order to legitimize imperial rule and the divine right to do so. It also included a legal system that exercised bias towards the elite by employing punishment appropriate not for the crime, but for the social status of the accused.[4] These political ideologies were clearly and broadly communicated through various media: coins, handheld billboards, proclamations in market places via images of

1. Van Eck, "Jesus and Violence," 112.

2. Malina, *Social Gospels of Jesus*, 16.

3. Gedaliah Alon observes that Emperor Vespasian (69–79 CE) decreed that all land in Palestine were his personal property, and could order them to be sold. See Alon, *Jews in their Land*, 1:6.

4. A detailed list is found in Freyne, "Urban-Rural Relations," 75–91. See also Horsley, *Jesus and the Spiral of Violence*, 15–34.

imperial figures, gods and goddesses, festivals announcing the birth of the emperor, and powerful imposing imperial buildings.[5]

With the destruction of the temple, the post-70 CE meant not only the loss of a house of prayer, but also of a center of identity, authority, and financial power, as well as a range of institutions and procedures connected with it. The Roman occupation of Judaea had huge consequences in terms of economy and land ownership. Furthermore, there were a lot of persecutions, apostasy and collaboration with the occupiers all of which disrupted society.[6]

The Jerusalem aristocracy was also undergirded by ideologies and interests, which they modified for the benefit of Rome. The Jews' great revolt against Rome in 66 CE led to the debacle of the year 70 CE, putting an end to Jewish political independence which had persisted in some degree since the return from Babylon.[7] In a "political-legal sense, the country ceased to be the land of the Jews. Even when the Romans later granted a form of national autonomy, this was given as to an *ethnos* that lived in the Roman province of Judaea."[8] An *ethnos* is "a socially and nationally distinct group with certain rights to administer its own internal affairs."[9]

The elite priestly houses comprehended God in terms of holiness (Lev 19:2), understood as the way in which God created the universe. God created the world through a spatial division—as "separate." The first chapter of Genesis fully expresses the divine order of the world by encoding various "maps" of lines that produce Israel's social space which God made for Israel to perceive and by which it was to abide. Hence, creation constitutes the original map of "purity" or holiness for Israel. "You shall be holy as I, the Lord your God, am holy" (Lev 19:2) became the norm that determined how Israel should replicate and continue the divine order already established by God's creation and holiness.[10] To replicate God's holiness was to separate the ritually clean and the unclean; a purity code that defined a society centered on the temple and its priests. Purity becomes a bound-

5. Carter, *Roman Empire*, 83–84.

6. Tomson, "Transformations of Post-70 Judaism," 98.

7. Alon, *Jews in their Land*, 1:5.

8. Ibid.

9. Tomson, "Transformations of Post-70 Judaism," 99. See also Alon, *Jews in their Land*, 1:41–85.

10. Neyrey, "Symbolic Universe of Luke Acts," 271–304, especially 177. See also Van Eck, *Galilee and Jerusalem*, 96–199.

ary marker of a sacred and social space. This theology (ideology) gave the temple elite control over the peasantry as well as the right to demand tithes and offerings.[11]

The elites of Jerusalem maintained their power and privilege by means of indirect rule, often compromising the life of their own people by taking the side of Rome. They controlled the land and temple economy (its taxes, tithes, offerings and sacrificial purity). They denied benefits to those who failed to tithe their produce, judging them "unclean and indebted" (*am ha-aretz le mitzvoth*).[12] They read the Torah with an emphasis on tithing and purity, for the purpose of serving the interest of the elites. They also ignored the widening gap between the rich and the poor peasantry leading to social tension and hostility. The leaders continued the major festivals in Jerusalem, the sacred space where both Judeans and Galileans met to renew their alliance to the temple and sacrificial system, once again requiring more taxes from the poor.[13]

The peasantry also had survival ideologies and interests, which were rooted in the liberation from slavery in Egypt and the gift of the land. The land belonged to Yahweh, who distributed it. Land did not belong to the Romans, to the elites or to the peasants. The land of Palestine was the Promised Land (Gen 12:1–3), which God gave as a blessing to the people of the land. Land was a sacred gift from God and remained God's. The peasantry therefore participated in pilgrimage festivals that celebrated Yahweh's liberating power in rescuing them from Egypt. They maintained the land as an inheritance, keeping it as Yahweh's. On this land, everyone could earn a living, practicing subsistence agriculture and putting away what they could for ceremonial needs.

Peasants sometimes failed to pay temple taxes because they had to pay an obligatory tribute to the Romans and Herodians.[14] Peasants avoided temple tithes since, unlike paying tributes that the leaders gathered through coercion, temple elites used persuasion, a different mechanism of power. G. Theissen distinguishes three forms of power: utilitarian, coercive, and persuasive. Through utilitarian power, an authority gains the support of their subjects by evoking expectations of advantages in exchange for pay in the form of money or natural resources. In coercive power, leaders use force

11. Van Eck, "Jesus and Violence," 114.

12. Ibid.

13. Ibid., 115.

14. Carter, "Constructions of Violence," 81–108.

that threatens health, possession, life, and liberty. Leaders use persuasive power to exercise power over their subjects by influence.[15] All three forms of power were abused by the Romans and their Jerusalem allies. They demonstrated utilitarian power by extracting taxes from the peasants for the sole benefit of the rulers and used coercive power to exploit and cause the submission of the peasants. Because of these abuses, the peasantry considered the Jerusalem elite's legitimate use of persuasive power as illegitimate.[16]

The peasants endured the oppression of the Romans and their allies, the local leaders. Sometimes the peasants rebelled, but the insurgences were violently quenched by Rome. Alon remarks that the Jews in Judaea, with the exception of those who were "close to the powers that be" (*mequravim la-malkhut*), never willingly submitted to the Roman yoke. For example, the Zealots and their political allies declared all payment of taxes to the Romans illegal, even on pain of death.[17] The struggles between the peasantry and the ruling aristocrats produced a space where signs of struggle continued to manifest among the peasants. John presents Jesus, addressing the needs of this oppressed community and winning a large following, raising fear among the local leaders that the Romans would become curious about him. This would lead the Romans to question the effectiveness of the local administration, putting their political positions at a risk.

Positioning Jesus' Signs in John's Gospel

In general Greco-Roman usage, signs (σημεῖα) denote things or processes that lead to insight or knowledge, by way of (typically visual) perception. For example, in Homer, σῆμα imparts knowledge through a series of developments that rely on visual phenomena. Signs can be marks for recognition, for example, Odysseus' scar (*Od.* 24:329–332), a monument (*Il.* 7:86), the turning point in a race (*Il.* 23:326), or a mark of individual achievement (*Il.* 23:843; Od. 8:192, 195). A sign is generally seen (*Il.* 23: 326–328 and *Od.* 8:192–198), although it can also be connected with an audible phenomenon (*Od.* 20.111). For Strabo, a σημεῖον can denote a mathematical or geographic point (*Geog.* 1.1.6; 1.4.1; 2.1.17), a signal beacon (*Geog.* 3.1.9), or the marks that record the least, greatest, and mean rises of the Nile

15. Theissen, "Political Dimensions," 227.

16. Ibid., 227.

17. Alon, *Jews in their Land*, 14–15. For details about the struggle against paying taxes to the Romans, see Mishnah Ned. III: 4.

(*Geog.* 17.1.48). This broad range of uses will be seen in the socio-political geography of Jesus' signs.

The Sanhedrin's accusation against Jesus concerns the way in which his "signs" configure space. Jesus performs many astonishing activities that attract public attention yet contaminate his relationship with political leaders. The resurrection of Lazarus becomes the crisis-inducing sign. After the resurrection of Lazarus from death, the chief priests and the Pharisees convene a council to address their fear that Jesus' performing of "many signs" (John 11:47; πολλὰ ποιεῖ σημεῖα) would eventually lead "all" (πάντες) to believe in him, provoking a Roman intervention which would be disastrous to the former's place and nation (11:48). Performing signs is not in itself a political activity, yet the council claims that Jesus' signs had adverse political consequences. The impact of such signs is moving beyond the religious dimensions to become a political and a social problem for the council members. The fears of the council are not misplaced; Jesus' signs impact their power and prestige. The many signs expand Jesus' geography of influence and his politics of place, raising the anxiety of the Judean leadership.

John's Gospel evidences the political consequences of Jesus' signs. On account of the signs, believers attempt to take Jesus by force to make him king (6:14–15). The crowd in Jerusalem, having learnt of the resurrection of Lazarus, proclaims him "king of Israel" (12:12–13). The crowd is excited about Jesus (12:17–19), yet the local leaders plot to kill Lazarus whom Jesus had raised (12:9–11). Killing Lazarus is "an easy solution to a complex socio-political problem."[18] The crowd understands the alternative geography of power and their attempt to crown Jesus as their king indicates a crisis of territorial legitimacy, reflecting the dynamics of the power relations among them. Jesus fulfills the functions of a true leader of the people.

Popular prestige is not the same as formal power, yet popular prestige accompanies formal power. The firstspace location in which Jesus' provides for the hungry crowd becomes a secondspace political site of struggle when, as interests clash, Jesus' popularity contravenes the formal power of the leaders. It is however, the thirdspace that allows not only the fulfillment of the needs of the people but their political liberation. The crowd recognizes Jesus as providing leadership towards liberation. Stephen Moore correctly proposes that "everyone" was starting to "believe in him," apparently

---

18. Umoh, *Plot to Kill Jesus*, 44.

as "the long awaited king of Israel," the one who would liberate Israel from imperial domination.[19]

The "many signs" of Jesus address the "lived experiences" of the people at the margins of society. In their diverse social situations of illness, death, poverty, and exploitation, individuals and communities exist in spaces of struggle. By raising Lazarus from the dead, Jesus not only liberates a bereaved family but also brings hope to a community dominated by Roman imperialism. Dominated people recognize liberation from oppression in any act that improves an aspect of their social life. This is perhaps the motivation for the attempt to crown Jesus king following his feeding of thousands of hungry people (6:15). It is therefore not out of place that Jesus' signs summon the community to see hope for a social revolution that would reestablish just, egalitarian, and mutually supportive socioeconomic relations.

By healing a man born blind (John 9), Jesus addresses both the needs of the individuals and the social relations in the society. The healings are not simply isolated acts of individual mercy but part of a larger project of social healing. Stories of these healings are retold in diverse spaces and point to the one in whom there is hope for an improved state of life. Jesus is thirdspatially present in the community as the one who liberates from physical illnesses. His restorative powers relieve the people from death-dealing domination by the Roman imperial rule. He heals the social injury caused by imperial violence and renews the "*esprit de corps* and cooperative spirit" in communities disintegrating under the impact of the imperial order.[20] "Jesus launches a mission not only to heal the debilitating effects of the military violence and economic exploitation, but also to revitalize and rebuild the people's cultural spirit and communal vitality. In healing the social "paralysis," he also releases life forces previously turned inward in self-blame."[21] In this way, Jesus instills hope in a seemingly hopeless situation.

Jesus carries out many other signs. John records the miracle at the wedding at Cana in Galilee in which Jesus changes water into wine (2:1–11). Jesus also cures the sick child of an official from a distance, which results in the officer's family believing in him (4:46–54). He cures a man born blind (9:1–12), explicitly referred to as a sign (9:3). As a result of this miracle, the man believes that Jesus was a "prophet" and a holy man from

19. Moore, "Romans Will Come," 342.

20. Horsley, *Jesus and Empire*, 126.

21. Ibid.

God. Jesus' raising of Lazarus is the last of the miracle stories in the Fourth Gospel described as a sign (11:1–44). Jesus boldly explains to his disciples beforehand that Lazarus is dead, providing an occasion for his disciples to believe (11:15). John narrates that, in addition to Jesus' disciples, the by-standers and many Jews come to believe in Jesus as the one sent by the Father (11:42).

These signs have both negative and positive social impact on the people who witness them. The crowd "follows" (ἠκολούθει) Jesus because it sees the sign of him healing the diseased (6:2). For the sake of the crowd, Jesus carries out another sign, this time on behalf of the hungry, multiplying the bread and fish and feeding the multitude (6:5). The people who benefit from the miracle (6:11–12) do not actually believe in him, but want to make him a king (6:15). When Jesus calls upon them to believe in him, they instead demand more signs (6:30). This is an indication that some of those who follow Jesus do not believe in him in a religious sense. Instead, they follow him because they see a leader who would resolve their social (6:31, 34) and political needs (6:15). Charles H. Dodd comments that the attempt to make Jesus a king (6:14–15) fits the turbulent conditions of the pre-70 Palestine.[22] While there is no evidence that Jesus was ever involved in any armed uprising against Rome, he was "not a pacifist preacher of religious ideals."[23] His ethos was neither political nor violent, yet he rejected and even provoked conflict with the ruling institution because of his opposition to violence in all forms: oppressive and repressive, political-economic and spiritual.[24] This demonstrates not only historical reality but a Johannine Christology in which Jesus is rejected by the world and its ruling powers as he does the will of his Father.[25]

Jesus encounters a marginalized and dominated crowd whose first concern is not theology but survival.[26] Jesus reinscribes the suffering people's spatiality by providing what was lacking in their experiences at the margins of society; they want to construct Jesus' space by raising him to a kingly status. Their hope is that as king, Jesus would continue to re-

22. Dodd, *Historical Tradition*, 213–17.

23. Horsley, *Jesus and the Spiral of Violence*, 319.

24. Ibid.

25. Rensberger, "Politics of John," 395–411.

26. The wretched condition of the people of Palestine under Roman colonialism is attributed to the various taxation schemes and other impoverishing strategies introduced by the Roman imperial government. See Mosala, *Biblical Hermeneutics*, 156–60.

configure their social and political geography. However, while Jesus' signs raise expectations among the common people, he sometimes disappoints them by not conforming to their expectations. The people fail to see that Jesus produces space according to God's will and not according to popular expectations of a messiah or political leader. As a result some of them abandon Jesus (6:66).

Jesus' signs create religious geography of belief for some, while configuring political geography for others. Thus, on one hand, signs could lead Jesus' friends and disciples to believe in him (2:11) and to recognize the revelation of God's glory and the glory of Jesus (14:4, 40). On the other, Jesus' signs could attract the crowd to follow him for reasons that are not religious (6:2; 14:5). His signs are subject to misinterpretation and misunderstanding, creating a conflicting geography. On account of his signs, the Jews are divided: some believe in him (11:45), others go away from him (11:46). The Pharisees are also divided: some Pharisees recognize Jesus as man of God through the signs (3:2; 9:16), others see in Jesus' signs a political provocation (11:47–48). Udo Schnelle observes that there was a "Christological schism" within the Johannine school as well, citing John 6:60–70.[27]

Jesus' signs reconfigure the social and political space of people from diverse walks of life. These include the Pharisee Nicodemus (3:2), the crowd (6:2, 12:8), pilgrims at a feast in Jerusalem (7:31), officials (perhaps of the imperial government) (4:46), authorities (12:46), outcasts of the synagogue (9:34–38), Jews (11:45–46), and his disciples and friends (2:11; 11:1–44). The political leaders could no longer ignore the social and political geography shaped by Jesus' signs. The council implies that its members are passive, through the rhetorical question "what are we doing? For this man performs many signs" (τί ποιοῦμεν ὅτι οὗτος ὁ ἄνθρωπος πολλὰ ποιεῖ σημεῖα; 11:47).[28] They seek to end their passivity by acting to end Jesus'

27. Schnelle, *Theology of the New Testament*, 679.

28. Raymond Brown interprets τί ποιοῦμεν ὅτι οὗτος ὅτι οὗτος ὁ ἄνθρωπος πολλὰ ποιεῖ σημεῖα (John 11:47 BNT) as deliberative with a rare use of the present tense, "what are we going to do?" now that this man is performing many signs. Brown, *Gospel According to St. John*, 1:438–39. He centers on F. Blass and A. Debrunner, for whom the question is "deliberative," in which case one would expect a subjunctive or a future tense. In this case however, we have a present indicative; the only case in which a present indicative is used in the deliberative sense. See Blass and Debrunner, *A Greek Grammar of the New Testament*, 185. I interpret with Barrett and Bauer, "what are we doing?" because it covers the "ironic" nature of John's writings, expecting the answer "nothing." ὅτι would then mean "for" or "because" implying that the council ought to be active but in fact

activities, lest "everyone will believe in him" (11:48), as the influence of Jesus, in fact, reaches a climax. The Pharisees then exclaim, "Look the whole
world has gone after him" (ἴδε ὁ κόσμος ὀπίσω αὐτοῦ ἀπῆλθεν; 12:19).
His sphere of influence is now "the whole world," spatially unlimited. The
extension of Jesus' social and political geography is measured not only in
terms of the increase of the number of people who have religious faith in
him, but also in his ability to attract "everyone" to himself.

Jesus' signs win him an enormous following, stoking the fears of the
Judean leadership to fever pitch. Indicating that the political consequences
of Jesus' signs would be detrimental to their place and their nation, the
council defines the signs as "out of place." The council thereby claims territoriality and exercises control over place and nation. The leaders' spatial
strategy is to affect, influence and control the space they define as their
own. Jesus' actions do not meet the expectations of behavior in the Roman
colonial space and in the space of Rome's allies from Jerusalem. However,
the council recognizes their failure to maintain territoriality over this space.
The decision at the meeting addresses this failure and is intended to ensure
the maintenance of territoriality by destroying Jesus' reputation.

The spatial effects of Jesus' signs play a more significant role in influ-
encing the decision of his opponents for his condemnation than is usually
acknowledged. Jesus' opponents react according to their evaluation of his
signs rather than to his theological position. The leaders' interpretation of
the spatial impacts of Jesus' signs play a leading role in the decision to kill
Jesus. The reason for his death is not his religious teaching; the cause of his
death is that perceived political understandings of space due to the leaders'
interpretations of his actions. Jesus' signs affect political space, and for this,
Jesus is put on trial.

Roman Space: The Power in the Name

The mere mention of the possibility of Roman retaliation creates a space of
unrest. The council moves to address Jesus' reputation in order to avoid a
violent outcome. Such unrest denotes the power of the name "Roman" and
demonstrates that actions based in fear were not uncommon in first-century

---

they are not. Barrett, *Gospel According to St. John*, 405; Bauer, *Johannesevangelium*, 155.
According to Bauer, ὅτι epexegetically explains why the council must stop sleeping and
immediately act. See *Gospel According to St. John*, 338.

Palestine. Reference to the name "Romans" (Ῥωμαῖοι; 11:48) constructs a landscape of insecurity among the most powerful Jewish leaders.

Andrew J. Overman discusses the impact of imperial forces on late first-century Palestine. He focuses on how imperial politics and the imposition of its own cultural symbols contributed to conflict, intergroup competitions, and fragmentation of Jewish society as each interest group competed to define the cultural boundaries, including collaborating with the imperial powers.[29] Jeremy Punt writes that "Roman imperial violence was all around, and pervaded every centimeter of first-century lives."[30] The Roman Empire was infamous for "the violent, brutal and cruel imposition of its imperial social engineering, especially after rebellion, whether through the local elite or directly."[31] Such violence ranged from the most incidental public punishment of criminals and perpetrators to the organized structured measures such as crucifixion.[32] Mass crucifixions acted as deterrent measures (Josephus, *Jewish War* 2.75; 2.241; 5.449–451).

Through spatial control, exploitation and violence, the Romans constructed regional spaces of fear. The Roman Empire was "aristocratic," meaning that a very small percentage of the population ruled everyone. The elite, two to three percent, shaped the social experience of the empire's inhabitants, determined the quality of their life, exercised power, controlled wealth, and enjoyed high status.[33] The Romans enslaved, oppressed, intimidated, and killed their subjects by torturing to death any rebel leaders.[34] The Roman Empire controlled resources and ruled the empire through coercion, the most effective measure of which was the Roman army.[35] They also controlled major forms of communication through the "the designs of coins, the building of monuments, and the construction of various buildings."[36] Through these activities, they shaped perceptions about themselves, producing their own social space as well as defining that of the dominated inhabitants.

---

29. Overman, *Matthew's Gospel*, 8–34.

30. Punt, "Violence," 27.

31. Ibid., 28.

32. Ibid.

33. Carter, *Roman Empire*, 3.

34. Horsley, *Jesus and Empire*, 15.

35. Carter, *Roman Empire*, 4.

36. Ibid.

Alliances between the Romans and the patrons in their various provinces served to maintain the *status quo* and the elites' interests, and contributed to the turbulence in the council over Jesus' fame. The Romans would have seen Jesus' notoriety as a danger to the empire and perceived Jerusalem authorities' failure to stop Jesus' infamy as poor leadership. Consequently, the leaders risked losing their political place.

Roman representations of space were tied to the relations that produce space and to the "order" which those relations impose. They exercised power and maintained territoriality through violence, the code that signaled their power. As Lefebvre argues, violence is an integral part of the "abstract space" of the dominant.[37] Violence explains the territorial reach of the name "Roman"; explicit reference to the name was a warning sign that their space was at a risk, and they should act immediately to avoid the disaster. The possibility of the arrival of the Romans sends a message of fear rather than relief to their partners, the local leaders in Jerusalem. The leaders would have liked to maintain a relationship with the Roman oppressors, for their own self-preservation. Both the Romans and the Sanhedrin operate in an ambience of mutual distrust, yet each tries to protect the interest of the other. This interest, which Caiaphas describes as an "advantage," is paramount for both parties, irrespective of the consequences for others. No wonder it does not matter to them "if one man should die," provided this advantage is preserved (11:50). The threat of losing place reminds the leaders of the fragility of their political position, demanding vigilance against anything that threatened their office.

Sanhedrin Space

The Sanhedrin (συνέδριον) was the highest "legislative and judicial" Jewish administrative body.[38] It comprised the Pharisees, the chief priests, and the high priest named Caiaphas, all influential Jewish leaders who were allies of Rome.

While in the time of Jesus (30 CE) the Pharisees had little political power, John (late-first century CE) characterizes the Pharisees' political space as authoritative and powerful. However, the Pharisees are still accountable to Rome.[39] The Pharisees question John the Baptist about baptiz-

37. Lefebvre, *Production of Space*, 56–57.

38. Von Wahlde, *Gospel and Letters*, 2:517.

39. Josephus writes that the Pharisees were a prominent and dominant group in

ing (1:24). Nicodemus, one of the Pharisees, visits Jesus at night and inquires about Jesus' identity (3:1–20). Jesus' activities are reported constantly to the Pharisees (9:13; 11:46). The Pharisees claim for themselves the authority to judge Jesus as bearing false witness (8:13), that Jesus is not from God (9:16), and that Jesus is a sinner (9:24). The Pharisees do not believe in Jesus (7:48), so the leaders who happen to believe in Jesus fear the Pharisees (12:42). Together with the chief priests, the Pharisees send officers to arrest Jesus (7:32) and issue an arrest warrant to the same effect (11:57). Their authorities allow them to request a band of soldiers from the Roman authority, who together with their own officers, follow the treacherous guidance of Judas and arrest Jesus (18:12–14). These incidences indicate that at the time of John, the Pharisee space is a dominant one.

In addition to the Pharisees, John includes the chief priests and the high priest as members of the Sanhedrin. They plot to kill Lazarus, on whose account many people have come to believe in Jesus (12:10). They take Jesus to Pilate (18:25) and cry aloud that Jesus should be crucified (19:6). They denounce Jesus in favor of Caesar (19:15). To the chief priests, Pilate hands over Jesus to be crucified (19:16). They complain to Pilate about the inscription that claimed Jesus as king of the Jews (19:21). The chief priests "had great influence among the people as well as with the

---

Judaism of the late first century. In the so-called death bed instruction of King Alexander Jannaeus to his wife (78 BCE), Josephus writes that Alexander advised his wife to securely retain the kingdom after his death, but to put some of the powers in the hands of the Pharisees for . . . "they had great authority among the Jews, both do to hurt to such as they hated, and to bring advantages to those to whom they were friendly disposed; for they are then believed best of all by the multitude when they speak any severe thing against others, though it may be out of envy at them" (Josephus, *Jewish Antiquities*, 3.15. 5). J. L. Martyn also remarks that the Pharisees had political authority both at the national and the local levels. See *History and Theology in the Fourth Gospel*, 84–88. G. Alon instead warns against generalization that portrays Pharisees as holding one political position. He comments that there were three political tendencies among the Pharisees of the late first century. The first group is the *Pharisee-Zealots* who hated the oppressive Roman occupation and cruelty and openly rallied people to war against the Romans. The second group consisted of the *moderates* who might be dubbed national realists. Unlike the zealots, they did not preach war as the only logical consequence of their patriotic ideology, but they were prepared to offer physical resistance in circumstances that seem to promise some chance of victory. They were capable of coming to terms with the Romans when such a step appeared either favorable, or on the contrary unavoidable. The third group is the *peace party* who from the very start rejected the possibility of victory, and therefore made no effort at all to wrest freedom from the Romans. See Alon, *Jews in their Land*, 94–95.

colonizing Roman imperial power."[40] Only those with access to Pilate could instigate the death of Jesus, making the chief priests suspect.[41]

The Sanhedrin's convening of the council points to a contested geography of power. They refer to Jesus as "this man" (οὗτος ὁ ἄνθρωπος) and focus on him as powerful and posing a political risk. "This man" makes Jesus secondspatially present though he is firstspatially absent at the meeting. It directs attention to an absent yet powerful person who continues to produce and reproduce spaces, posing a threat to the leaders. The council foresees and estimates that Jesus' geographical space would be maximized to the extent that "all" (πάντες) would believe in him, with the result that the political spaces of both the Jewish leaders and the Romans would be minimized. Believing in Jesus implies spatial allegiance to him; Jesus' winning of more followers would lead to an ordering of space that is not desirable either to the Jewish leaders or the Romans. It leads to a popular prestige which could establish a formal power. The believer space is the space of popular power yet as the Sanhedrin feared, popular power impacts formal power. There is a large oppositional spatiality from Jesus' supporters, which the council could contain only by eliminating Jesus.

By convening the council, the Sanhedrin announces its territoriality over the place and the nation. The possessive pronoun "ἡμῶν" (11:48) defines the place as belonging to the council members. The boundary of the Sanhedrin's place and nation is not demarcated by a material object such as a wall or natural phenomena. Instead, it is an immaterial boundary, a secondspace boundary defined by the word ἡμῶν. Jesus' territoriality defined by his activities clashes with the territory of the council members, which was also the territory of the Romans.

Jesus' signs provoke the Sanhedrin's need to continually redefine and maintain its territory, which resonates with Sack's comment that "a place or space might be a territory at one time and not at another."[42] The miracle

---

40. Sanders, *Jesus and Judaism*, 293.

41. Against Sanders who thinks that Jesus could have had significant conflicts with the Pharisees to warrant their seeking to get Jesus killed. See also Raymond Brown who holds the same position in his *Death of the Messiah*, 1:353. There is however evidence that people sought friendship with Rome to secure positions. See *Josephus, Jewish War* 1.2.1. This does not eliminate the possibility that the chief priests could do so to protect their political space. Alon and Tomson argue that the early rabbis had contact with Rome and exercised power, which would have affected Johannine memory of the Pharisees. See Alon, *Jews in their Land*, 13–17; Tomson, "Transformations of Post-70 Judaism," 91–117.

42. Sack, *Human Territoriality*, 19.

of the raising of Lazarus is a further impressive "sign." The resurrection of Lazarus is not just a sudden surprise , but follows many signs and belief in Jesus already witnessed (8:30–32), and it consolidates, confirms, and elevates these previous signs. The resurrection of Lazarus consolidates power to make Jesus instantly a threat to the space of the political elite. He was close to claiming their space. The Sanhedrin tries to use its spatial power to constrain the works of Jesus.

John understands the geography of power differently, and so proclaims that the death of Jesus will instead gather into one the children of God dispersed abroad (11:52). Spatial restructuring will take place when Jesus dies. The spatial power of the council is challenged as the narrator announces that Jesus' death would fulfill a plan that was not the Sanhedrin's.

Caiaphas moves the council to decide to kill Jesus with a typical Sanhedrin political expression, "It is advantageous for you." It is convenient for "you," members of the Sanhedrin, that this one man be killed. The Sanhedrin politics of expediency and compromise characterized the conduct of the ruling class in the Roman imperial context. Josephus testifies to this when he narrates that in revenge against the Samaritans who had killed a Galilean, the Galileans destroyed one Samaritan village. While the Galileans were matching towards Samaria, the leaders of Jerusalem gathered together and pleaded with the Galileans to go back to their homeland in order to avoid a Roman military intervention against Jerusalem. This would save "their land and temple," and their children and wives who were at great risk as the Galileans revenge the death of only one person (*Jewish War* 2: 232–246; see also *Jewish War* 2:345–401).

These examples demonstrate that the ruling class of Jerusalem (in John's narrative) is careful to avoid anything that could provoke Roman military involvement. The leaders in Jerusalem would execute their own people if their behavior is suspected of offending the Romans. The council's arguments for eliminating Jesus are primarily based on convenience and fear of a possible Roman military intervention that would place the leaders and the nation at a risk. The leaders have to compromise the values of Israel in favor of Roman interests. They demonstrate their predicament when, at the trial of Jesus, they shout "we have no king but Caesar" (19:15).

The Sanhedrin gathers in apparent response to pressure from Rome, demonstrating that Rome determines the Sanhedrin's space. To remain in their position of leadership, they have to be viewed favorably by Rome, as the relationship between the Sanhedrin and Rome was fragile. The Jewish leaders' survival strategy is to acquiesce to, if not actively cooperate with, Roman rule. Thus, it is not surprising that the populace view the leadership class with mistrust and contempt.[43] The weight of Roman oppression justifies the Jewish leaders' fear-based decision to eliminate Jesus, even though for selfish gains. Their decision is influenced by Roman pressures; their space is precarious and perilous. The opponents of Jesus are threatened not by Jesus' theological position, but by that which appears to undermine their political interest and their grip on the nation as their private property.[44] Roman imperial politics provide an ambience in which small aristocratic elites cooperate with the ruling powers, while the mass of people are marginalized. This contributes to a spiral of violence that arose from popular Jewish resistance to Roman institutional injustice and repression of the rebellions.[45]

Caiaphas' Space

John refers to Caiaphas as "the high priest that year" (11:49). As high priest, he is the head of the priests and the Sanhedrin. He was not just a member of the powerful group but holds the highest authority. He dominates the discussion of the council (11:49) and appears several times within the "death of Jesus narrative" (18:13, 14, 24; 19:11). Caiaphas, in the first century socio-political setting, was a Jewish religious authority. Together with the chief priests and the Pharisees, they "formed the ruling aristocracy [in Judea] who in alliance with Rome had immense political, social and economic power."[46] Therefore, it is not surprising that John presents a Jerusalem leadership that "acts like Roman prefects, or at least like a puppet aristocracy that serves as an interface between the procurator and the masses and thereby attempts to maintain the imperial *status quo*."[47] Their political space is primarily imperialistic; hence, the priests and Pharisees in the Fourth Gospel "command a police force (7:32, 45–52; 18:3, 12) and order their subjects to report treasonous activity (11:57). They also call witnesses, conduct inquiries and make rulings (1:19–25; 5:10–18; 9:13–34; 18:13, 19–24). These leaders violently abuse those who defy them (18:22),

43. Smallwood, "High Priests and Politics," 14–34.

44. Schubert, "Biblical Criticism Criticized," 385–402, esp. 395–96.

45. Kealey, "Political Jesus," 98.

46. Carter, *Pontius Pilate*, 39.

47. Thatcher, *Greater Than Caesar*, 52.

exile criminals from their community (9:22), convene council meetings to discuss political threats to the nation (11:48), negotiate directly with Rome (18:28–31), exhibit an elite 'sense of superiority' over the masses that they rule (7:47–49), and, "like the emperor, claim a divine sanction for their policies of domination (9:28–29; 16:2)."[48] The chief priests and the Pharisees are portrayed as "a powerful political party rather than as a group of individuals united by common religious interests."[49]

Caiaphas speaks bluntly and with much authority, showing that he is in control. He betrays arrogance when he challenges the council with a strong "you know nothing at all" (ὑμεῖς οὐκ οἴδατε οὐδέν; John 11:49), implying that while the council knows nothing, Caiaphas has the right answers. His superior space is defined by his office and places him in a position to accuse his fellow council members of knowing nothing. He is imperialistic like his Roman masters, courageously assuming superiority, defining his close associates as "ignorant" of what was politically expedient to them. Caiaphas, like his imperial masters, constructs his closest allies as ignorant. He counsels them that it is to their advantage that Jesus should die (John 11:49, 18:14). These are "shrewd words of political expediency, the sober weighing up of the situation, and the stark expression of the realpolitik."[50] His words, "it is better for you," directed to the council, demonstrate that what really matters is not the nation but their political space and maintaining the *status quo*.

The supremacy of Caiaphas and the political standing of his colleagues are at stake as Jesus' popularity grows. Their actions are prompted less by dispassionate concern for the well-being of the nation than for their own positions of power and prestige. Caiaphas operates from the perspective of political prudence in international realism (what will save the nation), as well as from the perspective of what is best for the ruling party ("it is

48. Ibid.

49. The possible exceptions seem to prove the rule: in John 3:1, Nicodemus is identified as a "Pharisee" but is also called "a ruler of the Jews." In 8:13, the Pharisees who question the validity of Jesus' "witness," seem to be members of the same group who had attempted to arrest him in chapter 7. In general while the Synoptics portray the Pharisees and Sadducees as distinct sects (Matt 12:38; 15:1–2; 22:34–46; Mark 2:23–24; 7:1–5; Luke 5:21; 13:31; 14:1–6). In John's account the Pharisees regularly appear with the chief priests rather than with the Scribes. See Thatcher, *Greater Than Caesar*, 52 and footnotes on p. 149. The Sadducees, scribes, and Pharisees are united in John because by 90 CE, the Pharisees/early rabbis did have political power, although they had little political power 60 years earlier.

50. Bond, *Caiaphas*, 132.

better for you"). The claim that national security is threatened by this political issue conceals the self-centered interests of the leaders. This argument secures the execution of Jesus and protects the interest and values of the imperialist regime. From that day on they plan to put Jesus to death (11:53). John does not say much about the planning aspect. However, the case is strong enough to allow the Roman authority to order the execution of the accused, as the Jewish leaders have no authority to put anyone to death. Roman imperial politics thus much influences Caiaphas' space, limiting Caiaphas' course of action.

Two statements deserve highlighting. First, the evangelist describes Caiaphas' statement, "it is better for one man to die," as a prophecy of that year's high priest. For John, the high priest "in his involuntary prophecy (11:51) is trapped in deep ignorance."[51] Caiaphas' space is nothing other than an office [high priest's] space to proclaim prophecies of God, implying that what Caiaphas thinks is within his powers is, in fact, not. His claim to save the nation from perishing is, in fact, a divine plan. By announcing the "prophecy," Caiaphas communicates a "divine necessity": Jesus must ($\mu\acute{\epsilon}\lambda\lambda\omega$) die.[52] Caiaphas is stripped of political powers and reduced to a mouthpiece that unknowingly announces God's plan. In opposition to Caiaphas, Jesus is in full control of the events leading to his death. By subverting the meanings of the events in question, John demonstrates that Rome's allies—the leaders in Jerusalem—could in no way interfere with Jesus' plan. Jesus is greater than these leaders and the Roman emperor they represent. This is the first level of Jesus' defeat of Rome.

Secondly, Jesus dies in order to gather together into one (a spatial image) the scattered children of God (11:51–52). Jesus is portrayed as the one who controls geography. His plan for the masses dispersed throughout the universe does not scatter them, like the imperialistic agenda which conquers, divides, and scatters the vanquished. His agenda is not a selfish political one based on what is expedient only to the elite leadership. His leadership is not a divide-and-conquer agenda as seen so often in separations of dominated people, but that which unifies the scattered children of God. Again, this statement qualifies and mocks the power of Caiaphas. He claims to know the reason why Jesus must die, but he has no knowledge of

51. Schnackenburg, *Gospel According to St. John*, 2:349.

52. I consider the verb $\mu\acute{\epsilon}\lambda\lambda\omega$ as expressing a divine necessity that Jesus "must" die, unlike the NA28 which translates that Jesus is "about to" die. This is to announce the absolute sovereignty of God over the events of the approaching death of Jesus.

the cosmic significance of the death of Jesus. Jesus' will to die is not meant to fulfill the selfish political motive of the leaders. Rather, its ontological reality is the achievement of universal unification. Caiaphas is not the influential, knowledgeable, powerful leader that he claims. His words are unintentional prophecies of a high priest, his decisions are part of the divine plan, and what he claims to know is in fact a half truth, or wrong information. In retrospect, his political space is limited, along with the political space of the Roman Empire that he represents.

The narrative continues to demonstrate the limitations of Caiaphas' space. In the trial and death of Jesus that follow, John mentions Caiaphas' name and office (or house) without specifying any detail regarding the effectiveness of this house in affecting the outcome. The prisoner is taken to Annas, the previous year's high priest described as the "father-in-law of Caiaphas" (18:13). That Jesus is led to the house of a deposed high priest exposes Annas' continuing influence on the high priestly office.[53] After some interrogation of Jesus, Annas sends him, bound, to Caiaphas (18:24). The text is silent about the investigations that Caiaphas makes. Caiaphas slowly disappears from the actively developing scene and reappears in the crowd of the accusers outside the *praetorium*, where he was not any different from all the other people in the crowd shouting "crucify him." Caiaphas and his office slowly retreat to the background, rendered insignificant.

The Fear of Losing Space

The fear of losing place and nation is strong, particularly among dominated people whose major resources are already under colonial domination. The Jerusalem leaders, the auxiliaries of Rome, fear that Jesus' activities could provoke a response from the Romans that would prove detrimental to their place and their nation. The political elite in Jerusalem is faced with a fight for survival in a hostile imperial environment. They explicitly assign a political motivation to their plot to kill Jesus, and focus on the signs of Jesus because they influence the political geography of the nation (ἔθνος; 11:48).

In addition to the sociological effects of Jesus' signs discussed earlier in this chapter, Jesus' signs cause σχίσμα[54] (division) among his audience

53. For more discussion of the influence of Annas the high priest, see O'Day, "Gospel of John," 806–7. A more detailed treatment is found in Chapter 5 of this book under the subtitle, Annas' space.

54. This word could be translated as "schism" but it seems rather too strong. On the

and population. Biblical scholarship often neglects this aspect, yet John enunciates three instances in which Jesus' signs caused division among the population: Jesus' address at the temple during the feast (7:37–44), the healing of a man born blind on the Sabbath (9:16), and the reaction of the people to the good shepherd discourse (10:19). These divisions threaten to undermine the authority of the political elite, signaling the potential loss of political control.

During the feast at the temple, Jesus addresses the people. His listeners are divided (σχίσμα) over his identity (7:40–44). Some of them think he is the prophet or the Christ, while others argue that the Christ could not come from Galilee. The disagreement reminds the reader that place matters. Jesus could not be the Christ because he hails from a location low in the hierarchy of places. Bethlehem ought to be the place of the Christ because the messiah must be descended from David.

John identifies Jesus' listeners as the crowd (ὄχλῳ; 7:43), amongst whom are officers sent by the chief priests and Pharisees to arrest Jesus (7:32). They do not arrest Jesus because in their opinion no one has spoken like him before (7:46). The officers recognize that there is something extraordinary in Jesus. The chief priests and the Pharisees reproach the officers for not carrying out orders, but at that point, even among the authorities who sent the officers, there is already disagreement. Nicodemus, one of the Pharisees, defends the acts of the officers with the argument that it is not lawful to judge a man before giving him a fair hearing (7:50–51). The remainder of the Pharisees reprimands the officers for being led astray like the crowd, and scold Nicodemus for behaving as if he were a Galilean. Galilee features again as the low-profiled place of a moderate people. The chief priests, the Pharisees, and the police strongly disagree over the course of action demanded by the principles of law and order. This is indicative of a political division among the leaders.

After Jesus heals a blind man on a Sabbath, some of the Pharisees accuse him of disrespecting the law of the Sabbath, while others refuse to endorse that accusation, leading to a σχίσμα (9:16). Matthias Rein remarks that because of Jesus' signs, some Pharisees believed that Jesus was from God.[55] Nicodemus, one of the Pharisees, announces to Jesus, "we know"

---

basis of the common usage in the NT and Apostolic Fathers, "division" seems to be a better translation. Paul describes the situation among the Corinthian community as a σχίσμα (division) (1 Cor 1:10; 11:18). See also 1 Clem 2.6, 46.5. In both cases, division is considered a very serious issue that could be rectified.

55. Rein, *Die Heilung des Blindgeborenen*, 88.

(οἴδαμεν) you are a teacher from God (3:2)." The first person plural refers to the Pharisees and supports the claim that the Pharisees' rejection of Jesus moves beyond a religious basis, as it seems that many Pharisees believe that Jesus is a teacher of religious truth.

In the discourse on the good shepherd, Jesus claims a special connection with God, his heavenly Father. The Jews are divided between those who think that Jesus was possessed by a demon and those who argue that Jesus words' and healing of a blind man indicate a reasonable man and a special person (10:19–21). This is yet another incident of a σχίσμα on account of Jesus' signs and words.

The incidences above show that the division caused by Jesus' teaching and signs affect people from diverse backgrounds. The divisions "cut across party lines, factional emotions and interests, and forecasted devastating consequences for the ruling class."[56] Division among the general public challenges the leaders' claim that they represented the common interest in their decision against Jesus. Unanimous opinion about him no longer exists. Within the ruling class, there is no consent on Jesus. Such strong disagreement among leaders demonstrates their incompetence in keeping the society united. A weak administration, incapable of maintaining social cohesion under imperial leadership, contributes to a loss of place. Umoh is right to suggest that the place in question is nothing more than the political posts of the members of the Sanhedrin.

Jesus' signs reawaken the consciousness of a dominated group who are beginning to judge for themselves what is right. An informed population is a threat to dictatorship. The people around Jesus are becoming aware of their own rights as human beings. Jesus awakens this in them, posing a threat to the colonial power and their Jewish auxiliaries. Disagreements among the populace over the identity of Jesus mean that they can no longer accept the position held by the authorities as unanimously correct. The people will decide for themselves about Jesus, a move which causes anxiety among the authorities and produces a political issue that has to be urgently addressed (11:47–57). The ruling elite see Jesus' signs as destabilizing society, and endangering their positions. Because they are accountable to the imperial power, their inefficiency could cost them their jobs. A politically-based decision motivates the leaders of the people (11:50), and explains why a religious motive is not given in the context of the decision to kill Jesus.

56. Umoh, *Plot to Kill Jesus*, 196.

Through his signs, Jesus introduces disunity and confusion to the nation. C. H. Dodd observes that Jesus' words caused κρίσις, a separation or judgment of those who heard them.[57] John's emphasis on the effect of Christ's presence and words is therefore deliberate. Even before the festival, some people are saying that Jesus is a good man while others complain that he is misleading the people (7:12). Society is divided among those who accept Jesus and those who do not. It is Jesus who constructs societal space. In the presence of Jesus, society cannot remain indifferent. Vis-à-vis the Empire as represented by their auxiliaries in Jerusalem, society has to decide whether it is for or against Jesus. The political impact of Jesus reaches an alarming state: if the Jewish aristocracy cannot preserve social stability among the population, then they risk losing their political space as the location of their political power, the nation, would be destroyed.

John employs irony throughout the Gospel. It is ironic, humorous indeed, that the chief priests and Caiaphas, in their very words, transfer the word "place" away from the common usage as their temple, to a most impermanent and improper abode: their will for political power! More positively, the transference of the word "place" *away* from the temple will result in the "place" being situated on the body of Jesus, who is being sacrificed for the nation. Through the space of Jesus, all people, the "whole" (v.50) nation, will be *gathered* into the "one" (v.52) place of Jesus, the Body of Christ.

Ideology of Place

Whether place in John 11:48 indicates a position of responsibility or the Temple/Jerusalem is an important debate, but more so is the unasked question concerning the role of ambiguity in the use of place. Caiaphas reminds the council members that because the place is in danger, common sense demands the elimination of Jesus in order to save many (11: 51). What is the effect of ambiguity of place in John's telling of this story? In language discourse, ambiguity and common sense are used to conceal ideologies and sustain existing power relations.[58]

The sociologist Harold Garfinkel writes of "the familiar common sense world of everyday life," a world built entirely upon "assumptions and expectations which control both the actions of members of a society and

---

57. Dodd, *Interpretation of the Fourth Gospel*, 352–53.

58. Fairclough, *Language and Power*, 64–90.

their interpretation of the actions of others."[59] Such assumptions and expectations are "implicit," pushed to the background, "taken for granted, not things that people are consciously aware of, and rarely explicitly formulated or examined or questioned."[60] The "effectiveness of ideology" depends on it being "merged with this common sense background in discourse and other forms of social actions."[61] When the ambiguity of Caiaphas' statement of having the "one man" killed (11:48) is interpreted through this "common sense" lens, it becomes evident that an "ideology of place" is being obscured through the ambiguity of the discourse. Place is taken for granted; the council is perhaps not explicitly aware of the place Caiaphas has in view, but they assume that Caiaphas argues for their advantage.

Place evokes a deep fear. The nation can be manipulated in the name of place as long as the arguments and actions serve the political space of the Jerusalem leaders concealed in the ambiguous τόπος. Jesus' death would then preserve the political advantage of the council; it would save the nation from destruction and, therefore, guarantee the council's continuous exercise of power. John, however, establishes that neither does Jesus wish the nation to perish, however, contrary to Caiaphas, Jesus does not wish to save the nation from perishing through the death of another person. He lays down his life to gather into one the scattered children of God (John 11:52, 12:32, and 10:15–16). This gathering creates a new space, discussed below.

Gathering the Scattered Children of God

The children of God are scattered to unspecified locations and will be gathered together in a place about which John remains silent. The text is also quiet about the identity of these children of God, and about the causes of the separation. This work does not address the identity of the "scattered children of God," other than to note that the category includes peoples from all ethno-geographies and histories who are open to believing in Jesus.[62] Instead, it focuses on how "scattering" and "gathering" indicate spatiality.

59. Ibid., 64.

60. Ibid.

61. Harold Garfinkel cited in Fairclough, *Language and Power*, 64.

62. This is in line with Lucio Cilia who holds that the scattered children of God are those who share the kind of historical situation of Jesus. He writes thus: "'I dispersi figli di Dio' sono dunque in riferimento a coloro che condividono la situazione storica di Gesù:

The Fourth Gospel records evidence of separation among the Israelite communities. In 4:20–23, the Samaritan woman asks Jesus about the right place of worship, offering the either/or possibility of either Jerusalem or "this mountain"–Gerizim. The Samaritan woman episode presents the case of a people separated by ethnic identity. While Jerusalem is the sacred space and center of Jewish identity, Gerizim is the sacred space and center of Samaritan identity. Jesus answers that true worship would no longer take place in Jerusalem or Gerizim but "in spirit." Swanson comments from a postcolonial perspective that this remark is "provocative because it posits the place-bound character of ethnic identity as something to be overcome in the newly opened placeless place of Johannine worship."[63] Because Jesus belongs to one of these two identities, it is reasonable to imagine that he does not want to abolish his ethnic identity. By proposing worship "in spirit," Jesus deconstructs the dualistic either/or tension and proposes an all-encompassing thirdspace place of worship "in spirit," where location no longer impedes.

Interpreting the "five husbands" of the Samaritan woman exposes the diverse significances of place. Schneiders interprets the husbands of the Samaritan woman as representations of past empires. In her reading, the current husband is the Roman Empire. She concludes that colonized Palestine "is a sick land" consisting of "a broken people" in need of healing, for the "whole society has been shaken, shattered and scattered."[64] Imperial ideologies and oppression had already separated a large number of Jews who lived in the Diaspora.

Soja challenges us to "think differently, to expand our geographical imagination beyond its current limits."[65] "Jews and Gentiles" as binary categories defining the first century world in which Jesus preached contribute to the spatial error of thinking dualistically. Assessing such geographies within simple binary categories leads to questions of inclusivity and exclusivity, of who belongs and who does not belong to a defined space. Thinking trialectically, John challenges the council to expand the implications of the significance of the death of Jesus. The council should consider what

---

i discepoli, i guidei che credevano in lui (ἔθνος); allargandosi, per anticipazione, a tutte le situazioni etnico-geografiche (guidei della diaspora-pagani) e storiche; tutti gli uomini che sarebbero aperti alla fede in Gesú." See Cilia, *La morte di Gesu*, 71.

63. Swanson, *To Prepare a Place*, 14.

64. Schneiders, *Revelatory Text*, 190–91.

65. Soja, *Thirdspace: Journeys*, 2.

is beyond their own political space, defined as "our [the council's] place," and what is beyond their ethnic boundaries, defined as "our [the council's] nation." In the same way, the leaders should extend their location of the scattered children of God beyond ethnic boundaries and imperial ideologies. Jesus' death would benefit the children of God scattered all over the world, i.e., Jews, Gentiles and more.

The children of God are not defined by one specific location; they are located in the imagined "space without margins," a secondspace without a specific firstspace location, but with a projection, a broader secondspace sphere which incorporates all earthly firstspaces. Thus, when John repeats Caiaphas' statement that Jesus would die for the nation (ἔθνος) and adds "not only for the nation but in order to gather together into one the scattered children of God" (τέκνα τοῦ θεοῦ: no longer for the λαός alone), John declares the council ignorant of Jesus' death, profanes their understanding of Jesus' death, and challenges them to extend their spatial considerations of the impact of the death of Jesus. Jesus' death would restructure earthly spaces in ways that benefit "all" people, without geographical limitations. In this restructuring of space, geography is no longer a barrier. The space is real and imagined and more.

In his *Jesus' Death and the Gathering of True Israel*, John Dennis argues that the gathering reflects "the restoration of the kingdom of Israel."[66] However, such an inscription generates immediate questions concerning real and imagined geographies. The children of God are scattered in diverse ethnic spaces by political oppression. Thirdspatially they would be liberated through the mediation of Jesus, the agent of restoration of the freedom of the oppressed people. In the death of Jesus, the children of God are no longer limited by boundaries and borders, they are without spatial limitations. This demonstrates that Jesus is the ruler of unlimited space, and therefore the "son of God," the ruler and "savior of the world," titles that were used for Roman emperors including Romulus the first king of Rome.

David Balch discusses the similarities and differences between Romulus and the Lukan Jesus.[67] My comparison of the Johannine Jesus and Romulus is to a great extent guided by Balch's work. While it is hard to know who the father of Romulus (and Remus) was, the Romans believed them to have been "sons of Mars" (Ἄρεος υἱοὶ γενέσθαι; *Ant. rom.* 2.2.3.). Like Romulus, Jesus is "son of God" (John 19:7). Romulus' grandfather

66. Dennis, *Jesus' Death and the Gathering of True Israel*.
67. Balch, "Jesus as Founder of the Church in Luke-Acts," 138–88.

instructed him about the Roman form of government, and Romulus followed his teaching (*Ant. rom.* 2.3.1; also 2.4.1; 28.1). Both Romulus and Jesus teach a "way of life and both maintain a degree of continuity with the past."[68] The Johannine Jesus teaches nothing but "the will of his Father" (John 6:38–40; 8:38; 5:30). Both Jesus and Romulus accept strangers into their space. Romulus offered asylum for suppliants, to protect those who fled from suffering harm at the hand of their enemy, and he granted them citizenship (*Ant. rom.* 2:15). Like Romulus, Jesus accepts strangers and instructs his followers to accept strangers (10:16; 11:52; 12:20–22). The major difference is that Romulus' final words emphasize his father's (Mars') values of "military preparedness and courage" aimed at making Rome the capital of the world (*Ant. rom.* 2.63.3), while Jesus' farewell words emphasizes his father's will to attain the unity of the children of God through his [Jesus'] death (11:52; 17:11). Jesus' followers do not fight with swords, with violence (John 18:10–11, 33, 36). The difference indicates that the Johannine Jesus had a better plan for the people, i.e., the unity of the children of God. Romulus had a selfish agenda of Roman military preparedness aimed at establishing Rome's rule over the world by force of arms. Romulus' plan was egoistic, with greed guiding his imperial ambitions.

Jesus' teaching and death symbolically destroys and replaces the spatiality defined by the Romans and their Jewish auxiliaries, including the significance of the offices of the Jewish leaders, the temple, the city of Jerusalem, and the nation. Moore argues that for John, the Jerusalem temple "must" be destroyed because it is destined to be replaced by the temple that is Jesus' body (2:19–22; cf. 4:20–21). Jesus himself would be the new temple and thus the new gathering place for the scattered children of God.[69] Jesus' body embodies the oppressed nation just as his body embodies the temple. The crucified body is an image of the nation; the resurrected body is the new reality, the new temple, the new place. In this, image becomes reality.

The significance of the death of Jesus is therefore the realization of a new community among the dispersed and distressed people of God, Jews and Gentiles. Tat-Siong Benny Liew observes that the purpose of John's Gospel is to build a community.[70] This idea of "community" finds a basis in Raymond Williams' and Anthony Cohen's definition of community. According to Raymond Williams, the lexical root of the word "community" is

68. Ibid., 158–59.

69. Moore, "Romans Will Come and Destroy Our Holy Place and Our Nation," 343.

70. Liew, "Ambiguous Admittance," 195.

"relations or feelings."[71] Anthony Cohen suggests that community, as a relational idea, is most concerned with boundary: where community begins and ends.[72] John's Gospel presents Jesus as part of a struggling dominated people. In his activities, Jesus attempts to restore the children of God into a unity in a global community where boundary is not a barrier. John therefore relates Jesus' death to the establishment of "one flock, one shepherd" (10:14–16) and to the 'gathering into one the dispersed children of God" (11:49–52). Jesus' farewell prayer confirms that community is the completion of his ministry and the primary purpose of his crucifixion."[73]

Ephraim as Secondspace

Jesus is condemned to die, so he withdraws to Ephraim. The multiple signs of Jesus affect his journey on earthly spaces. John announces that Jesus no longer went about openly or in public (παρρησίᾳ) among the Jews but withdrew to Ephraim, a town "near the wilderness" (ἐγγὺς τῆς ἐρήμου) and stayed there with his disciples (11:54). It was not uncommon for Jesus to leave Jerusalem and avoid public places after clashes with his opponents (7:1–4, 10; 10:39–40; 11:8). Jesus' withdrawal to the desert place before Passover indicates the explosive political atmosphere in and around Jerusalem. Places of Jesus' popularity become spaces of rejection, threat, separation and limitation. Jesus' places of fame become spaces of death.

Geographers have not located Ephraim, and John does not mention Ephraim elsewhere in his Gospel.[74] Karl Kundsin assumes that Ephraim was significant for the first Christians because Christian communities had settled there at an earlier date.[75] However, first century literature does not indicate this. Rudolf Schnackenburg writes that Ephraim is "probably the present-day village Et-taiyibe, about 12.5 miles north-east from Jerusalem as the crow flies, on a 2,600 feet elevation,"[76] however, this too, is specula-

---

71. Williams, *Keywords*, 75.

72. Cohen, *Symbolic Construction of Community*, 72.

73. Liew, "Ambiguous Admittance," 195.

74. Brant, *John*, 178.

75. Kundsin, *Topologische Überlieferungsstoffe*, 49–50.

76. Schnackenburg, *Gospel According to John*, 2:351. To him the village was previously called "afra", but this name, which in Arabic sounds like "misfortune" or "evil spirit," was changed (possibly by Sultan Saladin) into the present name of "Good," the place with a good name. Eusebius mentions the place and identifies it with Ephron, twenty

tion. Nevertheless, while Ephraim has no firstspace location, it generates questions concerning real and imagined geographies. Ephraim is a second-space marker without a firstspace location, a broader secondspace horizon which incorporates all earthly firstspaces where dominated people hide from the aggression of their oppressors. Ephraim is a secondspace realm of safety described as "near the wilderness." "Near the wilderness" implies distance from the common habitation where provisions are scarce. In this place, Jesus' experience of lack and suffering builds up the momentum and energy for liberation.

There is a progressive movement from places of terror to places of safety. Brant is right to propose that "Jesus chooses a location so far off the beaten path that few have heard of it."[77] As secondspace, it generates a political geography of safety and, as thirdspace, it becomes an experience of liberation for Jesus and his disciples. Significantly, this is the last time that Jesus withdraws to a lonely place to avoid arrest.

While Jesus is bodily absent from Jerusalem, he is secondspatially present in the minds of the pilgrims who, standing in the temple, look for him and ask one another whether or not Jesus will come to the festival (11:56). The festival space in Jerusalem is "out of place" for Jesus. By asking questions about Jesus' coming to Jerusalem, the pilgrims articulate that the political climate is perilous for Jesus, although their motivation for "looking for" him is unspecified. They are either his sympathizers or those who want to report him to the leaders. The verb "to look for" ($\zeta\eta\tau\acute{\epsilon}\omega$) likely refers to a search for a fugitive. The high priest's and the Pharisees' order that anyone who knew Jesus' location should report it so that they could apprehend him (11:57), indicates "reporters" were among those seeking Jesus. Brant puts it thus: "by forcing ordinary citizens to become informants, the Jerusalem authorities seek comprehensive surveillance comparable to the twentieth-century totalitarian states."[78]

Conclusion

John narrates the death of Jesus as the political power struggle of a dominated people in the Roman imperial context. Imperial pressure

---

miles north of Jerusalem (*Onom.* 90. 18ff). To Schnackenburg, it is the same "Ephron" mentioned in 2 Sam 13:23; 2 Chr 13:19; 1 Macc 11:34.

77. Brant, *John*, 178.

78. Ibid., 179.

exacerbates the conflict between Jesus and the Jewish leaders, and Rome's colonial occupation victimizes the leaders of Jerusalem. By seeking to eliminate Jesus, these leaders acknowledge the vulnerability of their place to the will of Rome. Roman presence also increases competition and animosity among the dominated community, and intensifies conflicts between different traditional groups. The council's decision to kill Jesus is governed by the selfish political gain of safeguarding their office and nation. The leaders are concerned about the nation primarily because it is the means through which they maintain their power. Jesus' death, however, transforms the socio-political space by restoring the children of God into a global community where boundary is not a barrier. In his death, Jesus constructs an alternative geography in which all become one in unity, regardless of boundaries.

By redefining the purpose of Jesus' death contrary to Caiaphas' definition and by claiming that Caiaphas' statement is a prophecy, John profanes Caiaphas' words and challenges Caiaphas' space. Caiaphas does not have control over his own tongue in matters pertaining to Jesus' mission. Jesus, on the other hand, is in control of everything, including his own death. John thus portrays Jerusalem's leaders as imperial agents with no power over Jesus. While these leaders realize that Jesus' spatial activities threaten their ideological hegemony and their own authority, their best efforts to control him through killing him fulfills Jesus' agenda and purposes while exposing their impotence. This is the first level of Jesus' challenge to the Roman world order.

CHAPTER 4

Locating the Place of Gathering

(John 12:20–36)

Introduction

John 12:20–36 is a transitional text bridging the decision to kill Jesus (John 11:47–57) and the Passion story (John 18—19). The passage is preceded by the text of Jesus' triumphal entry into Jerusalem (12:12–19), which reinforces the political stakes at play. A "great crowd" welcomes Jesus as the King of Israel, and both the crowd and Jesus himself fulfill scriptural tradition as they play their roles in the regal procession. In response, the Pharisees despair, noting that the "world" has gone after Jesus. These strong political overtones carry over into the first set of declarations of John 12:20–36: some Greeks approach Philip and request to see Jesus. To this request Jesus responds that his hour of "glorification," involving a death unto life and a lifting up, has arrived. He also announces that the "world," with its "ruler" overthrown, now stands in judgment; those who believe in the light will become children of the light; those who follow him (Jesus), who hate their life, will be honored by the father and will be with Jesus in the other world.

Considering these politically charged statements, what does the coming of the Greeks have to do with the coming of Jesus' hour? How does the horrible event of death on the cross become the event of glorification?

What are the effects of John's use of "glory" (δόξα) to refer to the tragic event of the crucifixion of Jesus? How does the crucifixion space become a place of gathering for all human beings? This chapter will answer these questions by looking at spatial constructions in the text.

The Greeks and Philip from Galilee

Among those who are "going up" (ἀναβαινόντων)[1] to worship at the feast are some Greeks ῾(Ελληνές). These Greeks come to Philip "from Bethsaida in Galilee" and ask to see Jesus (12:20). These Gentiles approach Philip, because he bears "a Greek name and comes from a predominantly Gentile area" and speaks Greek.[2] Philip relays the request to Andrew "from Bethsaida," and together they approach Jesus (1:44). Here lies a "brokerage chain" from Philip to Andrew to Jesus, indicating the status of those core followers who stand between Jesus and the public.[3] The mention of Philip's name and his place of origin recall John 1:43–44, where Philip was the first person sought out by Jesus himself to join his disciples.

Characterized as Greeks, these Gentiles are "out of place." They are "not Greek-speaking Jews but Greeks by birth," who have adopted Judaism as full or semi-proselytes. Brown writes that these Greeks are῾Ελληνές or Gentiles, not Ελληνισταί or Greek speaking Jews.[4] Their plan to worship God at the feast implies that they belong to the class known as "God fearers" who were not allowed to share in the eating of the Passover lamb.[5] "Travelers in the Greco-Roman era moved through a sacred landscape filled with sanctuaries and shrines, and to ignore the sanctity of a place by refraining from worship ran the risk of offending at least the residents, if not the local deity. Jerusalem stood apart from this norm."[6] Josephus describes a temple inhospitable to pagan "religious tourists," and notes that

---

1. Malina contends that "to go up" had become a term for pilgrimage and that the grammatical form implies habitual behavior. See Malina, *Social Gospel of Jesus*, 211.

2. Brown, *Gospel According to John*, 470.

3. Malina, *Social Gospel of Jesus*, 212.

4. Brown, *Gospel According to John*, 466. See also Beutler, "Greeks Come to See Jesus," 343.

5. Schnackenburg, *Gospel According to John*, 2:381. Josephus confirms that full or semi-proselytes liked to go to Jerusalem as pilgrims (ἀναβαινόντες, cf. John 7; 8, 10; 11:55) for the Passover (Josephus, *Jewish War* 6. 427).

6. Brant, *John*, 192.

the refusal of sacrifices offered on behalf of the emperor was a cause of the first revolt (*Jewish War* 2.409). Josephus also remarks that the veneration of Moses was widespread. He narrates the story of a group that came from beyond the Euphrates intending to make sacrifices. After a journey that lasted four months, they reached Jerusalem only to discover that they were not allowed to offer sacrifices. Out of reverence for Moses, they refrained from completing the rituals of the sacrifice which some of them had already begun (*Antiquities* 3.318–19). Jerusalem temple space is portrayed as inhospitable to strangers.

The Greeks seek the mediation of Philip, a member of the inner circle of Jesus' group. Philip is from Bethsaida in Galilee. Galilee is "strongly permeated by Hellenism and bordered on pagan areas."[7] Philip's name is Greek, and he comes from a city close to the Decapolis," making him "a suitable candidate to serve as a translator as well as a courier of the travelers."[8] Philip consults his countryman, Andrew (also a Greek name), and together they approach Jesus. That a group of Gentiles from a hierarchically less powerful place seek the mediation of two other individuals hailing from another low-powered space in order to reach the very influential and powerful Jesus signifies a socially fragmented society where hierarchical constructions of places are in full play. The lowly Greeks cannot but trust the lowly Galileans who geographically neighbor them. John explicitly connects the place of origin with power. Philip is portrayed as lacking confidence in his capacity to fulfill his roles when he seeks help.

The worshippers are "going up" (ἀναβαινόντων) in order to worship. Jerusalem is the firstspace location to which the group ascends. The Greeks' "going up" symbolizes the secondspace upward journey to be part of the prestigious Jesus movement. Thirdspatially, their "going up" signifies an elevation for a Gentile or semi-proselyte because by "going up," the worshippers are assured of attaining a new status of being "in place" by being drawn to Jesus. Interestingly, these Greeks who have gone for Passover worship focus on Jesus and not the feast. Jesus the Paschal Lamb becomes their object of worship, signaling Jesus' fame. When Jesus responds that the hour of glorification of the Son of Man has come (12:23), the Johannine double

---

7. Schnackenburg, *Gospel According to John*, 382. Against Mark Chancey who challenges the conventional scholarly view that first-century Galilee was thoroughly Hellenized. He holds that the great extent of Greco-Roman culture in the time of Jesus has often been exaggerated, arguing that the overwhelming majority of first-century Galileans were Jews. For details, see Chancey, *Myth of a Gentile Galilee*.

8. Brant, *John*, 192.

meaning indicates that he is already being honored by these Gentiles. The title "Son of Man" determines Jesus' spatiality with humanity and expresses Jesus' "feeling of an indissoluble connection with humanity, of which he will soon be the glorified representative."[9] Bultmann understands the title, in connection with its "grain-of-wheat epigram" (12:24), to be a direct answer to the request of the Greeks: "through his passion Jesus will become accessible for them as the exalted Lord."[10]

The Greeks' space is defined as a Gentile space, but the lowly Greeks determine the significant moment for Jesus to make the announcement. Previously, Jesus pointedly disavowed attempts to make other incidents the defining moments of his mission (2:4; 7:6, 8; 7:30; 8:20), issuing a pointed "not yet" and a firm "not this" when surface events in the narrative threaten to absorb the reader's full attention.[11] But the coming of the Greeks begins the overturning of the hierarchy of places. Both the Greeks and Philip are "out of place" in Jerusalem—their firstspace location—but "in their place" by being in Jesus' space. Jesus' firstspace location restructures the followers' location. His firstspace location will continue to restructure the believers' space, climaxing at the cross as the thirdspace location of liberation.

Attention to the geographical origin of the characters right at the beginning of the pericope is not accidental. Galilee is a humble firstspace location, a secondspace symbol of the acceptance of Jesus. The Fourth evangelist's descriptions of the movements of Jesus demonstrate that "Galilee is usually the point of arrival or departure" for the journeys of Jesus.[12] B. Olsson writes that "Jesus' journeys in John are centered on going to Jerusalem for the great Jewish feasts (2:13; 5:1; 7:1–10; 12:12)," and most of the dialogue occurs there, as well. Olsson notices four clusters of movements of Jesus in his public ministry. Galilee plays a decisive role in the first three of them.[13]

Fernando Segovia sums up the major events of the journeys to Galilee. In the first trip to Galilee (1:35–2:12), the group around Jesus continues to expand and people come to know his identity as they witness his miraculous deeds: "He is the one about whom the prophets wrote, the King of Israel, the son of God." Jesus' miraculous transformation of water into wine

9. Bruner, *Gospel of John*, 2:220.

10. Bultmann, *Gospel of John*, 424.

11. Tonstad, "The Father of Lies," 196.

12. Freyne, *Galilee, Jesus and the Gospels*, 117.

13. Olsson, *Structure and Meaning*, 27–35.

at a marriage feast reveals his glory, and the people's belief in him solidifies (2:11). Therefore, with this first journey, the "glory" or other-worldly character of Jesus is confirmed, leading his disciples to recognize his religious and political status.[14]

In the second journey, Jesus returns to Galilee (4:1–3), interrupted by a stay in the town of Sychar in Samaria (4:4–42). At Samaria, Jesus' miraculous knowledge about the woman at the well and his declarations about himself lead to "a fundamental affirmation about his identity—the Savior of the world." Jesus receives a broad welcome both in Galilee and Samaria. The sojourn in Sychar in particular yields a series of religious and political affirmations regarding his role and identity: "he is the messiah awaited by the Samaritans and the Savior of the world; he does the will of his father and offers life eternal to all; he supplants established patterns of worship through spirit and truth."[15]

The third geographical journey of Jesus involves a trip to Galilee (6:1—7:9) with a subsequent visit to Jerusalem (7:10—10:39). In Galilee, Jesus continues his marvelous deeds. He feeds a large crowd, and the people not only affirm Jesus as the prophet but also attempt to make him king (6:1–15). He calls on the people to believe in him—the bread from heaven—in order to earn eternal life. With this third journey, religious and political statements abound. Jesus expressly walks away from this offer of worldly "kingship." He announces that from a world that is evil nothing but hatred is to be expected. Only in him is the true bread from heaven to be found.[16]

While Jesus is well-received and becomes known amongst the people in his journeys to Galilee, his journeys to Jerusalem are challenging. According to Freyne, the journeys to Jerusalem have to do with Jewish feasts, but each occasion shows an increase in altercations between Jesus and his opponents. There is a "growing intensity of hostility with each visit as Jesus' challenges to the claims of Jerusalem become more explicit, climaxing in the final movement to his death." Freyne concludes that this hostility forms the backdrop to the various retreats to Galilee.[17] Jerusalem is unfriendly to Gentiles in addition to Jesus.

14. Segovia, "Gospel of John," 175–76.

15. Ibid., 178.

16. Ibid., 180.

17. Freyne, *Galilee*, 118.

Galilee is missing from the fourth movement, yet we read of some Greeks on a pilgrimage to Jerusalem requesting that a man [Philip] from Galilee connect them with Jesus (12:20–21). As discussed earlier in this chapter, the lowly Galilee now functions in a special way in the socio-political group of Jesus. Only the two disciples from Galilee (Philip and Andrew), both bearing Greek names, assume the privileged role of mediating between the Gentiles and Jesus, showing that Galilee is no longer a humble place but a space of power. Belonging to Jesus' space changes even the hierarchy of places. Coming from Galilee is no longer considered lowly, and no longer is being Greek a symbol of marginalization.

Jesus' response to the Greeks does not address the request they made, rather it is an interpretation of their physical presence. The presence of these Greeks announces that it is time for a more diverse community and to overcome social fragmentations in the society.[18] Jesus' death will achieve this, which will be his glorification as well as the glorification of the father. Brant writes that Jesus' death is necessary for the geometric growth of his followers.[19] By "glorification" he envisages the fullness of saving power which will be given him (13:32, 17:1–2) to "draw all people to himself" (12:32). Jesus intends that his death bear fruit for many (12:24), i.e., to provide rich fruit of unity to the divided community.

The movement of the Greeks toward Jesus and their need to be with him contrasts with the hatred of those who want to eliminate him. The Gentiles' requests in his favor provoke a cry against the injustice of Rome and its auxiliaries who are defined as "the rulers of this world" (12:31).[20] Earlier in the Gospel, Jesus repeatedly announces that his "hour" has not come (2:4, 7:30, 8:20). The hour of Jesus' death now arrives. This alerts us to see this occasion as the end of Jesus' mission both in timing and purpose.

18. The post-Jesus Johannine community went through a sectarian phase, but resisted sectarian dynamics, and became more inclusive. Its own capacity for inclusion and integration is a prototype of the later church. Boring, *Introduction to the New Testament*, 626.

19. Brant, *John*, 192.

20. Against scholars who argue that the ruler of this world is the devil. See Twelftree, "Exorcisms in the Fourth Gospel and the Synoptics"; Judith L. Kovacs, "Now Shall the Ruler of This World," 227–47. Seeking to demythologize, David Aune opposes the idea of the ruler of this world as "Satan," pointing out that in John the aliases "ruler of this world," "Satan," and "devil" designate a personal being, though he falls short of determining who the personal being is in this case. See Aune, "Dualism in the Fourth Gospel," 287. A detailed discussion of the identity of the ruler of this world is found later in this chapter under the sub-title "Dethroning the Ruler of This World."

The image of the grain of wheat illustrates the fruitfulness of Jesus' death; the point of the parable is that Jesus' death is necessary to bear rich fruit, both political and missionary.

The Greeks' coming signals Jesus' fast-approaching death and the inclusion of Gentiles in Jesus' mission. Jesus gives a political and theological explanation of the presence of the Greeks: as the first Gentiles, their arrival signals that Jesus' hour has come.[21] Beutler supports this view through Johannine texts that point to this inclusion and universality. In 10:16, while "the other sheep not of this fold" could refer to non-Jews in the sense of non-Judeans or to the Jews from the Diaspora or to the Gentiles, the latter is the most probable. In 11:52, the narrator's comment may carry a similar range but again, "the universalistic ring is strong."[22] Moreover, in the verse preceding our central text, i.e. 12:19, the Pharisees say: "You see that you can do nothing; look, the world has gone after him." The word κόσμος bears a typical Johannine double meaning: as the world is going to follow Jesus, in the next verse, the Greeks come to see Jesus, and John gives a lesson about following Jesus (12:26).[23] A universalistic sense of Ἑλληνές is underlined by Christ's "drawing all to himself" (12:32).

Jesus undergoes death to bring salvation to the Greeks and to all people. This facilitates the inclusion of the Greeks and the Gentile world into the people of God, which happens in fullness at the cross. "The hour has come" (12:23) creates not only a spatial gap but also intermediate earthly space. The time has arisen for finding a new relationship to this world. This new relationship is not merely between temporal and eschatological time, but is a spatial relationship geographically constructed by the coming of the Greeks. Jesus announces the time for a new spatial relationship that embraces all. The horizon expands from a single Israel to include other location markers like Greeks, Galileans and more. Jesus embodies this new progressive, inclusive, and global community.

Transforming the Crucifixion Space

As Jesus foretells his nearing death, he observes that he, the "Son of Man," is in the process of being glorified in the impending crucifixion. In the first century CE, death on the cross was not only one of the most horrific forms

21. Brown, *Gospel of John*, 466.

22. Beutler, "Greeks Come to See Jesus," 343.

23. Ibid.

of punishment in the ancient world but also a humiliating one. The crucifixion was the ultimate expression of Roman imperial power. It was the political space of a dramatic show of Roman power demonstrated in the brutality against criminals, particularly those who rebelled against Roman rule. According to James Scott, the crucifixion served as an instrument of the Roman Empire's totalitarian rule through the "physical deprivation" of bodies and "psychological denigration." The former refers to realities of "material exploitation" such as physical and sexual abuse, loss of goods and property, painful and unpleasant work conditions, while the latter relates to the issues of "dignity and autonomy."[24]

The crucifixion enacted both the "socially degraded status of the victim" and "Rome's conquest of the victim's nation."[25] Alan Kirk writes that "torturous deaths—such as the crucifixion was—can be highly symbolized forms of violence, with the disfiguring, distending, dismembering, smashing, and perforation of the human body routinized and choreographed to display and enact publicly the socially degraded state of the victim."[26] According to Pseudo-Quintilian, the Roman crucifixion was driven by the theorem: "every punishment has less to do with the offense than with the example." Hence, "when we [Romans] crucify criminals the most frequented roads are chosen, where the greatest number of people can look and be seized by this fear."[27]

Martin Hengel observes that crucifixion in the Graeco-Roman world was generally perceived as shameful since it involved a progressive humiliation of the victim and loss of honor.[28] It was regarded as one of the most horrific forms of punishment in the ancient world.[29] Cicero called it "that most cruel and disgusting penalty" and "the ultimate punishment" (*Orations* 2.5.165, 168). Seneca called the cross an "accursed tree" (*Epistles* 101:14), while in Justinian, the crucifixion was "the supreme punishment" (*Digest* 48:19). The crucifixion was the appropriate punishment for slaves

24. Scott, *Domination*, 22–23.

25. Kirk, "The Memory of Violence," 192; Pseudo-Quintilian, *Lesser Declamations*, 1:259. Pseudo-Quintilian's *Lesser Declamations* dates to about the second century CE. Accessed on January 6, 2014 at: http://searchworks.stanford.edu/view/7926843.

26. Kirk, "The Memory of Violence," 192.

27. Pseudo-Quintilian, *Lesser Declamations*, 1:259.

28. Hengel, *Crucifixion*, 22–23.

29. Ibid. The original German Edition of the work bore the Latin title *Mors turpissima crucis*, "the utterly vile death of the cross," a quotation from Origen in his commentary on Matthew 27:22.

(Cicero, *In Verrem* 2.5.168), bandits (Josephus, *Jewish War* 2:253), prisoners of war (Josephus, *Jewish War* 5:451) and revolutionaries (Josephus, *Jewish War* 17:295). Josephus also remarks that the crucifixion was "the most wretched of deaths" (*Jewish War* 7:6.4).

The violence of the cross went beyond physical punishment to "symbolic annihilation, with the destruction of the victim's flesh narrating Rome's capacity to suppress every threat to the state's entire sovereignty."[30] The destruction of the bodily space was figurative of Rome's conquest of the victim's nation. Thus Thatcher writes,

> Crucifixion was . . . a commemorative ritual and a symbolic reenactment of significant past events in the same way that the Eucharist is a symbolic reenactment of Jesus' last meal with his disciples. Specifically, every crucifixion reenacted Rome's conquest of the victim's nation. In this drama, the officiating soldiers played the role of the conquering Roman legions, while the person on the cross represented his entire people group, beaten, broken, and subjugated.[31]

This implies that, from the perspective of the Romans, the scourging and the crucifixion were intentional and explicit illustrations for the masses that any resistance against Roman rule would result in a painful and ignominious death.

From the perspective of Judaism of the first century, the crucifixion, with its suspension of the body of the victim on a wooden cross or stake, could be interpreted as a curse. Deuteronomy 21:22–23 stipulates that anyone who "hangs on a tree" is under God's curse. The Dead Sea Scrolls— 4Q169 (the *Pesher Nahum*; frags. 3–4, col. 1, lines 7–8) and 11Q19–20 (the *Temple Scroll*; col. 64, lines 7–13)—insist that the curse of the tree fell upon the eight hundred Jewish enemies of Alexander Jannaeus who were crucified as a punishment for their participation in a revolt in 88 BCE. The Temple Scroll reads:

> If a man slanders his people and delivers his people to a foreign nation and does evil to his people, you shall hang him on a tree and he shall die. On the testimony of two witnesses and on the testimony of three witnesses, he shall be put to death and they shall hang him on a tree. If a man is guilty of a capital crime and flees abroad to the nations, and curses his people, the children of

30. Thatcher, *Greater Than Caesar*, 93.
31. Ibid.

Israel, you shall hang him also on a tree, and he shall die (*Temple Scroll*, col 64, 7–13).

Both *Pesher Nahum* and *Temple Scroll* allude to Deuteronomy 21 as evidence that God affirmed the judgment of the earthly authorities by extending his own curse to the condemned. The sentiments are amplified in the Temple Scroll by the assertion that "hanging on a tree" is fit punishment for those traitors and those who curse the people of Israel, and in 4Q169 by the application of Nahum 2:13 to the victim as well: "'See, I am against you [the one crucified],' says the Lord of hosts."[32] Any witness to a Roman scourging and crucifixion would readily agree that God had abandoned the victim. The crucifixion was then seen as God's will. Considering that Roman imperial ideology considered the emperor as the leader desired by God, any rebellion against Rome's government would be a rebellion against God.

From the Roman and Judaism perspectives, Golgotha—the site of Jesus' crucifixion (19:17)—became the "ideal venue for Jerusalem crucifixions."[33] From a Roman point of view, Golgotha was the perfect place to tell the cross story simply because it was an elevated plot of ground that could be seen from many places in and around the Jewish metropolis, a veritable pulpit from which to proclaim the gospel of imperial power. In Jewish eyes, Golgotha was a good site for crucifixions because the unclean bodies of the cursed criminals would hang outside the walls, preventing pollution of the holy city. Deut 21:23 states that the corpses would "defile the land" if left to hang overnight.[34] Nailed to these two embedded narratives of enemies of the state and rejection by God, crucifixion victims were dehumanized and erased, discouraging any sequel to their stories.

The deterrence of public crucifixion served Rome's general strategy of "light interference in local politics" by encouraging the oppressed to do the

32. It is not completely clear whether the Temple Scroll and the Pesher Nahum quoted above used the phrase "hang on a tree" in reference to crucifixion, rather than to execution by hanging or to the public display of a corpse after execution—the scenario envisioned by Deut 21:22–23. Scholars today agree that both texts be seen as allusions to the crucifixion of eight hundred Pharisees by Alexander Jannaeus in 88 BCE, as narrated by Josephus in *Jewish Antiquities* 13:379–80 and *Jewish Wars* 1:96–98. For relevant evidence see Fitzmyer, "Crucifixion in Ancient Palestine," 498–507.

33. Thatcher, *Greater Than Caesar*, 94.

34. In the Gospel of Peter, Herod and the Jews demonstrate awareness of this problem and its implications for the timing of the death and burial of Jesus. See *Gos. Pet.* 2:3; 5:1; cf. John 19:31.

teaching for them. Scott writes that "in any established structure of domination, it is plausible to imagine that subordinate groups are socialized by their parents in the rituals of homage that will keep them from harm."[35] Citing the case of slavery, he observes that "it is in the interest of slave mothers, whose overriding wish is to keep their children safe and by their side, to train them in the routines of conformity."[36] I imagine that this would apply to Jewish parents who witnessed the crucifixion of a Jew on a Roman cross outside the walls of Jerusalem.

Given the above conception of the crucifixion, why are Johannine believers being asked to see in the event of Jesus' crucifixion his glorification by and to God? In other words, "to what end, for whom, and in what circumstances has this astonishing identification of Jesus' crucifixion as his exaltation and glorification been made?"[37] How does John transform this space of violence and shame into an attractive place to which all people are drawn and in which they experience liberation? By presenting the crucifixion as a place of Jesus' and God's glorification, John produces an attractive space to which believers are drawn and in which the marginalized envision their liberation from oppressive politics.

In her "Beauty, Sorrow, and Glory in the Gospel of John," Jo-Ann Brant wonders about "the ability of the artist to transform anguish into something sublime, something from which one does not retreat in fear."[38] She recognizes this in Michelangelo's *La Pieta*, the statue of Mary cradling the lifeless body of Christ in her lap.[39] To Brant, the author of the Fourth Gospel is another artist who draws upon the concept of divine glory, of which beauty is an essential dimension, to present Jesus' death on the cross as something beautiful in which the followers of Christ can see the presence of God within their affliction.[40] Similar to Brant, I argue that John makes the crucifixion space attractive by conceptualizing it through glory. Aside from the aesthetic dimension of glory, I examine the socio-political aspect of glory in order to ascertain how John transforms the geography of the cross from a space of violence into a positive place where the followers of

---

35. Scott, *Domination*, 24.
36. Ibid.
37. Boer, "Johannine History," 320.
38. Brant, "Beauty, Sorrow and Glory," 83.
39. For a detailed discussion, see Brant, "Beauty, Sorrow and Glory," 83.
40. Ibid., 84.

Jesus recognize the presence of God in their sufferings and envision their liberation from oppressive Roman imperial power.

Scholars define John's use of "glory" (δόξα) or the verb "to glorify" (δοξάζω) in diverse ways, some of which are examined here. G. B. Caird writes that in John, the verb "oscillates between 'to give honor, respect or praise' or to bring to a position of honor and clothe with [heavenly] splendor."[41] In Bruce Malina's view, "glory" functions within the ancient "honor and shame" systems in society, designating either a "desirable status in the social hierarchy" or denoting a certain way of "appearing" that corresponds to a superior position.[42] As a social status, "glory" appears in discussions describing everything from evoking recognition to establishing high status such as wealth (Gen 31:1), belongings (Job 19:9) or payment (Num 22:17), etc. Consequently, the verbal expressions "to give glory" stand for social recognition, as for example, when God calls forth recognition of himself as God by his mighty deeds (Exod 14:4). As a way of "appearing" that corresponds to a superior position, "glory" primarily concerns the appearance of God. Wherever he appears, his "glory" is present, for example, on Mt. Sinai, in the tabernacle, or in the temple. Like Malina, Jerome Neyrey understands glory in light of honor and shame as cultural forces, laying emphasis on "glory" as a function of social status. To him, 'glory' means Jesus' worth, honor and status.[43]

Brant makes a number of important observations about the meaning of glory. She comments that Neyrey's survey "does not address the emphasis upon Jesus' glory as a manifestation of divine presence and a possible distinction between human and divine glory."[44] She distinguishes between God's glory from glory sought by human beings:

> The Johannine Jesus constantly juxtaposes God's glory and the glory sought or gained through acknowledgement by people (5:41, 44; 7:18; 8:50). John uses forms of the verb to see θεάομαι (1:14, 32; 4:35; 11:45) and ὁράω (11:40; 12:41) to describe the act of looking at or perceiving God's glory. The narrator proclaims, "We have beheld [ἐθεασάμεθα] his glory, the glory as of an off-spring" (1:14). Jesus proclaims, "whoever beholds [or looks at] me,

41. Caird, "Glory of God," 265–77.

42. Malina, New Testament World, 28–50.

43. Neyrey, Gospel of John, 45.

44. Brant, "Beauty, Sorrow, and Glory," 87. Brant's remarks are based on Alexander Tsutserov's work on glory, grace and truth in the Gospel of John. See Tsutserov, Glory, Grace and Truth, 218 and 241.

beholds the one who sent me" (12:45; see also 14:9). John refers to a quality that both Jesus and God possess rather than the act of granting God a status. In order to exist, honor must be acknowledged (it is socially constructed), but divine glory is an aspect of God that is evident or perceptible to humanity.[45]

To Brant, in John "faith makes possible the perception of divine presence in Jesus."[46] The glory of the Son is evident only to those who seek God's glory and who do not look at the worldly standards of honor. It is even more challenging to see God's glory in the cross event, which normally signifies an absence of God and the presence of human cruelty. Followers can distinguish the crucifixion space of Jesus from other crucifixion spaces which they had seen previously through the lens of faith in Jesus. Faith in Jesus enables them to envisage any crucifixion space thereafter as a space of struggle and liberation.

When Jesus' followers perceive God's glory through faith, they construct their new spatial relations through this experience. Witnesses come to understand the crucifixion of Jesus in a new way, just as they also come to a new view of their lived experience of suffering. God's glory transforms the cross into thirdspace, where the marginalized people's lived experiences are given hope in the liberating power of the cross of Christ. When God manifests in glory on the cross, the cross is transformed from a cursed space (where God is absent, signifying abandonment) into a place of God's presence and blessing.

The glory of God is a relationship. Ashton argues that the glory of God is not something God possesses in God's self-independent of the world God created and from which God receives praise. Glory "expresses the impressions he makes on humankind when he manifests his power to them. For example, God's justice may be said to imply a relationship: in this case the relationship with those to whom he reveals himself."[47] In the case of the crucifixion, God's glory impacts the relationship between Jesus and the marginalized people. The followers begin to see salvation in the cross as the crucifixion space is translated by God's presence. God's positioning at the cross reminds the Romans of who the true God is, contrary to the ideology of a deified Roman emperor. Glory therefore becomes a tool of resistance as well.

45. Brant, "Beauty, Sorrow, and Glory," 87.

46. Ibid., 88.

47. Ashton, *Understanding*, 472–73.

The true Johannine paradox is that glory is manifest in Jesus' death, a death that Jesus' opponents intended to be inglorious, something shameful and hideous from which Jesus' followers would turn away in dismay. By calling it a place of glorification John renders the sad and sorrowful event attractive. He transgresses the boundaries of a defined role of the cross to attract believers to it, where Jesus becomes a voice for the voiceless bodies abused and dehumanized at the cross. Humanity should focus on Jesus because he is their voice against the oppressor. Brant notes the importance of John's focus on the bodily space of Jesus in his moments of agony:

> Whereas the Synoptic tradition treats the crucifixion as the fulfillment of Isaiah's comment "there was no beauty in him to make us look at him, nor appearance that would attract us to him" (Isa 53:2–3) and trains the eye away from the cross itself, John continuously draws his audience's eye to Jesus' body. Pilate commands, "Behold the man," pointing to Jesus' lacerated, bleeding body (19:5). John describes Jesus bearing his own cross (19:17). We see the soldiers disrobe Jesus before gambling for his garments (19:23). We see Jesus drink from the vinegar-sopped sponge and then the final indignity to his body, a spear thrust into his side from which pours out his blood and water (19:34). These are all sights from which one would normally avert one's eyes.[48]

Elaborate spatial constructions spotlight Jesus' bodily space and portray it as dehumanized—adding poignancy to Jesus' death—only to redefine the space as the place of glory. Jesus is not in an ungodly crucifixion space, abandoned to doom and its forces, but in a welcoming space of divine presence bearing hope of unity for the children of God dispersed in various modes and places by imperial politics. Rome made use of the crucifixion to arouse in the crucified victim's followers doubts about the goodness, beauty or meaning of the victim and his convictions. By transforming this ugly death into something desirable, John subverts Rome's intent. Death on the cross is no longer abandonment by the gods; it is no longer devoid of the beauty that draws the love of the gods. Just as Jesus gazes down from the cross upon the afflicted and lifts them up, God gazes down upon the cross and lifts up the crucified and dethrones the oppressor.

---

48. Brant, "Beauty, Sorrow and Glory," 93–94.

Dethroning the Ruler of This World

Jesus announces the consequences of his death. He calls it "the hour" for the "judgment of this world" and for "expelling the ruler of this world" (12:31). Raymond Brown writes that "the prince of this world" is a Johannine term for "Satan."[49] Interpreting the "ruler of this world" as Satan, Judith Kovacs reads Jesus' death on the cross as the climax of the cosmic battle between Jesus and forces of evil, represented by Satan.[50] Graham Twelftree agrees with Kovacs though, unlike Kovacs, he compares the Fourth Gospel and the Synoptic Gospels in order to support his case.[51] While the Synoptics are full of exorcism stories, John intentionally eliminated the exorcism stories in order to dissociate Jesus from exorcism.[52]

Twelftree claims that the Fourth evangelist deliberately suppressed the exorcism traditions for three reasons. First, from a literary point of view, John preferred miracle stories that are "spectacular and relatively uncommon," an indicator that Jesus' acts exceeded the religious leaders of his time.[53] Hence, he performed miracles such as turning water into wine, feeding a multitude, raising the dead, etc. Twelftree claims that in the ancient society and even in the Synoptics, exorcisms are portrayed as relatively unspectacular.[54]

Second, John may have been theologically uncomfortable with the inherent ambiguity of exorcisms. Twelftree argues that the Synoptic story of casting demons by the power of the prince of demons, "Beelzebul," indicates that ancient exorcists drew their powers from a wide range of supernatural sources (Matt 12:24; Luke 11:15). John instead characterizes Jesus' miracles as "signs" of his divine identity, as exorcisms could not prove that Jesus was the "Son of God." Even in the Synoptics, exorcisms signify "the realization of the kingdom," not something about Jesus' nature.[55]

Third, John may have omitted exorcism stories because he intended to characterize the whole ministry of Jesus as a battle with Satan and especially

---

49. Brown, Gospel According to John, 468. See also Bruner, Gospel of John, 718.

50. Kovacs' work is discussed in chapter one of this work. For details see Kovacs, "Now Shall the Ruler of This World," 227–47. See also Dennis, "Lifting up of the Son of Man," 677–91.

51. Twelftree, "Exorcisms," 137.

52. Ibid.

53. Ibid., 137–38.

54. Ibid.

55. Ibid., 139–40.

to localize the devil's defeat in Jesus' death. Hence, "the cross event" becomes the "grand cosmic exorcism" in the Gospel of John.[56] This means that for John, "the lie of Satan's control of this world is far more pervasive than the possession of some individuals."[57]

Twelftree claims that the cross is the focal point for Christ's battle with Satan. His arguments are based on John 12:31; 13:2, 27; and 16:11. Just before Jesus retires to the upper room with his disciples, hours before his death, he claims that the "ruler of this world" will be "cast out." Shortly after this reference, we hear twice that the devil has inspired Judas to betray Jesus (13:2, 27), thus setting in motion the events that lead to the agony of the cross. In the farewell discourse, Jesus reassures the disciples that the Holy Spirit will affirm his victory by bringing judgment on the ruler of this world, a final proof that the evil one has no power to stop Christ's mission. Twelftree concludes that in John's account, the cross essentially replaces the synoptic exorcism stories as the battleground for Christ's combat with the devil.[58]

While Twelftree is convincing about John's omission of the exorcism stories, he is less convincing that the cross story is a replacement for the exorcism stories. Thatcher objects to Twelftree's arguments by using the same texts on which Twelftree bases his arguments. Thatcher observes that the verb "to cast out" (ἐκβάλλω) in 12:31 is the only instance that "might refer to exorcism," as elsewhere it could refer to "excommunicating someone from a religious community."[59] A closer look reveals that it is not actually the devil that is being "cast out" when Jesus is "lifted up" on the cross but rather "the leader of this world" (ὁ ἄρχων τοῦ κόσμου τούτου; John 12:31–33). This individual reappears at 14:30, where Jesus says he would like to tell his disciples more but cannot so do because "the ruler of this world is coming." Again in 16:11, Christ promises that the spirit will bring judgment on the

56. Ibid., 140–41.

57. Ibid.

58. Ibid., 141.

59. While the verb ἐκβάλλω appears six times in the Gospel of John, other than in 12:31 in which it might refer to exorcism, the five other occurrences refer to excommunication instead. Thus at 2:15 Jesus "casts out" money exchangers from the temple; in 9:34–45, twice the verb is used to describe the blind man's excommunication from the synagogue. At 6:37 Jesus promises that all who come to him will never be "cast out," rather he will "lead out all his own" sheep to safe pasture (10:4). The Johannine Jesus thus enacts the Synoptics' "first will be last" principle by casting out Caesar while drawing in the world's rejects. See Thatcher, *Greater Than Caesar*, 121 and 160.

world because "the ruler of this world has been judged." Perhaps because John regularly portrays the world as morally corrupt and hateful towards God and believers, Twelftree assumes that John uses the title "ruler of this world" as a "moniker for the devil,"[60] not unlike the references to Satan in Ephesians (2:2; 6:12). Combining these references with the words "cast out" at John 12:31 suggests that Christ's battle with Satan will take place at Golgotha and that Jesus' death will effect the ultimate exorcism.[61]

Each of the references cited above strongly point to the "the ruler of this world" sayings as references specifically to the forthcoming trials and crucifixion. When Jesus says that "the ruler of this world will be cast out" when he is "lifted up" (12:31–32), he is referring to what the Roman soldiers will do to his body. In the same way, Jesus says that "the ruler of this world is coming" to silence him (14:30), referring to the Romans coming to arrest him (18:3, 12) and Pontius Pilate putting an end to his preaching. When in 16:8–11 Jesus says that "the ruler of this world" has been "judged about judgment," he is referring to Rome's responsibility for his own violent death (19:11). The events of Golgotha then become a reference to the ruler of this world, the reigning Roman Emperor.[62] Considering that double meanings are a stylistic feature of the Gospel of John, it is not out of place to consider the "the ruler of this world" as the devil and to suggest that the Roman Emperor is the symbolic devil.

Scholars commonly describe the "judgment of this world" as language of mythological imagery. Stripped of this imagery, the subject of judgment is the human world, inhabited by unbelievers and haters of Jesus. According to Brown, this is a realized eschatology wherein the very presence of Jesus in the world is a judgment provoking people to judge themselves as they decide either for or against Jesus.[63] John says that the ruler of this age will be driven out (ἐκβληθήσεται; 12:31), "is coming" (14:30) and has been condemned (κέκριται; 16:11). In these statements, John announces this world's most critical moment. In the context of the "political drama that is unfolding in the minds of the crowd and the Jewish authorities, Jesus initially appears to sound a battle cry for the overthrow of Roman occupation. Yet set within the narrative that Jesus has been telling, his pronouncement takes on a different meaning. Brant observes that ἐκβληθήσεται can also

60. Ibid., 121.

61. Ibid.

62. Ibid., 121.

63. Brown, *Gospel According to John*, 147.

mean to "be exposed."[64] In light of the crucifixion, "the ruler of this world will be shown to be powerless."[65]

John also uses the same word "ruler" to denote the Jerusalem leaders (3:1; 7:36, 48; 12:42), who are agents and children of the devil (8:44–47). The reference to the "coming ruler" refers to Jesus' coming meeting with the Jerusalem elite and Pilate, the Roman governor. John attributes their hostility towards Jesus to their being children of the evil one, the devil. The architect of evil impels the Romans to dominate and rule with cruelty, and their auxiliaries continue to work for and fulfill the agenda of the oppressor by choosing to kill Jesus. Jesus' death on the cross will become a focal place. The rays of his glorification on the cross will shine through the antagonism that exists among the various groups of dominated peoples, and between the imperialist leaders and subjects.[66]

Responding to both the crisis situation of the Johannine Jesus in the Roman imperial context and the Johannine community's minority situation, John highlights the universal and fundamental change which takes place in the "lifting up of the Son of Man" (12:32). The death of Jesus on the cross transforms the conflict between Roman imperial power and their auxiliaries and Jesus by challenging the world's allegiance to the imperial divide-and-conquer power system. As both the believers in Jesus and non-believers focus on the cross, they see in the dead body on the cross an indication that their liberation is at hand. In fact, the leaders of this world are exposed by the crushing weight of evidence brought to bear on Jesus' person and program by his life and death. Jesus' death exposes the leaders and their evil plans. In his death, Jesus' followers—the oppressed people who believe in his leadership—see the extent of the oppression, are inspired by Jesus, who sacrifices his life for them, and move towards him.

God's judgment stands over the leaders of "this world" of Caesar. Confident that the present Roman imperial order stands under this judgment, Jesus announces that his death will initiate the trial of Rome and its allies. In contrast to the people waiting quietly for God to liberate them from Rome and rebuild their community, Jesus is involved in a social project to instill

64. Brant, *John*, 194.

65. Ibid.

66. Sandra Schneiders, leaning heavily on the Wisdom of Solomon in her interpretation of the Gospel of John, sees one group of Jews persecuted by another in the context of Rome, a situation similar to the Johannine community in conflict with the Pharisees in John, for example, John 9. For details see Schneiders, *Johannine Resurrection*, 97–113, esp. 110–13.

hope in the community and to rebuild the life of the subjected peoples. The Roman rulers and their auxiliaries are already condemned by God, accomplished as the crucifixion defeats the demonic Roman powers and inaugurates the geographical space in which the Roman powers—and the social and psychological structures based upon them—undergo a progressive de-legitimization. As Rudolf Schnackenburg puts it, "the ruler of the world encounters the final rejection, loses his sphere of influence, becomes powerless—over those who look up in faith to the crucified Jesus and let themselves be 'drawn' to him."[67]

As firstspace, the cross is a space of violence, a physical spatiality that is comprehended in empirically measurable configurations. It is situated outside the city of Jerusalem, protecting the center from its horrors while terrifying the margins with its awful spectacles. The social production of this firstspace is a historical unfolding, an evolving sequence of changing geographies that results from the dynamic relations between the Romans and the dominated people of first century Palestine. The crucifixion constructs new behaviors.

The cross is also a symbolic secondspace, a world of rationally interpretable signification. It not only parades the physical bodies that are abused but also sends a message of fear to the dominated people. It is designed to deter any rebellion against empire. This is the imagined geography which becomes a reality, as the image or representation defines and orders reality in the empire.

By defining the cross as the place of "glory," John deconstructs the firstspace and secondspace mode of thinking about the crucifixion space, making it a thirdspace of new possibilities. It becomes Lefebvre's "possibilities machine," a recasting of Proust, a Madeleine for a *recherche des espaces perdus*, a remembrance-rethinking-recovery of spaces lost . . . or never sighted at all.[68]

Founding a Political Community at the Cross

In chapter three, I discussed the Sanhedrin's concern for the safety of their place and nation. The expressions "our place" and "our nation" imply both inclusion in and exclusion from the place. Inclusion into the group is facilitated by meeting conditions of spatial belonging. The council's designation

67. Schnackenburg, *Gospel According to John*, 2:392.
68. Lefebvre, *Production of Space*, 26–27.

of the space as theirs discloses inclusivity and exclusivity. Only those who belong have access to privileges in this space. Behaviors that jeopardize the space at risk should be curtailed. This space demands a selective reduction in diversity to homogeneity as behaviors in this space are shaped by the norms defined by Rome and its allies. The space is intolerant to heterogeneity as it appears to exclude the "other" who is considered "out of place" and dangerous to the nation. According to Zipporah G. Glass, constructs of homogeneity "sustain the marginalization of heterogeneous identities while simultaneously setting the parameters of power and the privileges of access to power in homogenizing enterprises."[69] The Palestine peasants find themselves marginalized in their own land. The nation and place belong to the Romans and the local leaders. The peasants are the "other," in a liminal space.

The peasants belong to the nation, yet their inclusion does not provide full access to the benefits of social, economic or political inclusion. Glass refers to this as a "de facto exclusion," often masked by the appearance of a cohesive socio-political context, in this case the nation state.[70] Achebe observes that such exclusionary categories remain hidden until political, economic or social space becomes contested within the nation. Contesting space within nations shifts the focus of attention from overt manifestations of external invading and colonizing forces to the progressive and subtle internal forces of colonization.[71]

William Edward DuBois points out the "non-national character or ambiguous political status of the colonized peoples."[72] This ambiguity resolves only when the imperialist—"the master nation"—either integrates their colonial subjects into the polity, or allows them to become independent,

69. Glass, "Building toward Nation-ness," 154.

70. Ibid., 156. Glass writes that in modern states two primary principles have acted to exclude the colonized "other," namely, the principle of *ius sanguinis* (nationality by blood descent) which acts formally to exclude from citizenship mostly immigrants and "mixed blood" progeny resulting from interactions between nations and foreign blood. The second principle is de facto exclusion where statutory citizenship does not provide for full access of the benefits of social, economic and political inclusion. This is the situation of the peasants in first century Palestine. They have a statutory citizenship, yet are deprived of benefits. The political elite in Jerusalem care about their "advantage" and that of their Roman Empire.

71. The exclusionary categories are explicit after protests and fights against the British imperialists in Umuofia, led by Okonkwo and a few elders. For details see Achebe, *Things Fall Apart*, 192–207, esp. 203.

72. DuBois, "Negro and Imperialism (1944)," 155.

free peoples.[73] DuBois, located in the African-American context, explains that African-Americans were citizens already in the 1880s, yet it was not until after the civil rights movement in the 1960s that selective and limited enfranchisement was attained. Their continuing struggle with assimilation confirms DuBois' statement that black people in America are "a nation without a polity, nationals without citizenship."[74] Such might have been the situation of the peasants in first century Roman Palestine.

For dominated people, a nation is not a community of people whose members are bound together by the sense of solidarity that arises from a common culture and a national consciousness. Instead, a nation is a community whose solidarity comes from what is expedient for the local and colonial leadership. In such a nation, diversity is strangled because it poses a threat. Postcolonialism enables the recovery of solidarity, a common culture, and a national consciousness that re-inscribes heterogeneity. In doing so, it displaces those strategies which—in the past and in the present—have characterized empire.[75] This is the project that Jesus undertakes. In his death on the cross, Jesus inscribes the heterogeneous progeny. He gathers "all people" from diverse nationalities and cultures into a global community in which boundary no longer hinders and in which everyone is privileged to access power. In Jesus' global nation, he disables the need for a common culture and replaces it with the need for common values (defined by Jesus as the will of his Father). In Jesus' nation, the political process of nation-building creates the capacity to transcend the particularism of culture nation, and maintains the nation as a political unit with a common will and purpose.

Jesus' insistence that whoever follows him will be with him wherever he is (12:26) initiates the formation of this global community. The place "where I am" (ὅπου εἰμὶ ἐγὼ) emphasizes that the initiative and power come from Jesus. His bodily space is the focal point that attracts. The place where "I am" indicates the sacred place where God is present.[76] The one "lifted up" has the power to restore what is lost. He gathers a society, socially fragmented by imperialism, to where he is, in order to work out their liberation. Even in his death on the cross, the society will gather together

---

73. Ibid.

74. DuBois, "Souls of White Folk," 49.

75. Glass, "Building toward Nation-ness," 154.

76. "I am" in the Old Testament is the divine name. In Jesus' days, uttering the name of God was prohibited (Josephus, *Antiquities* 2.275–76; 1QS 6.27—7.2).

as one suffering people, and as a new group with hope for a new life. At the cross, Jesus and his followers re-inscribe heterogeneity. Imperialist values do not form this new society, but rather the will of God, shown to Jesus' followers by the Spirit (John 14:15–24).

Jesus' confession, "now my heart is troubled" (12:27), signifies the self-giving aspect of his death. The advent of Jesus' time of death leaves him anxious, but, in spite of his anxiety, Jesus embraces it as a sacrifice that carries with it an element of pain. As such, he does not ask to be delivered from it. For Jesus, "now" denotes both the punctual awareness of the death that awaits him (12:27) and the critical moment to manifest his power by driving out of the ruler of this world (12:31). He articulates the understanding of his mission in the statement, "for this reason I have come to this hour" (12:27).[77]

Jesus characterizes the hour of his death as the glorification of God's name (12:28). According to Schnackenburg, God's name stands for the essence, the holiness, the inviolable will, and also for the mercy and love of God. "Jesus revealed 'God's name' to his disciples as referring to his holiness (17:11), 'justice' in the sense of mercy (17:25) and love."[78] God will glorify God's name by reinstating the Son in heavenly glory and by making his death fruitful for the world.[79] A voice from heaven assures Jesus and the listeners of the glorification, "I have glorified it, and will glorify it again" (12:28). God's name is glorified in Jesus' missionary activities, however God will also be glorified in Jesus' death. The glorification occurs in a contested space. Sigve Tonstad puts it thus, "the glory that is to be affirmed comes in counterpoint to glory that has been denied."[80] Jesus faces serious opposition, which climaxes in being killed. The glory manifested in his death is therefore a manifestation of power that has been refuted.

A voice from heaven confirms that the Father has glorified his name and will glorify it again. "Heaven" calls attention to the different levels of power that are conferred by different spaces on their occupants and travelers. Heaven is a place of superior power when compared to earthly spaces and their occupants. The "voice from heaven" thus confirms Jesus' unparalleled

77. The Good News Bible beautifully puts it, "that is why I came." J. H. Bernard translates it thus: "and yet for this very purpose, I came." See Bernard, *A Critical and Exegetical Commentary*, 2:437. Both translations clearly express Jesus' full knowledge of what awaits him; he foresees and accepts even death as part of the struggle.

78. Schnackenburg, *Gospel of John*, 387.

79. Ibid., 388.

80. Tonstad, "Father of Lies," 199.

power, in contrast to those whose fame is announced by earthly voices. The voice confirms Jesus as a superior traveler, reminding the crowd of his superior origins—"from above" (3:34, 8:26). The voice highlights the power of Jesus through its claims that it has glorified Jesus and will continue to glorify him. Jesus is involved in a real struggle and show of power.

The voice from heaven recalls John's emphasis on the power of Jesus, a traveler who originates in heaven, roams the earthly spaces exercising power over its creatures, and returns to heaven. In John 3:13, "no one has ascended into heaven except the one who comes from heaven, the son of man . . ." John makes explicit the relationship between power and place of origin by announcing,

> The one who comes from above is above all; the one who is of the earth belongs to the earth and speaks about earthly things. The one who comes from heaven is above all. He bears witness to what he has seen and heard, yet no one receives his testimony; . . . the Father loves the son and places all things in his hands" (3:31–32, 35).

As Musa Dube observes, constructing the spatial origins of Jesus as "from above," "from heaven," and emphasizing that the Father has placed all things in Jesus' hands emphatically elevates the authority of Jesus over all other notable cultural figures and over their earthly spaces of authority. The out-of-this-world spatial origin functions precisely to take control of this world, as a power over earthly powers rather than other human beings.[81] By constructing this highest and most unique place of origin, John highlights the superiority and capability of Jesus over Rome and its allies. He claims for Jesus power where it is not guaranteed or where is has been denied or lost. Jesus' power is supported and proclaimed by a voice from the realm of power—heaven—that has glorified and will glorify Jesus. The voice declares the politics of divine approval, challenging the Roman politics of the divine emperor. The superiority and authority over all things makes Jesus the right person to restructure the peasant space disfigured by Roman oppression.

Some of the bystanders assume that the "voice" is thunder. Others think an angel has spoken to Jesus (12:29).[82] Whether they perceive it as

81. Dube, "Savior of the World," 119–120.

82. Adolf Schlatter holds that the picture of the people, understanding nothing and floundering in superficial conjectures ["Lightning!", "Angel!"], is meant to stimulate deeper reflection by the readers and to disclose the theological nuances behind the light/ Angel remarks: "the double judgment about the event mirrors at the popular level the

thunder or an angel, such a booming voice would herald either death, judgment, or both (Sophocles, *Oedipus* col 1463). Jesus therefore clarifies that
the voice is not for his sake but for the sake of the listeners (12:30). By
claiming that the voice is not for his sake but for the crowd's, the Gospel
adopts the colonial ideology of disinterest and lays claim to the natives.[83]
Here, the master's tool is effective; the heavenly voice confirms Jesus as the
voice of the marginalized people. The dominated people whose heaven and
earth remain invisible, suppressed, and unknown, now have an ally in Jesus,
as confirmed by the voice from heaven—the most powerful of all spaces.

After being confirmed by the heavenly voice as the superior traveler,
Jesus announces that the critical moment has come for the leader of this
world to be expelled (ἐκβληθήσεται; 12:31, see also 14:30, 16:11). In the
political drama that is unfolding in the minds of the crowd and the Jewish authorities, Jesus appears to call for an overthrow of Roman occupation. According to Jo-Ann Brant, his pronouncement takes on a different
meaning when set within the narrative that Jesus has been telling. The verb
ἐκβληθήσεται can also mean "to be exposed." In the crucifixion, the ruler of
this world is exposed as powerless. Even death does not prevent the world
from being drawn to God's son."[84] With an emphatic "I," Jesus says, "And I
when I am lifted up from the earth, will draw all to myself" (12:32). John
links this directly to Jesus' death by pointing to these words as an indication
of the kind of death Jesus would die (12:33).

The verb "lift up" (ὑψόω) combines the sense of physical elevation
on a pole or cross with an exaltation in honor. It does not refer to Jesus'
exaltation to heavenly majesty.[85] The "lifting up" idea builds upon various

---

difference between the theology of the Sadducees and that of the Pharisees. Both groups
were far from thinking that a divine work or speech was present. By the one group [the
Sadducees] the event could have been worked through nature [Lightning] and by the
other [the Pharisees] through the spirit world between human beings and God [Angel]."
See von Schlatter, *Evangelist Johannes*, 270.

83. Ideology of disinterest is an imperial ideology that under the guise (rhetoric) of
serving solely the interest of the dominated people (duty to the natives) conceals all the
gains it seeks from the land of a colonized population. In Achebe's *Things Fall Apart*, the
District Commissioner (DC) addresses the elders claiming that the imperial power has
brought peaceful administration to Umuofia so that the natives may be happy; the DC
comments that in all his years, all he has done is toiling to bring civilization to different
parts of Africa and the DC has decided to write a book entitled, The Pacification of the
Primitive Tribes of the Lower Niger. See Achebe, *Things Fall Apart*, 194, 208, 209.

84. Brant, *John*, 193–94.

85. Moloney, *Signs and Shadows*, 193.

intertextual echoes: Jesus' opponents lift him up (8:28) as the serpent is lifted up on a pole (3:14). John reminds the reader of this motif in 18:32, where Jesus claims absolute power in all spaces by drawing all to himself. "All" people from "all" places will be drawn to Jesus in his death; the power of Rome fragments society while that of Jesus unites. Jesus is "lifted up" to die by crucifixion, the Roman form of execution.

The crucifixion space is one of marginality, a frontier that is meant to protect the center, the Roman space. Crucifying prisoners in liminal spaces outside Jerusalem secures and protects the center, the political leaders of the time. The liminality of these spaces makes them candidates for the development of thirdspace visions.[86] When the political authority in Jerusalem "lifts up" Jesus from the earth, it attempts to sever the ties that Jesus has created with the world following him. Yet to Jesus, the cross provides an occasion for new and varied forms of bonding, and he draws all people to himself. Jesus indicates that this marginal space will be a space of critical exchange, host to new and radical happenings. It is a space for oppositional practices and resistance to every oppression, including Roman rule. Jesus creates at the cross a new politics of location that supersedes divisive Roman politics.

In his death on the cross, Jesus creates new real and imagined places where diverse oppositional practices meet. By claiming to draw all people to himself, Jesus claims the crucifixion space as a place of radical openness. It becomes a context from which to build communities of resistance and renewal that cross boundaries of all oppressively "Othering" categories such as race, class, and culture. The marginality of the cross constitutes the center of the new community, one that is abidingly global as it disorders, disrupts and transgresses the center-periphery Roman approach to relationships. When Jesus is crucified on the cross, he initiates a new politics of location, a radical perspective that pushes against oppressive Roman boundaries and accepts "all" in his politics.

The crucifixion space is not a safe place, yet it is at this marginal space that a community of resistance is created, where its decolonized visions, analyses and practices are defined in the teachings of Jesus and in the farewell discourse (John 13—17). Jesus envisions a world in which unity exists in diversity, symbolized by the arrival of the Greeks seeking Jesus (John 12:20). He also envisions a new leadership that serves its subjects (John 13). By declaring and demonstrating that a leader washes the feet of the

86. Soja, *Thirdspace: Journeys*, 83–105.

subjects, Jesus is involved in oppositional practice. This oppositionality reaches its climax when Jesus asserts that he has "conquered the world" (ἐγὼ νενίκηκα τὸν κόσμον; 16:33) even before the Romans arrest him, and that the ruler of this world will be expelled through his own death (12:31–33). Jesus claims control over himself and over agents of Rome. Rome and its allies are victims of Jesus' divine politics. In his life and death, Jesus demonstrates God's defeat of earthly empire. Jesus is bold enough to signal the fall of Rome, an assertion that indicates power.

Jerusalem is the capitol and the center of power. Outside of the city walls, Rome crucifies its victims. Geoffrey Bennington observes that "frontiers exist to define and protect the center."[87] In his crucifixion, Jesus establishes another center at the margins. Spatially, it indicates a shifting boundary. If, however, as Geoffrey Bennington suggests, a frontier can also be the region that permits the greatest contact between heterogeneous peoples, then it is also the region where diversities flow through its center.[88]

The crucified Jesus on the cross constructs a new community of believers by drawing them to the cross space. Believers in Jesus are moved to see the shameful cross event differently, indicating a shifting boundary dividing the frontiers of the Roman Empire. In this division, the frontiers evolve into a new center as a community that occupies the very space that it divides. Jesus is himself the embodiment of this new community, which he shapes according to his guidelines and values. The new space includes "all" people denoting universality. Jesus' death does not separate him from his followers but creates new conditions and new relationships. The expectation of the believers creates an anticipatory space, as foretold by Jesus.

Jesus' prediction that he shall be lifted "from the earth" (ἐκ τῆς γῆς; 12:32) reinforces this spatial conception. "Lifting up" is associated with elevation and signals the earth as the departure point. John emphasizes the cross as the place of glorification and the beginning of Jesus' saving rule (cf. 19:37). Jesus does not only draw people to him on the cross, but configures a better spatiality (relationship) for the scattered community. In this new community, all are welcome, Jew and Gentile alike in a unified identity. The crucifixion space opens up the possibility of a sphere of universalism that stands above racial, ethnic and cultural particularism, one that incorporates "all people" or "everyone" (πάντας; 12:32). Elsewhere, John expresses universalism as an incorporation into the children of God (1:12;

87. Bennington, "Politics," 21.
88. Ibid.

10:16; 11:52). The formative process of the political community climaxes in Jesus' death on the cross. This community exceeds both the real and the imagined. Its reality comes from the power of the cross for Jesus' followers as a symbol of their liberation, both spiritual and political. It is an imagined political community as it carries a particular vision and generates authority through its claims to unite the children of God.

Followers of Jesus thus recognize themselves and their experience in the lifting up of Jesus onto the cross, even though the horrific lifting up of Jesus would have caused his believers to rethink their allegiance to him. Simone Weil writes, "[those] struck down by affliction are at the foot of the cross, almost at the greatest possible distance from God."[89] Yet John reveals that Jesus' alignment with God's will bridges the gulf between suffering and the divine presence (3:16–17; 12:27–28).[90] Believers in Jesus are asked "to see in the outward event of crucifixion [of Jesus' and their own], the inward meaning of exaltation."[91] They are to remain steadfast amidst the life-threatening persecutions that may come with their struggle for liberation. The followers of Jesus are to reject the δόξα (glory) of Rome's world in favor of the greater δόξα of God (12:43).

Conclusion

This study has revealed that the coming of the Greeks to see Jesus presages the inclusion of the Gentiles into the new community of Jesus, and the formation of the previously scattered children of God into an all-encompassing global community of the children of light. This chapter exposed the identity of the true rival of Jesus, namely the reputed "ruler of this world" who "is cast out" (12:31), "judged" (16:11), and who now "has no power" over Jesus (14:30). Only the Roman emperor could claim such a dominion over the earth in the first century. Consequently, Jesus' declaration that this leader is made powerless issues a strong political challenge to his listeners, who must decide either for continuing oppression under Rome or for Jesus. Jesus thus becomes a political challenge to Rome and a candidate for crucifixion.

While the crucifixion is a cruel and shameful death, meant to deter observers, John points out that Jesus' crucifixion is unlike other crucifixions.

89. Weil, "Love of God and Affliction," 442–44.

90. Brant, "Sorrow, Beauty, Sorrow," 95.

91. Boer, "Johannine History," 320.

The cross of Jesus is a Roman political space transformed into a place of the ingathering of all humanity by means of the glory that ties God to the space.

The concept of glory carries two consequences for the spatiality of the crucifixion and for the Jerusalem leaders and their Roman masters. First, by characterizing Jesus' death on the cross as the event in which God is glorified, John creates an attractive space from this otherwise shameful space of violence. This space draws all people of all races and nations to form a community that resists dominions. In this thirdspace, the dominated people of all races and nations envisage their liberation and are drawn together in unity. The very act intended to prevent the world from going after Jesus instead makes it possible, defeating the Jerusalem elites and Rome.

Secondly, by redefining the crucifixion space as an attractive space of glory, John profanes the normal public meaning of the crucifixion and turns upside down the greatest tool of imperial power. Christ defeats Rome and its Jerusalem allies by transforming the cross into a space of attraction and unity for believers in Jesus, a space that resists all forms of socio-political oppression. In this space, boundary no longer separates. This is the second phase of John's presentation of the death of Jesus as the defeat of Rome.

CHAPTER 5

Spaces of Struggle and the New World Order

(John 18:1—19:22)

Introduction

Jesus' final journey travels through the earthly spaces of the garden where he is arrested, the house of high priests where he is interrogated, the praetorium where he is tried, and Golgotha where he is crucified. This section of the narrative of Jesus' death is commonly known as the Passion Narrative, which comes from the Greek word *pathos*. Aristotle defines pathos as "an action resulting in destruction or distress such as death on the stage, agony, or other forms of affliction" (*Poet.* 1452b.12), and as a tragic action that arouses pity and fear (*Poet.* 1453b.32). The Fourth Gospel ends in Jesus' death, determining it as a Passion Narrative, yet preceding story dissuades the reader from pitying Jesus or from becoming fearful and attempting to avoid a similar fate. In the various spaces of struggle—the garden, the courtroom and at the cross—John presents Jesus' triumph. I argue that by telling the story of Jesus' death as a triumph, stripped of any suffering, John passively resists empire and forms an alternative space–a community that stands for its values even at the cost of losing life.

The Garden Space (John 18:1–11)

In their work on the Johannine metaphor of Jesus as the vine in John 15:1–8, Gabriele Elsen-Novák and Mirko Novák observe that the symbolism was influenced by ancient Mesopotamian image of the vineyard as part of the artificial "garden of paradise."[1] Since a flourishing garden was always a symbol of fertility in the dry regions of Mesopotamia, it was seen as a place of pleasure and became a synonym of civilization. All the attributes of legitimate leadership were represented in such gardens. The Sumerian kingship ideology based on the twofold functions of the king as gardener, and as protector of the herds and hunter of wild beasts. Moreover, as representative of Tammuz, the king had to celebrate the rebirth of fertility of nature after the dry months in the rituals of holy marriage. The paradise gardens and their ideological meaning were familiar to the inhabitants of Palestine in the period covering the formation of the New Testament. During this time, the vine became part of the "artificial paradise" and one of the symbols of paradise. The vine metaphor hence represented paradise garden, fertility, power, civilization and order. In this line therefore, Jesus was associated with a charismatic king as representative of God on earth, but also with the Mesopotamian and Levantine fertility god, who underwent a yearly cycle of death and rebirth.[2]

Francesca Stavrakopoulou remarks that gardens played a notable role in royalty's socio-political promotion and propaganda. A number of Neo-Assyrian kings created monumental gardens which were "visually impressive" and "horticulturally prestigious" in their collection of trees and plants gathered from the furthest reaches of the empire, demonstrating the royal mastery of other peoples, their gods, and the produce of their lands.[3] The breadth and variety of vegetation found in the garden were a "a reflection of the social and political role" through which these spaces demonstrated a ruler's reach and domination.[4] In the same way, the luxurious Roman imperial gardens were particularly splendid and magnificent, with plants serving both decorative and nutritional aims, meant to legitimate absolute power.[5]

1. Elsen-Novák and Novák, "Ich bin der wahre Weinstock," 183–206.
2. Ibid., 183.
3. Stavrakopoulou, "Exploring the Garden," 6.
4. Ibid.
5. Di Pasquale and   Paolucci, eds., *Il giardino antico*, 108. See also Boatwright,

David Balch however observes that the Romans loved to place in their gardens marble or bronze statues of barbarians they had defeated, portrayed as they receive punishments.[6] While the sculpture demonstrates the strength of Rome, their presence in the gardens transforms the space into a site of struggle. Both the Eastern *paradeisoi* and the Western Roman *horti* were violent spaces where animals killed each other, and human beings fought with animals or each other.[7] Tacitus and Suetonius write that the *horti* represented Nero's perversion as emperor and exposes abusive imperial acquisition of private property in Rome (Tacitus, *Ann.* 11: 31; 15: 33; Suetonius, *Nero* 22). To Boatwright, from the first century through the second century CE, the *Horti* remained liminal spaces where politics and diversions could both flourish, and other polarities could be negotiated.[8] Michel Foucault is right when he describes the ancient garden as "a special otherworldly site" that illustrates the aspects of "simultaneity and liminality" which characterize heterotopic spaces, a "contradictory site" that contained an impossible mix of flora not naturally found in the same habitat.[9] The gardens were violent spaces and spaces of struggle.

From the above discussions of Elsen-Novak and Novak, Jesus' garden across the Kidron valley could as well be considered a "palace garden," not because Jesus had a palace in the vicinity, but because just like the Mesopotamian kings who claimed to be an extension of the deity, Jesus identified himself as divine. Garden spaces were not available to commoners; the mere possession of such a space reveals Jesus' socio-political capabilities. If the garden was a political space for discussing political issues, the garden across the Kidron valley could as well be suspect as a place of grooming opposition to political leadership in the Roman imperial world.

On the day of his arrest, after supper, Jesus and his disciples cross the Kidron valley and enter (εἰσῆλθεν) a garden (18:1)—an architectural space.[10] The garden is described as "an enclosed open-air structure" (18:1–

"Luxuriant Gardens," 72.

6. Balch, "Church Sitting in a Garden," 220. Commenting on sculpture in Cima and Talamo, *Gli horti di Roma Antica*.

7. Elsen-Novák and Mirko Novák, "Ich bin der wahre Weinstock," 190–92.

8. Boatwright, "Luxuriant Gardens," 82.

9. Foucault, "Of Other Spaces, Heterotopias," 25–26.

10. James Resseguie identifies two types of settings namely, the architectural and topographical settings. Architectural settings refer to human made structures such as a well, temple, synagogue, tomb, pool, sheepfold, garden, praetorium, door, courtyard, and so forth. Topographical settings are demarcations on a physical map, such as sea,

11, 26).[11] The garden is the domain of Jesus and his disciples, a social, political and spiritual expression of their power and prestige. John notes that Jesus and his disciples frequently visit the garden (18:2), to whence they would withdraw from the crowd, indicating the group's separation and particularity. This firstspace (physical space) separation from others highlights the group's secondspace separation—an ideological separation from others. The firstspace ordinary geography becomes a secondspace social and political geography. The garden stands out from the surrounding spaces, manifesting its exclusivity to Jesus and his disciples.

James Resseguie considers the space inside and outside the garden to be safe and dangerous respectively. Inside the garden, the disciples of Jesus are safe while outside they are exposed to trouble and danger.[12] Considering that gardens are spaces of struggle, both inside and outside remain liminal spaces. Thatcher refers to the garden as "a place of intimacy, an intimacy that Judas himself once enjoyed."[13] Intimacy in this space of struggle, if any, is very temporal as seen in Judas' betrayal of his master. Judas leads the police to arrest Jesus because, as a member of the group, he knows the place very well (18:2). Judas, however, departed from the fellowship of the last supper (13:30) thereby abandoning both the firstspace physical garden and the secondspace ideological security of the group. He "went out" (ἐξῆλθεν) from the presence of Jesus, committing a spatial apostasy that symbolized the end of his being a follower of Jesus. The idea agrees with Rudolf Schnackenburg who refers to Judas' departure as "an outward expression of inward apostasy, a falling back into the darkness far from Jesus (8:12; 12:35)."[14]

Judas approaches the garden with a group of strangers described as a "cohort" (σπεῖρα), and officers (ὑπηρέται) from the chief priests and Pharisees (18:3, 12). Σπεῖρα is the technical terminology for a cohort—a unit of 600 Roman troops (Polybius, *Hist.* 11.23.1). It refers to the "complete body of Roman troops permanently garrisoned in Jerusalem."[15] The presence of

---

mountain, desert, river, plain, cities, etc. See Resseguie, *Strange Gospel*, 61.

11. Thorsen, "Gethsemane," 2:997–98.

12. Resseguie, *Strange Gospel*, 68.

13. Thatcher, *Greater Than Caesar*, XVI.

14. Schnackenburg, *Gospel According to John*, 2:75.

15. Crossan, *Who Killed Jesus*, 80–81. Incidentally, John is the only evangelist who mentions that Judas came with a band of Roman soldiers. The Synoptic Gospels indicate that Judas brought with him a crowd (ὄχλος; Matt 26:47; Mark 14:43; Luke 22:47).

Roman soldiers suggests prior collaboration between Jewish and Roman officials, as a cohort of six hundred soldiers is a disproportionately large number for the arrest of one man accompanied by eleven disciples. Stephen Moore remarks that "John floods the garden with Roman troops, cramming them in shoulder-to-shoulder and cheek-to-jowl, eliminating any possibility that this time Jesus and his disciples can escape arrest."[16] This large number of soldiers points to the popularity of Jesus, to the political leaders' fear of him.

The arrival of these strangers situates Jesus within the spatial practices of the Roman Empire and their allies in Jerusalem. Their presence puts the struggle in action; Jesus experiences betrayal, his followers experience anxiety and grief. Jesus is not bothered by the spatial interference of the apparent aggressors. He has known all things that were coming upon him yet he "went out" (ἐξῆλθεν; 18:4) to singlehandedly foil the redoubtable threat. By facing the invaders, Jesus demonstrates his resolve to lay down his life in the face of this threat. This corresponds with John's ideology of the good shepherd who "lays down his life" for his sheep (10:11). Jesus' "going out" lays down the conditions for his disciples' release, fulfilling still another saying that "he did not lose a single one of those whom" he was given (18:9). By narrowing down the spatiality (firstspace) between him and the arrest party as he goes out, Jesus confronts the ideological (secondspace) spatiality of the strangers.

He questions the arrest party by asking whom they seek (18:4). Their answer, "Jesus of Nazareth," (18:5) means more than distinguishing Jesus from others with the same name. The mention of "Nazareth" signals "derision and contempt" toward Jesus, as evident elsewhere in the Fourth Gospel (1:46; 19:19).[17] Jesus comes from a lowly place in the hierarchy of places. To the question, Jesus responds "I am he" (ἐγώ εἰμι; 18:5)," which Brant argues is Jesus' straightforward acknowledgment that he is the one whom the arrest party seeks. It is also a theological statement:

In Jesus' days, uttering the name of God was prohibited (see *Josephus, Antiquities* 2.275–76; 1QS 6.27—7.2). The LXX does not translate the name YHWH, a first form of the verb "to be" but instead uses "Lord" (κύριος). The Greek word ἐγώ εἰμι does not necessarily refer to the divine name, but the arrest party's response points to the theological significance: "they fell to the ground." Josephus describes the name as τὸ φρικτὸν ὄνομα τοῦ θεοῦ

16. Moore, *Empire and Apocalypse*, 53.
17. Brant, *John*, 235.

(the tremendous name of God), something that causes one to shudder in religious awe (*Jewish War* 5.438). [18]

The arrest party therefore collapsed in a submissive posture before the divine being.[19] Their falling to the ground indicates a low and weak spatial standpoint. The fall defines their spatiality as inferior to the divine spatiality of Jesus.

John writes that Judas the betrayer "was standing" (εἰστήκει) with the arrestors (18:5). Standing with the arrest party demonstrates Judas' new socio-political stance. Peter reacts violently, cutting off the ear of one of the high Priest's servants, Malchus. Peter's reaction seems impulsive and naïve considering the presence of such a large number of soldiers of the "cohort." Surprisingly, the soldiers to do not react to punish Peter. Could the fall have weakened their morale? Liminality and simultaneity of actions and meanings and possibilities are now in full play. A space of common gathering has been invaded and constructed into spaces of uncertainty, interrogation, looming violence, and eventually transformed into a space of active violence. The different characters, both from Jesus' group and the arrest party, continuously produce and reproduce the garden space according to their needs. Jesus is, however, in full control of every scene, including the spatial behavior of his own group. His rebuke of Peter continues his production of the space, an attempt to transform the garden into a space of non-violence.

Jesus constructs all spatialities even as he tells his arresters to let his followers go free (18:9). His arresters obey him. In fact, Jesus' control is so encompassing that he hands himself over to the arrest party. Despite the superiority of the raiding group in number and quality as soldiers, Jesus wields spatial superiority by determining his arrest. He is perceptive of his fate (18:4), he fells the cohort with his own instance of the divine name "I am" (18:5–6), and he reprimands Peter for interfering with God's plans that are inescapable (18:10–11).[20] In Anton Dauer's words, Jesus is the "Herr der Situation"—the master of the situation.[21]

---

18. Ibid.
19. Ibid.
20. Resseguie, *Strange Gospel*, 68.
21. Dauer, *Passionsgeschichte*, 39–40.

Annas's Courtyard and Caiaphas's House (John 18:12–24)

The arrest party leads Jesus to the courtyard of Annas, the father-in-law of the current high priest, Caiaphas. It was unusual for the prisoner to be taken to a retired high priest for interrogations. In Gail O'Day's view, Annas' interrogation demonstrates his influence on the administration of Caiaphas. Annas reigned as high priest for approximately ten years (6–15 BCE) and he ensured the succession of five sons and a grandson to the position of high priest.[22] That his son-in-law also became priest is therefore unsurprising. Annas' participation in the interrogation of Jesus protects the political space of his son-in-law, which is threatened by Jesus' popularity. Camillus Umoh comments that during his term of office, Annas had a friendly relationship with Rome, winning the confidence of the emperor and following a politics of external stability.[23] With his predecessor still exercising much authority during Caiaphas' reign, John portrays Caiaphas as a weak high priest whose political space is reduced to a figurehead. Caiaphas' political space is constructed by Annas, his mentor and father-in-law. Annas appears at this point as a powerful person to whom Caiaphas answers, yet both priests answer to Rome.

The soldiers bind Jesus and send him to Annas (18:12–14). By binding Jesus, the authorities declare their control over his bodily space. Interrogating Jesus, the retired high priest asks vague questions concerning Jesus' teachings and his disciples (18:19). Jesus defiantly responds that Annas should interrogate his accusers (18:21). The high priests' guard recognizes the disrespectful response and slaps Jesus. Jesus becomes even more defiant, asserting that he has spoken rightly (18:23). While the leaders appear to exercise control over Jesus' body by locking him in chains, Jesus is third-spatially free and active as he refutes oppression and claims his innocence.

The courtyard, part of Annas' house, is an enclosed space. The territorial character of the house is designated by walls that demarcate its boundaries and a doorkeeper (θυρωρός; 18:16) who restricts access.[24] Peter is left standing outside the courtyard door (18:16) while the anonymous disciple,

---

22. O'Day, "Gospel of John," 806–807.

23. Umoh, *Plot to Kill Jesus*, 82.

24. Robert Sack defines Territoriality as "the attempt by an individual or group to affect, influence, or control people, phenomena, and relationships, by delimiting and asserting control over a geographic area." Three essential facets of territoriality are classification of area, communication of boundaries, and enforcement of access. See Sack, *Human Territoriality*, 19. On the essential facets of territoriality, see pages 21–22.

who is "known to the high priest" (18:15), enters with Jesus. John does not clarify the relationship of the anonymous disciple with the Jewish leaders, but it is one of privilege. His plea with the maid at the door brings Peter in. In this space, Peter is the one on trial. He must demonstrate an allegiance either to the high priest or to Jesus.

Peter enters in and stands (ἑστὼς; 18:18) warming himself near a charcoal fire, together with the slaves and attendants who are presumably members of the arrest party. Peter's spatial stance is associated with defection and recalls Judas' being "with them [the arresters of Jesus]" (μετ᾽ αὐτῶν) outside the garden (18:5). Asked if he is a disciple of Jesus, Peter denies it (18:17, 25, and 27), confirming the negative significance of his spatial stand. Brant holds that the intent of Peter's actions have "shifted from loyalty to Jesus to his own comfort and security."[25] This spatial setting contrasts the faithful follower and the wavering disciple. When offered an opportunity to be in the inside space with his master, Peter instead demonstrates that he is "with them" (μετ᾽ αὐτῶν)—not with Jesus. Peter's situation exemplifies that inside space indicates a character's commitment.

At the house of Annas and the courtyard of Caiaphas, Jesus does not face a formal Jewish trial. While Annas questions Jesus' teaching and disciples, John is silent about any interrogations in Caiaphas' courtyard. Responding to Annas' questions, Jesus answers that he has spoken "openly" (παρρησίᾳ) to the world, and that he has taught in the synagogues and in the temple where all the Jews come together (18:19). Jesus' bold and open speech demonstrates that he will not participate in public games. Jo-Ann Brant writes:

> Jesus' description of his openness should not be confused with the sort of transparency that is named as a value in modern political rhetoric. In the ancient context, this sort of frankness and absence of dissimulating courtesy is normally reserved for the circle of friends. Jesus is acknowledging that he spoke dangerously, without regard for his personal safety. So his present situation does not catch him off guard. He seems to anticipate the accusation that he has spoken sedition, an act that usually occurs behind closed doors.[26]

Jesus demonstrates that he is deliberate in his speech and aware of its consequences. He is so bold that he even calls for witnesses and a trial

25. Brant, *John*, 240.
26. Brant, *John*, 240–41.

(18:21), with the result that an attendant slaps him in the face. This challenges Jesus' dignity, which Jesus restores by questioning the righteousness of his interrogators. Jesus continues his control even at the house and courtyard of the priests.

The Praetorium Space (John 18:28—19:16)

From the house of Caiaphas, the authorities lead Jesus to the praetorium—the Roman governor's official residence and the architectural space of trial. The inside space of the praetorium is clearly differentiated from the outside space. To remain ritually pure for the Passover feast (18:28), the Jewish authorities do not enter the praetorium.[27] By remaining outside the praetorium, the Jewish leaders characterize the inside Roman space as unholy. Purity and impurity serve as boundary markers in the trial of Jesus and determine the dynamics of the trial. During the trial of Jesus, the Roman governor travels back and forth between the outside and inside space. The governor's space is considered unholy, thereby defining the governor himself as "morally inferior."[28] From the moment Jesus' opponents lead him to the court, the governor is challenged and, ironically, placed on trial.

Roman imperial politics impact the discourses inside and outside the praetorium. Outside, the subordinate Jews and the dominating Roman governor openly interact, in what Achebe describes as public lies, characterized by the public support of a social system that is privately hated, (as exemplified in Achebe's study of the dominated people of Umuofia).[29] James Scott refers to similar situations as a "public transcript."[30] Public transcripts serve the interest of the powerful, and the survival tactic of disingenuous behavior characterizes the public life of a dominated people. Like their subjects, the masters flatter the other in public venues while hiding their true feelings behind a mask of propriety that implies satisfaction with the status quo.

---

27. In the second-temple Israel it was known that the temple at Jerusalem would be polluted when a non-Israelite conqueror sacrificed an unclean animal there (see 1 Macc 1:54; 2 Macc 6:1–2). The undoing of this pollution was commemorated at *egkainia*, the feast of the rededication, which John 10:22 cites as the occasion of one of Jesus' arguments with the Jerusalemites. A holy place may be made polluted and then re-sanctified. See Neyrey, "Spaces and Places," 62.

28 Thatcher, *Greater Than Caesar*, 71.

29. Achebe, *Things Fall Apart*, 201–5.

30. Scott, *Domination and the Arts of Resistance*, 1–2.

When their colonial masters are absent, for instance at village meetings, the people of Umuofia talk, gesture, and engage in practices contrary to what they profess in the presence of colonial administration. These are covert forms of resistance that undermine the Umuofia people's public gestures of deference.[31] Scott refers to these as "hidden transcripts."[32] In private space, the mask of formality is lifted. The domination of public and private discourse requires this duplicitous behavior.

Outside the praetorium, the public transcripts for both Jews and Pilate are uttered. "Offstage," hidden transcripts take place when Pilate interrogates Jesus inside the praetorium. I follow Raymond Brown's seven divisions of Pilate's alternate movements inside and outside the praetorium during the trial, although I name them in line with what I consider to be the major theme for the sake of this work. Below are Browns' seven divisions with my own headings:[33]

1. Outside (18: 28–32): Death as a fulfillment of Jesus' word

2. Inside (18:33–38a): The un(worldly) kingship of Jesus

3. Outside (18:38b–40): The illusory "not-guilty" verdict

4. Inside (19:1–3): Geography of the torture of Jesus

5. Outside (19:4–8): Territorial reach of the title "Son of God"

6. Inside (19:9–11): Direct clash of powers in private space

7. Outside (19:12–16a): Occupying God's space

Scene One: Death as a Fulfillment of Jesus' Word (John 18:28–32)

The interrogations open outside the praetorium as Pilate addresses the Jewish leadership (18:28–32). By remaining outside the praetorium, the Jerusalem leaders undermine Pilate's space as unholy, yet only Pilate will enable their desire for the death penalty for Jesus. That the one portrayed as morally inferior decides a case before the morally superior evidences Johannine irony. Pilate's question "what accusations do you bring against this man?" is answered rhetorically, "If this man were not a sinner we would not

---

31. Achebe, *Things Fall Apart*, 201–205.

32. Scott, *Domination and the Arts of Resistance*, 1–2.

33. Brown, *Gospel According to John*, 858–59.

have handed him over" (18:29–30). By this response, Jesus' accusers render Pilate's question ridiculous.

Tension arises in the outside space as Pilate asks "the Jews" to take Jesus and to try him by their own law. Jesus' accusers respond that the law does not permit them to put any man to death. This is a normal "public" conversation in which the will of Rome prevails. The reply challenges Pilate, who should know the law better. The leaders do not mention any specific accusation against Jesus, but they demonstrate that they respect the Roman law and that this case demands a death penalty. John then reminds the reader that all these happens "to fulfill the word which Jesus had spoken to show by what death he was to die" (18:32).

By describing the death as a "fulfillment of Jesus' word" and as a "fulfillment of Scripture," (19:23–25, 28, 36–37), John deprives the Jewish and Roman authority of responsibility for their action. While they may claim success in eliminating an opponent, John informs the world that Jesus' death is the climax of a divine plan. The private transcript of the Gospel sends the message that the circumstances of Jesus' death are not a display of Roman authority over a rebellious Jewish figure, but rather the inevitable climax of a divine drama that was written at the dawn of creation. In Thatcher's words, "prophecy thus becomes an antidote for the imperial power."[34] Consequently, Jesus' death on the cross does not put him under a divine curse, since it fulfills scripture. John strategically responds to empire by describing the death as "according to Scripture," thereby contradicting the normal imperial meaning of the cross.

Scene Two: The (Un)Worldly Kingship of Jesus (18:33–38a)

Inside the praetorium, a private space in which the governor faces Jesus, Pilate asks him whether or not he is "King of the Jews." In the public space, Pilate feigns ignorance of the charge against Jesus, yet the release of a cohort of soldiers to arrest Jesus presupposes a governor's office well-informed of Jesus' case. Inside the praetorium, the governor is on top of his game. He knows the accusation. By asking about Jesus' kingship, Pilate "seeks grounds to accuse Jesus of *Lex Iulia de maiestate*, sedition against the imperial authority of Rome."[35] The accusers' public silence on this matter is

34. Thatcher, *Greater Than Caesar*, 99.
35. Brant, *John*, 243.

suspect and Pilate may have therefore wanted a public official pronouncement of the accusations against Jesus.

Jesus counters Pilate's question by asking whether this is Pilate's pronouncement or one that other people have told him. His mockery of Pilate
over his failure to probe into the specifics of the case demonstrates the private nature of this transcript. Jesus responds harshly to the imperial agent
in a private space, the same type of response that earned him a slap in the
face in the public space of the high priest's courtyard (18:19–22). Pilate's
retort, "Am I a Jew?" attempts to distance himself from the accusation while
claiming that this particular struggle for power is intra-Jewish.

Jesus admits that he has a kingdom but "not of this world" (18:36).
"This world" is Rome's space and "not of this world" is Jesus' space. While
Jesus claims that his kingdom is "not of this world," his activities critique
the world of the Roman emperor. His announcement of "judgment" on
this world and its leadership (9:39; 12:31; 16:11) demonstrate the effect of
his kingdom on Caesar's world.[36] As long as the space of "this world" and
that which is "not of this world" intersect, claims that Jesus' space of power
does not affect Caesar's are untenable. Jesus' reign is unfamiliar to the Roman governor. As such, the Roman governor cannot decide whether Jesus
is a threat to the status quo (guilty) or not (innocent). It is not surprising
that the Roman governor distances himself with the rhetorical question
of whether he is a Jew. In John's view, however, "Jesus has come to define
Pilate's place in the cosmic scheme of things and we quickly learn that this
is a very low place indeed."[37] Jesus' final statement inside the praetorium
clarifies this: "those who are of the truth" belong on Jesus' side. Pilate's friv-
olous response, "What is truth?" (18:38), indicates that he neither belongs
on Jesus' side nor does he understand Jesus' reference, "revealing his moral
inferiority to the man he stands to judge."[38]

The theme of Jesus' kingship dominates the trial of Jesus (John 18:33–
40; 19:14–15, 19–22). John exclusively references the title "King of the Jews"
(βασιλεὺς τῶν Ἰουδαίων) throughout the trial, except in a single reference
to the "Son of God" in 19:7. The term βασιλεὺς ("king", "emperor") occurs

36. Against scholars who hold that the kingdom of Jesus poses no immediate threat
to Caesar's reign. Matthew Skinner, for example, holds that Jesus' kingdom exists in the
same space and time as the emperor's, but his reign is an altogether different kind, one
unfamiliar to the world and to Pilate and posing no threat to Rome's interest. See Skinner,
Trial Narratives, 96; Moore, *Empire and Apocalypse*, 50–52.

37. Thatcher, *Greater Than Caesar*, 75.

38. Ibid.

no less than eleven times and the term βασιλέα ("kingdom," "kingship," "empire") appears three times.[39] Their occurrence amidst tense argument between Pilate and Jesus indicates John's characterization of the charges against Jesus as political. Moore raises the possibility that John places Jesus' kingship "front and center only in order to depoliticize it."[40]

Jesus' kingship remains ambivalent throughout the Johannine trial and crucifixion narrative (18:33–40; 19:14–15). No one may claim with certainty what the kingdom "not of this world" is. His kingship becomes an object of "mockery and mimicry" as the soldiers crown Jesus with thorns (19:2–5) and as Pilate presents Jesus to the crowd on the day of preparation for the Passover, saying, "Behold your King!"(19:14–15). Yet, like any other trial, John's Roman trial disallows an ambivalent verdict.

Upon being questioned by Pilate about his [Jesus'] kingship, Jesus answers that his kingdom (βασιλεία) is "not of this world" (οὐκ ἔστιν ἐκ τοῦ κόσμου τούτου). If his kingdom were of this world, his servants would fight so that he might not be handed over to "the Jews" (18:36). "This world" as a firstspace refers to the dominion of the Roman emperor. It is a space of physical struggles, where power is obtained through physical wars. Jesus denies this earthly authority. A. E. Harvey suggests that the dialogue between Jesus and Pilate is carefully designed to demonstrate that the former's kingship does not confer secular authority.[41] The next verse appears to confirm this interpretation, as Pilate asks Jesus, "So you are a king?" and he responds, "You say that I am king. For this I was born, and for this I came into the world, to bear witness to the truth. Everyone who is on the side of truth hears my voice" (18:37).

A "dualist" interpretation of Jesus and Caesar's kingship, each with his own sphere of authority (in heaven and on earth respectively), is common. Neither sphere overlaps with the other nor—theoretically, at least—should one come into conflict with the other.[42] Francis Moloney remarks that Jesus becomes incarnate not to assume power in "the world" but to allow his followers to escape from it, leaving the power structure proper to it untouched.[43] Rensberger and Cassidy assume that the sovereignty possessed by Caesar and the sovereignty claimed by Jesus each exist in differ-

---

39. Moore, "Romans Will Come," 332.

40. Ibid.

41. Harvey, *Jesus on Trial*, 88.

42 Richey, *Roman Imperial Ideology*, 158.

43. Moloney, "Johannine Theology," 1417–26.

ent ontological (heaven versus earthly) or moral (violent and non-violent) spheres and are ultimately disconnected from one another.[44] This dualistic approach implies that the Roman emperor's world does not conflict with that of Jesus in any way.

Yet the text (18:33–38) does not support a bipolar division of these two worlds. Jesus proclamation that he was born and came to the world for a kingship that witnesses to the truth does not exclude an overlap or intersection of the spaces of the two kingdoms. Jesus' kingdom is not very "unworldly" as John claims. Jesus' kingdom instead involves a production of space and authority that does not rely on a force of arms (18:36), as the Romans do, but on the proclamation of the "truth." It is the production of a community—a social sphere where truth rules. Jesus' kingly role bears witness to that truth. Truth as such is not always amicable; hence the common English saying "the truth is bitter." Jesus is the gadfly that keeps the earthly authorities awake. As long as Jesus' kingdom is of truth, he cannot claim that it is completely unworldly.

Jesus' kingdom resists the category of duality by its presence as a thirdspace "not of this world," yet also of this world and more. Pilate's declaration that he is ignorant of what truth is pronounces that he does not belong to Jesus' community of truth. This is a defeat for Pilate and a loss to the Roman Empire. Jesus' social space is neither produced by force of arms nor is his enthronement realized through fighting, exemplified by Jesus' non-violent actions in the gardens during his arrest as he rejects Peter's use of the sword and openly surrenders to the arrest team.[45] Jesus knows that the crucifixion space will transform the outcome and trigger a change. The cross will be the site of victory despite the apparent defeat by death. Jesus will be crowned king when he and God are glorified in his death on the cross.

Jesus' space is defined by truth. Those who belong to this space do not escape from this world, but continue to live in a way that wins more followers.[46] They must continue to produce spaces where truth rules. These are

44. See Rensberger, *Johannine Faith*, 96–100; Cassidy, *John's Gospel*, 48–49.

45. Against Cassidy who holds that Jesus' order during his arrest that the disciples do not resist "emphasized that he himself was consciously choosing to drink the cup which the Father had given him (18:11)." Cassidy does not see any ethic of non-violence implied in this yet acknowledges that John does not promote a violent resistance to Rome. Cassidy, *John's Gospel*, 48.

46 Against Francis Moloney's conviction that the followers of Jesus escape from this world.

Lefebvre's counter-cultural "lived experiences"—spaces of representation—that draw people out of a "world" mentality and into a truth community. The truth community is loyal to Jesus, whose rule supersedes every form of power. Believers must show what Jesus' kingdom looks like. When believers create this space, the death of their master on the cross is no longer an end. The master continues to live in the spaces based in his principles. Believers in Jesus live in the world and experience challenges, and they will survive if they continue to create an alternative society where truth rules. Jesus' kingship does not flee the principles of the Roman Empire but challenges them.

A "spatialized" reading of the world deconstructs Moloney, Cassidy, and Rensberger's interpretation of a Johannine binary opposition of heaven and earth, and reconstitutes them by properly recognizing their position within the production of space. This results in thirdspaces, which are "both similar and strikingly different."[47] Jesus' followers remain in this space yet order it, provoking what Soja calls "an-Other world"[48] beyond the ontological division of heaven (οὐρανός) and earth (κόσμος).

The lived experience of Jesus' followers constitutes a thirdspace, a space of social struggle and radical openness that seeks to make "this world" different without escaping it. It is a space for struggle, liberation and emancipation. The territories of Rome and Jesus are not two separate and contrasting spaces, heaven and earth, or above and below, without any intersection. Jesus' proclamation of truth constantly bridges the space between "this world" and "Jesus' world." The "either-or" dualistic space of heaven and earth is actually "heaven and earth and more"—a thirdspace. Firstspace heaven and firstspace earth each has their own spatial ideologies which constitute their secondspaces. Jesus' ideology of truth bridges the gap between these secondspaces by producing a space that is inclusive and open to all.

Wayne Meeks raises another important aspect of Jesus' kingdom. Its origins are "not of this world" (οὐκ ἔστιν ἐκ τοῦ κόσμου τούτου; 18:36). He translates "τοῦ κόσμου τούτου" as a genitive of origin, suggesting that Jesus' kingship does not derive from the world but from God.[49] Since Jesus' kingdom does not originate in the world, it is not established by earthly

47. Soja, Thirdspace, 61.

48. Soja, Thirdspace, 34. See also "Thirding-as-Othering," 60–70.

49. Wayne Meeks understands the phrase τοῦ κόσμου τούτου as a genitive of origin. See Meeks, Prophet-King, 63. NA 28 adopts the reading he "withdrew" (ἀνεχώρησεν; John 6:15) rather than he "fled" (φεύγω).

power but only by the power of God. Because of this, Jesus flees from those who seek to make him king by force (ἁρπάζειν; 6:15).[50] Jesus is king but his kingship neither depends on nor is inspired by the powers of this world. While the spatiality of Jesus' sovereignty is of this world, his sovereignty is not. Hence, Jesus responds to Pilate: "You would have no power over me unless it was given you from above" (ἄνωθεν; 19:11). Jesus does not deny that he has a sovereign domain in this world but he asserts that the power of Pilate over him can only exist because it comes from above.

By describing the spatiality of his kingdom as from above, Jesus claims the superiority of his reign over the kingdoms of this world. He does not deny that he has power over this world but derides Pilate and Caesar's entire kingdom as "imperfect and derivative, a pale shadow of the true and supreme power of the Father and of the Son."[51] The power claimed by Pilate derives from God and is limited to earthly space, just as Pilate's power from Caesar is limited to Judea and is a power ultimately in service to God.[52] Pilate is subject to Jesus because, through Jesus, he is subject to the power from above. If he decides to allow Jesus' crucifixion, he is simply fulfilling what was designed by God. While Jesus' kingdom does not compete with Caesar's kingdom, it is the origin of Caesar's kingdom and shapes it according to the values of the truth community. As Bultmann comments,

> If [Jesus'] βασιλεία does not enter into rivalry with political organizations of this world, his claim nevertheless does not allow the world to rest in peace, for it concerns every man, and so stirs up the sphere within which the state establishes its order. For the βασιλεία is not an isolated sphere of pure inwardness over against the world, it is not a private area for the cultivation of religious needs, which could not come into conflict with the world.[53]

However, Bultmann works from a dualistic worldview that thirdspace interpretations deconstruct. Dualism guides Bultmann's understanding of the dynamics at work in Jesus' response: "this world of sin" is criticized by that of Jesus "from above." However, Jesus' kingship is not as "unworldly" as it appears to be. Instead, "this world" thirdspatially becomes a space for the practice of truth values, hence the production of a different social space with different values that spur change in Caesar's world. It is therefore not

50. Meeks, *Prophet-King*, 63–64.

51. Richey, *Roman Imperial Ideology*, 163.

52. Ibid., 163–64.

53. Bultmann, *Gospel of John*, 657.

surprising that the accusations against Jesus emphasize the political implications of his activities.

John's decision to emphasize the most political aspect of Christ's person appears intentional when placed in the social context of the Johannine
community. The fundamental decision placed before Pilate, Jesus' accusers,
and the rest of the world is not the easy separation of kingdoms and separation of powers. These separations would make it possible for the Johannine
Christians to live comfortably with Rome while following Christ. John does
not advocate a separation of kingdoms and powers, for in his Gospel he
does not say "render unto Caesar what belongs to Caesar and unto God
what belongs to God" as the Synoptics do (Matt 22:21; Mark 12:17). Had
John included this clear separation in his Gospel, the argument for a dualistic interpretation of a "kingdom not of this world" would be more tenable.

Scene Three: The Illusory "Not-Guilty" Verdict (18:38b–40)

After Pilate fails to understand what Jesus means by truth, he walks outside
the praetorium to the crowd (18:38–40). He announces a "not-guilty" verdict, but this announcement does not end the trial. The governor does not
release the man he had pronounced "not guilty," but asks the crowd whether
he should release for them "the King of the Jews or Barabbas," according to
the custom of releasing a prisoner during the Passover (18:39).[54]

The Aramaic name "Barabbas" means the "son of the father."[55] For
the Johannine author, Jesus is the son of his "heavenly Father." Gil Bailie
remarks that the choice is between Jesus Barabbas (son of his father) and
Jesus bar Abba (son of his Father).[56] The theological irony is explicit.
Barabbas is identified as a λῃστής (brigand), meaning that he is a "revolu-
tionist Jewish nationalist" committed to overthrowing Roman occupation
through violence. The irony is that zealots such as Barabbas have learned
to use violence from their "spiritual father," the Roman tyrant—the mur-
derer—whom they hope to overthrow.[57] As son of his Roman tyrant father,
Barabbas' space of violence is constructed by the violence he witnessed in
dealing with his colonial father.

54. On the background of this custom and its historicity, see Brown, *Death of the
Messiah*, 1: 814–20.

55. Bailie, *Violence Unveiled*, 223.

56. Ibid.

57. Ibid., 224.

Pilate's use of the title "King of the Jews" is counterproductive, if his intention is to release Jesus. Such a title would only increase the anger of an already angry crowd and would mock both Jews and Jesus, particularly given Pilate's previous declaration of Jesus' innocence (18:38). In this context, the crowd's demand for Barabbas' release serves Pilate's political purpose in two ways. First, it gives him the occasion to scourge and crucify "the king of the Jews" as a public example of the futility of resistance. Second, it portrays the Jews as a rebellious people who would prefer the pardon of a λῃστής (bandit or highway robber) over a man found not guilty.[58] These events take place in public space, following the normal public transcript for interactions of subjects with a Roman imperial ruler. Pilate is seemingly in full control of the Jews and apparently in control of Jesus as well.

Scene Four: Geography of the Torture of Jesus (19:1–3)

Inside the praetorium, Pilate has Jesus scourged. Torture is not uniquely characteristic of empires although they are inseparable. In his *Things Fall Apart*, Achebe writes that the best tool of the imperial power is the whip. Even in a society where elders and leaders are highly respected, empires bring shame on the society by brutalizing the elders. In Achebe's view, the relationship between violence and empire is symbiotic, fundamental and central.[59]

After the crowd vocalizes its preference for a robber, Pilate takes Jesus and has him scourged (19:1). The text is silent about the intensity of this flogging but Josephus, recounting the flogging of a different Jesus (son of Ananias) before a different Roman procurator (Albinus), graphically describes that "he was flogged till his bones were laid bare" (*Jewish War* 6.5.3). Josephus also claims that some of Albinus' Galilean enemies were scourged "until the entrails of them were exposed" (*Jewish War* 2.21.5). In line with such reports, we assume, despite John's silence, that Pilate had Jesus severely tortured.

Elaine Scarry remarks that torture involves three phenomena, which, if isolated into separate and sequential steps would occur in the following order: the infliction of pain, its objectification, and its denial.[60] Pain is an event that happens within a person, inside the body. It belongs to

---

58 Thatcher, *Greater Than Caesar*, 76.

59. Achebe, *Things Fall Apart*, 194–95.

60. Scarry, *Body in Pain*, 28 and 57.

"an invisible geography" that, however portentous, has no reality because it has not yet manifested on the visible surface of the earth. In torture, this pain continually amplifies within the person's body, and is also amplified in the sense that it is "objectified, made visible to those outside the person's body."[61] In the very process of inflicting pain in the body of the prisoner, torture "bestows visibility on the structure and enormity of what is usually private and incommunicable, contained within the boundaries of the sufferer's body."[62] Torture aspires to totalize pain and, like pain, continually multiplies its resources and means of access until the room and everything in it becomes a giant externalized map of the prisoner's feelings.[63] At such a level, torture can be easily seen because it has "dimensions and depth, a space that can be walked around in though not walked out of."[64]

Every sense of the body—sight, hearing, touch, or taste—manifests the prisoner's pain.[65] When pain is externalized, the objectified pain is denied as pain and is read as power, a translation made possible by the obsessive mediation of agency.[66] Denial occurs as objectified elements of pain are translated into the insignia of power, the conversion of the enlarged map of human suffering into an emblem of the regime's strength.[67] Scarry's brief description of torture deepens our understanding of the socio-political geography of Jesus' torture.

The motivation for Pilate's decision to flog Jesus is not specified. Matthew Skinner holds that it is an "inquisitional torture," meant to extract truth from the man in custody.[68] For Jennifer Glancy, it is a "penal torture" occurring prior to the crucifixion as in Mark's and Matthew's Gospels.[69] Pilate's proclamation to the crowd that he finds no basis for a charge against

61. Ibid., 27.

62. Ibid.

63. Ibid., 55. Torture involves the conversion of every conceivable aspect of the event and the environment into an agent of pain. It is not accidental that in the torturer's idiom, the room in which the brutality occurs was called the "production room" in the Philippines, the "cinema room" in South Vietnam, and the "blue lit stage" in Chile: built on these repeated acts of display and having as its purpose the production of fantastic illusions of power, torture is a grotesque piece of compensatory drama. See ibid., 27–28.

64. Ibid., 55.

65. Ibid., 56.

66. Ibid., 28.

67. Ibid., 56.

68. Skinner, *Trial Narratives*, 98.

69. Glancy, "Torture," 107–36.

Jesus rules out behavior stemming from frustration or a desire to placate the Jews (19:4). Scourging is an expression of Pilate's ability to use force and to shape the proceedings, as well as an attempt at "unmaking Jesus' world."[70]

After scourging Jesus, the soldiers plait a "crown of thorns" (στέφανον ἐξ ἀκανθῶν; 19:2) and put it on Jesus' head. By crowning Jesus' already pained body with thorns, the soldiers amplify the pain in Jesus' body, objectifying it and stretching further the geography of the torture. The soldiers and the authorities deny Jesus' pain as power when they dress Jesus in "purple robes" (ἱμάτιον πορφυροῦν; 19:2) and mock him as "king of the Jews" while striking him with their hands (19:3). This behavior towards Jesus expresses the irony of Johannine space, as his robes and title do not befit the way he is treated.

Subject to multiple forms of physical torture, Jesus' body is the third-space in which God becomes identified and fully implicated in the life of those who live at the margins of society. Jesus foregrounds bodies that are brutalized daily by forces of domination and gives voice to those unheard and neglected. Jesus' bodily space functions as Scarry's "body in pain," wherein the powerless are voiceless bodies subject to pain and domination by the bodiless voices of those in power. Scarry enumerates a series of mechanisms through which the voiceless body in pain can be transformed into a bodiless voice of power. Most generally, the human subject seeks to alleviate pain by giving it a place in the world through verbal articulation and in the Judeo-Christian tradition, God authorizes humans to divest themselves of their bodies and seek power through the making of material artifacts, including language. In Christian interpretations of death, the resurrection privileges the verbal category over the material by endowing humankind with an immortal voice.[71] The cross is the climactic event in which Jesus embodies all human oppression and liberation.

Scene Five: Territorial Reach of the Title "Son of God" (John 19:4–8)

Chinua Achebe writes about the territorial reach of names and titles. He mentions the titles of the two leaders in a power struggle. The district commissioner argues that imperial rule brings a peaceful administration to the

---

70. Borrowed from the subtitle of Elaine Scarry's *Body in Pain*, "The Making and Unmaking of the World."

71. Scarry, *Body in Pain*, 233–34, 219.

colonized people of Umuofia for their happiness, and therefore they should cooperate with colonial rule. He reminds the revolutionary elders that "any rebellion is a crime in the dominion of the queen, the most powerful ruler of the world."[72] The queen's great rule over the earth defines the spatiality of the queen's power and is intended to elicit the submission of her subjects.

Okonkwo, the leader of the revolutionary natives, was the "greatest wrestler" in the nine villages. He had also taken two village titles and shown incredible prowess in two intertribal wars.[73] At village meetings, Okonkwo is very concerned about titles that people have achieved. At a kindred meeting, he rebuts a man contradicting him with, "this meeting is for men," since the man has no titles.[74] Names and titles define territory and power.

Outside the praetorium, Pilate displays a brutalized prisoner to show that he finds "no guilt in him" (19:4). His interjection, "Behold the man!" invites the crowd to focus on Jesus' maltreated body. Presenting a tortured, bruised and bleeding prisoner dressed with thorns to the crowd to convince them of his innocence is ridiculous. That Pilate proclaims no guilt in Jesus is an imperial political lie in a public space. The game continues when, in response to the cries of the chief priests and the temple guards that he crucify Jesus, Pilate demands that the crowds deal with Jesus themselves (19:6). Pilate knows that imperial law precludes such an action and the response of the leaders simply expresses the Jewish leaders' reliance on Pilate (19:7).

The interrogations continually focus on Jesus' claim to kingship. At this point, the crowd levels another accusation against Jesus: he claims to be "son of God." In this title, a Christological claim is brought to a political arena. In stating the purpose of his Gospel, John asserts that it is written so that the reader "may believe that Jesus is the Christ, the Son of God" (20:31), centering on the title "son of God" as the focus of Johannine Christology. However, the author of the Fourth Gospel did not create this title. E. P. Sanders observes that in the Jewish context, the title "son of God" does not mean "more than human" or even the (collective) "son of God" as in Hosea 11:1 or Exodus 4:22 (Israel is my first-born son).[75] However, the specific title "Son of God"—universally rendered *divi filius*

---

72. Achebe, *Things Fall Apart*, 194.

73. Ibid., 3–8, esp. 8.

74. Ibid., 26.

75. Sanders, *Historical Figure of Jesus*, 161. Psalm 2:7 refers to Israel's king as "son of God."

in Latin—referred to the Roman emperors of the first century beginning with Augustus, whose full name after 27 BCE was *Imperator Caesar divi filius Augustus*. Ordinary Romans were simply called, for instance, Marcus Tullius Marci filius Cicero."[76]

Augustus promoted of his own apotheosis and authority under the banner of the divinity of his adopted father Julius Caesar, a practice repeated by his successors: "As Augustus was the son of the god Julius, and Tiberius of Divus Augustus, so was Nero the son of Divus Claudius and Domitian the son of Divus Vespasian."[77] The assumption of this title by an emperor was immediately communicated throughout the empire by its inclusion on coins and public monuments.[78] Statues in public places and the prevalent use of coins powerfully promoted the emperor's divinity, even in the provinces, as evidenced in the Synoptic Gospels (Matt 22:21; Mark 12:17; Luke 20:25).

The title "son of God" was therefore territorial. Jesus' use of the title may have represented a clash of cultures, conflicting geographies, and counter ideologies. Culturally, the same title has diverse connotations in two cultures, namely, Judaism and Greco-Roman. Yet Jesus' use of this title becomes a thirdspace of resistance by providing a meaning that is Jewish, Greco Roman and more. Out of the clash of cultures emerges a thirdspace. John's presentation of Jesus as "Son of God" challenges the Greco-Roman and Jewish understanding and promotes Jesus as the "Son of God" par excellence. In this presentation, the Johannine community becomes the in-between space that disrupts and displaces the hegemonic colonial narratives of cultural structures and practices. This is Lefebvre's social space and Soja's thirdspace.

Elsewhere in the Fourth Gospel, Jesus as "Son of God" is used diversely nine other ways. Jesus applies the title to himself three times (John 3:18; 10:36; 11:4) and the remaining six occurrences are placed on the lips of the main symbolic witnesses to Jesus' divinity: John the Baptist (1:34), Nathanael (1:49), the Samaritan woman (5:25), Martha (11:27) the leaders of the synagogue (19:7) and the evangelist himself (20:31). Each of these instances articulate the identity of Jesus.

Lance Richey observes that the history of each speaker on this list evokes a unique significance for the members of the Johannine

---

76. Galasterer, "A Man, a Book, and a Method," 15.

77. Ibid., 73.

78. Taylor, *Divinity of the Roman Emperor*, 131.

community.[79] First, the figure of John the Baptist is significant for bringing his followers into the Johannine community.[80] Second, Nathanael is described as "an ideal Israelite" (1:47) and most probably represents the true Israelites who believe in Jesus and recognize him as king.[81] Third, in John 5, the Samaritan woman's portrayal presents the Samaritan people as part of a world estranged from God.[82] Fourth, in John 11, Martha is held up by John to mirror the faith of his readers, where Martha's faith proves its worth in a critical situation.[83] Fifth, the chief priests and officers in John 19, representing the Jews in the synagogue who persecute the community, ironically call Jesus "Son of God" as they denounce him to Pilate.[84] Sixth and finally, the Jewish testimony in John 19 is then sealed by John's confession in 20:31, revealing the purpose of the preceding narrative of Jesus' life, death and resurrection, namely, that Jesus is in fact the Son of God.

When we place the list within the Johannine community's historical context, we realize the true identity of Jesus (albeit ironically in the case of the Synagogue Jews). The list represents every major group confessing Jesus' identity. In the course of the Gospel, the entire social world, including John the Baptist, believing Jews, Gentiles, Johannine Christians, synagogue Jews, the leaders of the community (in the person of the evangelist), and even Jesus himself, acclaim him as the son of God. The artistry and theological work is here evident.[85]

The universality of the confession of Jesus as "son of God," enables every reader to relate to the Gospel and to Jesus. This universality also reveals that the Roman emperor is the true rival of Jesus, the "ruler of this world." John's use of the title "son of God" indicates to Jesus' followers that Jesus is a figure of universal significance and the real "son of God," not Caesar.

Other than "son of God," John also presents Jesus as "savior of the world" (John 4:42; 1 John 4:14), another title used by the Roman emperor. Using titles proper to the emperor may be a strategy for resisting imperial rule. Both Jesus and the Roman emperor are presented as the "son of

---

79. Richey, *Roman Imperial Ideology*, 97.

80. Brown, *Community of the Beloved Disciple*, 69–71.

81. Barrett, *Gospel According to St. John*, 184. Against Brown who argues that there is no evidence that Nathanael is a symbolic figure.

82. Koester, "Savior of the World," 669.

83. Schnackenburg, *Gospel According to Saint John*, 101.

84. Duke, *Irony in the Fourth Gospel*, 133.

85. Richey, *Roman Imperial Ideology*, 98.

God" and "savior" of unlimited spaces. Through these titles John indicates to his readers that the real "savior of the world" and "son of God" is Jesus. John's Christology counters Roman ideology and negotiates the Roman occupation.

Scene 6: Direct Clash of Powers in a Private Space (John 19:9–11)

Pilate reenters the praetorium for the last time and asks Jesus, "Where are you from?" (19:9). He is not asking for Jesus' place of birth or citizenship but expects to hear about Jesus' claim to be "son of God"—an inquiry about Jesus' ultimate origin. If Jesus is "son of God" then he is likely a great challenge to the Roman Emperor, who uses the same title. "Son of God" becomes a title upon which Pilate places much interest.[86] Jesus gives no answer to the question, but not as a self-defensive evasion. According to Thatcher, within the context of the ancient Roman culture, Jesus' refusal to speak would indicate either deference to or rejection of Pilate's authority. In the Fourth Gospel, Jesus' refusal to speak is a gesture of defiance, a symbolic expression of his authority to disregard the governor's queries.[87]

When Pilate claims authority over Jesus by challenging his refusal to speak, Jesus responds that Pilate would have no authority over him if it had not been given "from above" (19:11). In Thatcher's view, the idea that Pilate's authority is given from above rationalizes a peaceful coexistence between God and Caesar.[88] In other words, Caesar's kingdom is given from heaven by God; the two do not contradict each other. This is consistent with Roman political theology, since Roman propaganda argued that the gods supported Roman rule in order to rationalize imperial ideology. However, considering that Jesus asserts that he himself comes "from above," he may as well claim to be the source of Caesar's power. This means that Caesar is answerable to Jesus.

The contention that Pilate rules only by God's sanction implies that Pilate's power is "solely contingent on God's whim," that Pilate can "serve

---

86. Against Thatcher who holds that this should not be a question of Pilate's interest given that he had earlier on indicated that he does not intend to pass judgment on matters of Jewish faith, remembering Pilate's offer to hand over Jesus to the Jewish leaders to try them by their law when they claimed they had a law and according to that law Jesus must die. In this way Pilate is basically accepting his "incompetence" in matters of Jewish tradition. See Thatcher, *Greater Than Caesar*, 77–78.

87. Ibid.

88. Thatcher, *Greater Than Caesar*, 80.

as an unwitting pawn in the cosmic theme of redemption," and despite the fact that he is carrying out his part, God will still regard Pilate's involvement in the death of Jesus as 'sin' and will punish him accordingly.[89] Given this, the sincerity of Pilate's claim to release Jesus is doubtful. It was likely uttered to heighten the tension between Jesus and his fellow Jews rather than a genuine claim to release the one who has claimed that the Roman emperor's agent stands under God's judgment (19:11).

Scene Seven: Occupying God's Space? (John 19:12–16)

Soon after Pilate claims he wishes to release Jesus, the crowd shouts out to him, "If you release this man, you are not Caesar's friend" (19:12). I argue that here Pilate is leading the crowd to explicitly declare its allegiance to Caesar in a public space, performing a political game and mocking the dominated populace. Through their public lies and insincerity, both Pilate and the crowd achieve what they desire.

The expression, "friend of Caesar" (φίλος τοῦ Καίσαρος), here depends on the Roman context, and not a Jewish OT background.[90] Dominic Cuss references attestations for that title from the Hellenistic period under the Seleucids and Lagids, though meaning varies. Augustus adopted the title for imperial usage.[91] The Latin equivalents, amicus Augusti or amicus Caesaris, were expanded to include members of the imperial family. Consequently, Tacitus was able to expand the expression *amicorumve Caesaris* to include the friends of Drusus, the son of Tiberius (*Ann.* 1:27).

The title was likely honorific rather than official. Cuss explains that Suetonius refers to the "friends" of the emperors, and together with those references made by Tacitus and Dio, each emperor had his cohort

---

89. Ibid.

90. The expression "friend of 'x'" (φίλος τοῦ 'x') as a title is not very common in the OT, yet it is not completely absent. In 1 Chr 27:33, there is reference to Hushai the Archite as "the king's friend," and in 1 Macc 15:32, Athenobius is said to be the "friend of the King." Proverbs 25:1 mentions "the friends [men] of King Hezekiah," Dan 3:27 speaks of the "King's friends [counselors]." None of these except Daniel 3: 27 suggest a titular usage of the expression. In the NT, the formula is rare. In Luke 7:34 (Matt 11:19), we read of Jesus as "a friend of tax collectors and sinners" hardly meant to honor him. James 4:4 does identify a "friend of the world" with an "enemy of God," and calls Abraham a "friend of God (φίλος τοῦ)." The precise Johannine usage φίλος τοῦ Καίσαρος has no parallel in Scripture. See Richey, *Roman Imperial Ideology*, 167.

91. Cuss, *Imperial Cult*, 45–46.

of friends. This practice was adopted to suit the needs of the empire, and reflected the changing position of "friends" to include the performance of official or semi-official functions, something not part of Hellenistic practice.[92] According to Sherwin-White, this usage, originally political rather than personal in Republican usage, becomes markedly official in imperial documents, connoting that the referent is the official representative of the princeps.[93] Throughout the first century, the increasing significance of the honorific title indicates that friends of the emperor enjoyed a particular intimacy with him, and that the title of friend was conferred for imperial gratitude for things such as loyalty.[94]

According to Smallwood, in Judea under Roman rule, the title's frequent use secured the position of the Herodian dynasty by connecting it to the authority of the emperor and the benefits he brought:

> With the return of peace and the stability to the empire after Actium, Herod was at last eternally secure: the threat from Cleopatra had been removed, the problem of a choice of loyalty between rival Roman warlords had been resolved, and his position had been confirmed by the undisputed master of the Roman world. The two things now required of him by Rome were efficiency in his internal administration and loyalty to Octavian, who trusted him politically and liked him personally. The next two decades were years of material prosperity and imperial favor for the king who styled himself "friend of Rome" and "friend of Caesar."[95]

Agrippa continued the practice of openly allying Judea with the emperor, with the result that Gaius (Caligula) honored him with a formal treaty of alliance and, until his death in 44 CE, he ruled a kingdom larger than his grandfather's as "Great king, friend of Caesar and friend of Rome."[96] Helen Bond's observation that "coins of Herod Agrippa I frequently read *Philokaisar*, a designation that Philo also gives him (*In Flaccum*, 40) indicates that the title might have been commonplace in the imperial provinces of the first century.[97] Bond remarks that Pilate himself may have been called

---

92 Cuss, *Imperial Cult*, 46–47. See also Barrett, *Gospel According to St John*, 543.

93. Sherwin-White, *Roman Society and Roman Law*, 47.

94. Cuss, *Imperial Cult*, 49.

95. Smallwood, *Jews under Roman*, 70–71.

96. Ibid., 192.

97. Bond, *Pontius Pilate*, 190.

a "friend of Caesar" although there is no attestation external to the gospel of John.[98]

Many scholars have speculated that Pilate received this appellation through the patronage of Sejanus.[99] If so, the charge, "You are not Caesar's friend" would have increased pressure on Pilate. Yet this may have as well been a strategic move by Pilate: he goes outside the praetorium to taunt the already angry crowd with the threat to release Jesus, maneuvering them to publicly acclaim their loyalty to Caesar, consequently evoking even greater loyalty from "the Jews" who demand a Roman execution for Jesus. A population that "has no king but God" now has "no king but Caesar." Pilate's threat to release Jesus is a political game, through which he leads "God's nation" to publicly declare that Caesar occupies God's space. However, the crowd also wins. Their acclamation of Caesar as the only King is the public transcript of a dominated people, a survival strategy. Through this lie, the crowd maneuvers Pilate to grant their wish, i.e., the condemnation of Jesus. The public transcript reveals the complexity and contradictions of life under imperialism.

Golgotha: A Thirdspace (John 19:17–22)

John locates the place of Jesus' crucifixion at Golgotha—the place of the skull (19:17). In chapter four, I discussed Golgotha as the ideal venue of crucifixion both from the Roman and Judaism perspectives. From a Roman point of view, Golgotha is the perfect place to tell the cross story. As an elevated plot of ground that could be seen from many places in and around the Jewish metropolis, it is a veritable pulpit from which to proclaim the gospel of imperial power. From the point of view of first-century Judaism, Golgotha is an appropriate site for crucifixions because the unclean bodies of the cursed criminals would hang outside the walls, preventing the pollution of the holy city. Deut 21:23 states that corpses defile the land if left to hang overnight. Viewed from the Roman and first-century Judaism perspectives crucifixion victims—enemies of the state and rejected by God—were dehumanized and erased, discouraging any continuation of their stories. The act of crucifixion erases their first and second spaces.

98. Ibid.

99. Spicq, *Agape dans le Nouveau Testament*, 3:239–45, Schnackenburg, *Gospel According to St. John*, 3:262; Cuss, *Imperial Cult*, 48; Brown, *Death of the Messiah*, 1:693–95.

John emphasizes that Jesus carried his own cross to "the place of the skull, which is called in Hebrew, Golgotha." Roman tradition called for the flogging of the condemned person in preparation for the crucifixion. The victim would then carry the patibulum, the transverse beam, to the site of execution (Plautus, *Mil. glor.* 359–60). Jesus carries his own cross, unlike in the Synoptics where Jesus is so much weakened by the flogging that Simon of Cyrene is conscripted to carry Jesus' cross. Brant suggests that in the Fourth Gospel, Jesus carries his own cross "in order that no one else suffers as a consequence of his arrest" and to demonstrate that Jesus "moves forward at every step sustained by his resolve."[100]

John also presents the crucifixion scene in a way that controls the eyes of the mind to move back and forth only to focus on Jesus' body. "They crucified him, and with him two others, on this side (ἐντεῦθεν) and on that side (ἐντεῦθεν), then in the center (μέσον) Jesus (19:18)." The scene is vague: Jesus is crucified with these two other criminals, about whom John says nothing. John's explicit focus on Jesus in the middle calls attention to the body that is reconstructing the crucifixion space.

Pilate places an inscription (τίτλον) on the cross that reads, "Jesus of Nazareth, the King of the Jews" (19:19).[101] Τίτλον (Latin titulus) was a common feature of Roman punishment which served to inform the public and shame the offender. Suetonius describes a public banquet in Rome at which Caligula has a slave's hands cut off and hung around his neck, while a placard describing his offence is carried before him as he is paraded among the guests prior to being executed (*Cal.* 32:2; see also *Dom.* 10:1; Dio Cassius, *Hist.* 54.3:6–7; 73.16:5). In Jesus' case, the title was offensive to the Jews, whose political leaders protest against it (19:21). That a possible king of the Jews might come from Nazareth, a lowly place, appears to be an intentional insult.

Golgotha was outside the city, yet near enough for people to see and to be intimidated by Roman cruelty. The location enables the highest possible number of Jews to read the title. Moreover, the title's Hebrew, Greek, and Latin translations (19:20), make it accessible to everyone. Pilate creates this provocative scene, which the Jewish political leaders immediately protest. By refusing to alter it, Pilate mocks the Jewish people. By refusing to make

---

100. Brant, *John*, 251.

101. On Pilate's inscription on Jesus' cross, "King of the Jews" (John 19:19 and Mark 15:25), Dahl comments on it as authentic, and the first time that *Christos* (King) and cross were united. See Dahl, *Crucified Messiah*, 10–36.

the requested change, Pilate affirms Jesus as king over those whom Pilate oppresses, but demonstrating that he, like Caiaphas, is a puppet who has no control over his own tongue. On the cross then, Pilate announces Jesus as king of the dominated people. The three languages and the content of the superscription point to the universality of Jesus' reign.[102] The languages of the inscription constitute an element of thirdspace, as it moves through barrier of language and ethnicity demonstrating the universality of the people who are drawn to Jesus as he is lifted up on the Roman cross.

Jesus is executed by crucifixion—the Roman theater of cruelty which humiliates its opponents and reassures the execution's advocates that the condemned indeed deserve their punishment. For Jews, crucifixion brought an added stigma since the law reads "anyone hung on a tree is under God's curse" and will "defile the land" if left there overnight (Deut 21:23). Yet crucifixion was the subject of comedy and satire and not of serious Roman literature (See Suetonius, Cal.57.4; Plautus, Mil.glor.372; Josephus, Ant. 19:94), and a Greco-Roman audience would have been startled that the cross would become a symbol of Christianity.

David Balch, writing on the crucifix on the Palatine, agrees with Maria Antonietta Tomei, that the first visual representation of Christ dying on a cross that was drawn on a wall may be a graffito found on the Palatine hill, now exhibited in the Palatine Museum. It sketches a man on the cross who has the head of an ass. To the left of it, is a sketch of a man who raises his hands toward the figure on the cross, and a graffito underneath the two figures reads "Alexamenos adores God" (dates to the first half of the third century CE). The picture mocks the Christian worship of a crucified Lord.[103] The crucifixion space was therefore a dishonored space in the face of the world. John instead presents Jesus' crucifixion neither as a humiliation nor as a dishonor. It is a place that glorifies Jesus and God. The crucifixion space represents the climax of the politics of place in the Fourth Gospel. It reveals the extreme cruelty of Roman imperial politics yet it represents one of the greatest of challenges to imperial rule. By redefining the crucifixion space, John profanes both the political ideology and the theological entities in the Roman cross, defeating Rome and its Jerusalem-based allies.

Ultimate spatial restructuring is located in the death on the cross, with consequences for all spaces. It is not a space where the heavenly replaces the

---

102. Brant, *John*, 252.

103. Balch, *Roman Domestic Art*, 104; Tomei, *Museo Palatino*, 104–5 #78. See also Brant, *John*, 232–33. Brant's location of the graffito "near Circus Maximus" is inaccurate.

earthly, nor where the "not-of-this-world" replaces "this world," but a novel hybrid spatiality, exceeding both the real and imagined. Jesus' activities continue to construct spaces even at his death. Jesus at the cross does not abide by simple rules of proximity and distance, or of death and life. He is firstspatially absent through death on the cross but maintains a thirdspace presence. His status on the cross structures the socio-political life of believers and the proclamation of space. The will of this crucified man interprets and organizes this space.

In his death, Jesus functions thirdspatially. Death does not reduce him to inactivity. In his thirdspatial irreducibility, he continues to direct his followers in this horrific time of Roman rule and tyranny against them. Christ is absent and active but cannot be reduced to either of these poles. Such irreducibility expresses the "and more" that exceeds dualities and is constitutive of thirdspace. Christ who is raised on the cross governs the production of space on earth. He is both powerfully exalted/raised on the cross and powerfully active among believers thirdspatially. The cross is a thirdspace filled with liberating potentialities, a place in which an alternative social order is established.

In his death, Jesus announces the formation of a new community, a thirdspace community of liberation, an alternative society, a counter culture opposed to the politics of Rome in all its various forms. Jesus' death on the cross draws people out of the world to himself, to the marginal space of the dominated people, creating a community of resistance regulated by decolonized visions, analyses and practices. This community is loyal to the crucified king, whose rule supersedes every form of earthly power. As loyal followers of the world's creator, they are empowered to criticize the world's injustice and violence. This criticism takes the form of a visible demonstration of the teachings of Jesus in their lived experiences in various spaces.

The new community is "a community of friends," formed from Jesus' greater love that lays down life for friends (15:13).[104] Jesus chooses friendship as a model of service for his new community. Sandra Schneiders argues that friendship is "the one human relationship based on equality."[105] In perfect friendship, the good of each is truly the other's good, and so, in seeking the good of the friend, one achieves one's own good. In such an equitable friendship, domination is excluded as it arises from, expresses,

---

104. Schneiders, *Written That You May Believe*, 184–201 esp. 193–94.
105. Ibid., 193.

and reinforces inequality.[106] Believers model and reflect Jesus' kingdom by washing each other's feet, for leadership is service (13:4–5, 12–15). Jesus reverses the Roman political logic from being served to serving others, thereby challenging Rome's spatial behavior that considers it inconceivable for an emperor or any leader to wash the feet of his subjects. Jesus demonstrates passive resistance.

Conclusion

In his death, Jesus claims and exercises power—absolute power—in both the religious and political spaces simultaneously. He invalidates and displaces the existing institutions and authorities, values and norms, ideals and goals, while promoting and placing alternative authorities and institutions, norms and values, goals and ideals in their Roman imperial context.

Firstly, Jesus challenges Rome and the Jerusalem aristocracy by claiming his death as a fulfillment of Scripture. By this, John reminds Pilate and Rome that the circumstances of Jesus' death are not, in fact, a display of Roman authority over a rebellious Jew but rather the inevitable climax of a divine plan as written in the Sacred Book. The use of "according to Scripture" contradicts the normal meaning of the death and renders the authorities' understanding of his death flawed. Pilate is the ultimate loser in the trial. From the moment when Jesus is handed over to him, the leaders in Jerusalem define his place as unholy, implying that he is also morally inferior. Outside the praetorium, the crowd challenges Pilate's judgment while inside his own residence Jesus defies his words, challenges his leadership, and announces the formation of a community built on truth. Pilate has no idea what truth is. He is in fact the ultimate loser in this trial. This is the final stage of the defeat of Rome.

Secondly, Jesus' followers are called upon to produce their space by adopting practices of transformation shaped by Jesus' purpose. They have no safe alternative to generate transformation, such as the ballot or by forming political parties. Johannine Christians are to form alternative communities with practices that provide life-giving alternatives to the destructive Roman ones. Followers of Jesus must show the world what Jesus' kingdom looks like by imitating the way Jesus lived in their treatment of one another and in their response to the world. By refusing to grant allegiance to Caesar, the Johannine Christians fulfill the first stage in their

106. Ibid., 194.

liberation, the liberation of their consciousness, delegitimizing the oppressor's rule and authority over the lives of the oppressed, and opening up the possibility of a new allegiance. By giving allegiance to Jesus, the followers lay the groundwork for nonviolent resistance to any oppressive force, and to any ideology that would support the role of a Caesar. John paves the way for justice by removing from injustice the aura of sovereignty with which it surrounds itself and by pointing the way to a better alternative.

The Johannine Christians are colonized subjects engaged in private behaviors that express their dissatisfaction with the status quo. Through hidden transcripts—opposing the official versions of reality, the dominated people alleviate the emotional strain of submission and seek to restore some of the dignity they have lost through their forced compliance with the norms of the elite. Hidden transcripts achieve this by mocking and reversing the public behaviors that reflect the values of the great tradition— they create an alternative moral universe, a "world turned upside down." [107]

107. "The World Turned Upside Down" is an English ballad first published in the middle of the 1640s as a protest against the policies of the then British parliament relating to the celebration of Christmas. Parliament believed the holiday should be a solemn occasion, and outlawed traditional English Christmas celebrations. It is ironic that when the young American army under Washington defeated the British at Yorktown, the final battle of the Revolutionary War, the British band played the song "The World Turned Upside Down." See http://en.wikipedia.org/wiki/The_World_Turned_Upside_Down, accessed on February 15, 2014.

General Conclusion

In the five chapters of this book, I presented interpretations that not only contribute to Johannine studies but also carry important implications for future research. I proposed that in the Fourth Gospel, Jesus death is presented as a political event occasioned by Jesus' production of space. His construction of spaces positively impacts his society while it negatively affects the political authorities. The leaders interpret his activities as a challenge to their political space. In an attempt to mitigate political risk to themselves, they eliminate Jesus.

In the first chapter, I exposed the gap left by an exclusive focus on soteriological significance, and provided the rationale for a political reading of the death of Jesus. In John's account of Jesus' death, he emphasizes the political implications of the story. In John 11:48, he introduces a specifically political motivation to the plotting of the Jewish authorities. During Jesus' trial, the political element is accentuated: Jesus claims to be the king of the Jews, thereby contesting the authority of the Roman Empire (John 18:3, 36–37, 39; 19:12, 15, 21). To underscore Jesus' sin, the crowd's affirmation of loyalty to Caesar evokes faithfulness to the Roman Empire, which Jesus does not share (John 19:12–15). Finally, at the crucifixion of Jesus, Pilate insists on crucifying Jesus as the awaited political liberator, despite the chief priests' resistance to the inscription, "Jesus of Nazareth, the king of the Jews" (John 19:19–22). Jesus is portrayed as a threat to place and national security, and fear of the Romans becomes the motivating force in the decision to kill Jesus. It is a situation of powers conflicting at the site of imperialism.

In the second chapter, I critically examined Johannine studies that have considered the importance of the notion of place. I developed a methodology for a postcolonial geographical reading of the death of Jesus that uses John's construction of diverse places in the narrative. I proposed Henri Lefebvre's and Soja's theories of space as the means for broadening our understanding of space beyond the physical dimension. In Lefebvre's view, space is physical, mental and social. Soja refers to these dimensions respectively as firstspace, secondspace, and thirdspace. This new way of envisioning geography exposed a wider spatiality in John than has been hitherto imagined. I argued that when John's Gospel redefines spaces in the narrative of the death of Jesus, it produces new spaces for new social situations. This revolutionary reading of the Fourth Gospel deconstructs the dualistic interpretation of reality in John and suggests a trialectic consideration of space. The commonly held dualistic interpretation of Jesus' "not of this world" kingdom as an opposition between "heaven" and "earth" is replaced by a creative thirdspace that is heaven and earth and other.

In the third chapter, I proposed that the significance of this text lies in the space between the decisions that the council makes in the logic of eliminating a political threat and what John understands it to be. When John writes that the death of Jesus will unite a separated people, he contradicts the intent of Caiaphas and the council, making them ignorant pawns of the divine. Under the divine plan, Caiaphas does not control even his own tongue. This challenges the authorities of Jerusalem and the Roman Empire they represent. This is the first stage of John's defeat of Rome, as Rome's strongest ally among the local leaders of Jerusalem is defeated.

In the fourth chapter, I suggested that Jesus being "lifted up" refers to his immediate death and to his exaltation as he becomes the point of unity for the global truth community formed by his teachings and supported by his values. The Greeks' journey to Jesus highlights the inclusion of Gentiles into the new community of Jesus, underscoring an all-encompassing global community formed from God's previously scattered children. I have also suggested that the true rival of Jesus, the reputed "ruler of this world" who "is cast out" (12:31), "judged" (16:11), and who now "has no power" over Jesus (14:30), is the Roman emperor. Consequently, when Jesus publicly declares that this leader is made powerless, he is issuing a strong political challenge to Rome that endangers his life.

Jesus' death transforms socio-political space by reuniting the children of God in a global community where boundary is not a barrier. This global truth community thinks and analyzes from a decolonized perspective, and is capable of working out its liberation from all forces of oppression. Jesus' kingship leads an oppressed community into a liberation of awareness and opens up the possibility of a new loyalty. By giving allegiance to Jesus, the followers engage in passive resistance to all oppression, and to every imperial ideology. John removes the self-claimed mantle of sovereignty from injustice, thus paving the way toward justice.

The community's liberation is possible if, through faith, they see God's glory in Jesus' death and remain in the truth that Jesus proclaimed during his lifetime. Glory transforms the crucifixion space, shaping it into an attractive space where marginalized people gather for liberation from empire in all its various forms. The cross, as the place of God's glorification, encourages John's audience to recognize the presence of God even in crucifixion. Through new eyes of faith, the followers of Jesus see their everyday spaces of struggle (their own crosses) in the light of God's active presence and liberation. By presenting the crucifixion as a space of gathering for all peoples, John profanes the normal meaning of the cross and defeats the empire's greatest tool of oppression—the cross. This is the second level of Rome's defeat.

In the fifth chapter, I discussed the garden space, the courtyard of high priests, the praetorium space, and the crucifixion space. I proposed that Jesus is always the one who produces and reproduces space. As such, he determines his arrest in the garden, is defiant to Annas the high priest in his own courtyard, and contradicts every statement of Pilate during the trial, turning apparent losses into gains. Even his death revolutionizes the very understanding of death. He continues to construct believers' spaces even in his death. When Jesus is king, enthroned on the cross, he draws all people to himself. He is "truth incarnate," who influences the production of truth space, to which the world responds. Those who belong to the truth belong to Jesus. Pilate's ignorance of truth eliminates him from belonging to the truth community of Jesus. This is a loss for Pilate and the empire he represents, because Jesus creates a new world order that exposes the Roman world order as "world disorder," the third level of defeat of empire.

John's narrative presents Jesus' space as a thirdspace that empowers the marginalized. Jesus not only challenges the Roman imperial power but is also ethically committed to creating a just world. He challenges the Roman politics of divine sanctioning by presenting himself as the "son of God." The Roman exaltation of the state, in the person of the emperor, over God, in the person of Jesus Christ, inspired John to write his Gospel as a polemic against Roman ideologies and its absolute sovereignty in the world. However, rather than promoting a popular revolution against the

Romans that would be unsuccessful, John's Gospel attempts a systematic reversal of the political logic of the Romans. The reservation of "power" to Christ alone, the bestowal of the titles "son of God" and "savior of the world" on Jesus, and the confrontations with Pilate in the Passion Narrative all suggest that the Fourth Gospel aims at the very center of Roman power. Moreover, by challenging Caiaphas and by redefining the cross space, John challenges a historically and socially specific political system. John's Jesus resists by opposing the official version of reality, by reversing the political logic of Roman imperialism, and by creating an alternative community.

John's presentation of Jesus as a passive resister of the empire undergirds a theology of non-violent resistance. Whether the Johannine model of Jesus' leadership can be emulated is unclear. The task of Christian theologians is to reconceive the role of Christian theology in the socio-political sphere. Roman dictatorship is not a viable model, yet neither is Jesus' authority as presented in John's writing. John's narrative confers absolute power to Jesus. Jesus comes to his own people and he is above all. This absolute sovereignty complicates the problems confronting political theology: given that John's theology was formed within and against an autocratic and decidedly non-democratic society, are these ancient paradigms of political authority that John incorporated into his Christology to be abandoned as historical relics? Reading trialectically presents Jesus' kingship as a third-space of possibilities, an open space that shapes a new leadership with society's values at heart.

This book does not address the farewell speeches of Jesus (John 13—17), although I mentioned that the Johannine Jesus defined some values for his community including leadership as service in the model of friendship, and noted that Jesus proposes love and unity as basic for his community. How might interpretations of the farewell discourses change through a reading of Jesus' death as a polemic against Roman imperialism? How might these interpretations be further influenced by incorporating perspectives of social and political geography? These are future avenues of research.

Bibliography

Achebe, Chinua. *Things Fall Apart*. New York: Anchor, 1994.

Allen, John. *Lost Geographies of Power*. Oxford: Blackwell, 2003.

Alon, Gedaliah. *The Jews in their Land in the Talmudic Age (70–640 CE)*. Translated by Gershon Levi. Jerusalem: Magnes, 1980.

Appold, M. L. *The Oneness Motif in the Fourth Gospel*. WUNT 11. Tübingen. Mohr Siebeck, 1976.

Aristotle. *Nicomachean Ethics*. Translated by H. Rackham. LCL 73. Cambridge, MA: Harvard University Press, 1926.

———. *Poetics*. Translated by Stephen Halliwell. LCL 199. Cambridge, MA: Harvard University Press, 1995.

Ashcraft, Norman and Albert E. Scheflen. *People Space: The Making and Breaking of Human Boundaries*. Garden City, NY: Anchor, 1976.

Ashcroft, B. Griffiths, Gareth Tiffin, and Helen Tiffin, eds. *The Postcolonial Studies Reader*. London: Routledge, 1995.

Ashton, John. *Understanding the Fourth Gospel*. Second edition. Oxford: Oxford University Press, 2007.

Augustus Caesar. *Res gestae divi Augusti: ex monumentis Ancyrano et Antiocheno Latinis, Ancyrano et Appolloniensi Graecis*. 2nd edition. Edited by J. Gagé. Paris: Les Belles Lettres, 1960.

Aune, David E. "Dualism in the Fourth Gospel and the Dead Sea Scrolls: A Reassessment of the Problem." In *Neotestamentica et Philonica: Studies in honor of Peder Borgen*, edited by David Aune, et. al., 281–303. NovTSup 106. Boston: Brill, 2003.

Bailie, Gil. *Violence Unveiled: Humanity at the Crossroads*. New York: Crossroad, 1995.

Bal, Mieke. *Narratology: Introduction to the Theory of Narrative*. Translated by Christine van Boheemen. Toronto: University of Toronto Press, 1995.

Balch, David L. "The Church Sitting in a Garden (1 Cor 14:30. Rom 16:23. Mark 6:39–40. 8:6. John 6:3, 10. Acts 1:15. 2:1–2)." In *Contested Spaces: Houses and Temples in Roman Antiquity and the New Testament*, edited by David L. Balch and Annette Weissenrieder, 201–35. WUNT 285. Tübingen: Mohr Siebeck, 2012.

———. *Roman Domestic Art and Early House Churches*. WUNT 228. Tübingen: Mohr Siebeck, 2008.

Barclay, John M. G. "Deviance and Apostasy: Some Application of Deviance Theory to the First-Century Judaism and Christianity." In *Modeling Early Christianity: Social-scientific studies of the New Testament in its context*, edited by Philip F. Esler, 114–57. London/New York: Routledge, 1995.

Bar-Efrat, Shimon. Narrative Art in the *Bible*. London: T. & T. Clark, 2008.

Barrett, C. K. *The Gospel According to St. John: Essays on John*. London: SPCK 1982.

———. *The Gospel According to St John: An Introduction with Commentary and Notes on the Greek Text*. 2nd edition. Philadelphia: Westminster, 1978.

———. *The Gospel of John and Judaism*. Translated by D. M. Smith. Philadelphia: Westminster, 1975.

Bassler, Jouette. "The Galileans: A Neglected Factor in the Johannine Research." *CBQ* 43 (1981) 243–57.

Bauckham, Richard. *Jesus and The God of Israel: God Crucified*. Grand Rapids, MI: Eerdmans, 2009.

Bauer, Walter. *Das Johannesevangelium*. HNT 6. Tübingen: JCB Mohr Siebeck, 1933.

Bennington, Geoffrey. "The Politics and the Institution of the Nation." In *Nation and Narration*, edited by Homi Bhabha, 121–37. New York: Routledge, 2006.

Bernard, J. H. *A Critical and Exegetical Commentary on the Gospel According to John*. 2 Volumes. ICC. Edinburgh: T. & T. Clark, 1985.

Beutler, Johannes. "Greeks Come to See Jesus (John 12:20f)." *Bib* 71 (1990) 333–47.

———. "The Identity of the Jews for the Readers of John." In *Anti-Judaism and the Fourth Gospel: Papers of the Leuven Colloquium, 2000*, edited by R. Bieringer, D. Pollefeyt, et. al, 229–38. Assen: Royal Van Gorcum, 2001.

———. "Two Ways of Gathering. The Plot to Kill Jesus in John 11:47–53." *NTS* 40 (1994) 399–406.

Blass, F. and A. Debrunner. *A Greek Grammar of the New Testament and other early Christian Literature*. A Translation and Revision of the Ninth-Tenth German Edition Incorporating Supplementary Notes. Chicago: Chicago University Press, 1961.

Boatwright, Mary T. "Luxuriant Gardens and Extravagant Women: The *Horti* of Rome between Republic and Empire." In *Horti Romani: Atti Convegno Internazionale Roma, 4–6 Maggio 1995*, edited by M. Cima and Eugenio la Rocca, 71–82. Bulletino della Commissione Archeologica Communale di Roma Supplementi 6. Rome: L'Erma di Bretschneider, 1998.

Boer, Martinus C. de. "Jesus' Departure to the Father in John: Death or Resurrection?" In *Theology and Christology in the Fourth Gospel*, edited by G. van Belle, J. G. van der Watt, and P. Maritz, 1–19. BETL 184. Leuven: Leuven University Press and Uitgeverij Peeters, 2005.

———. "Johannine History and Johannine Theology: The Death of Jesus as the Exaltation and Glorification of the Son of Man." In *The Death of Jesus in the Fourth Gospel*, edited by G. van Belle, 293–326. BETL 200. Leuven: Leuven University Press and Uitgeverij Peeters, 2007.

———. *Johannine Perspectives on the Death of Jesus*. Contributions to Biblical Exegesis and Theology 17. Kampen, The Netherlands: Kok Pharos, 1996.

Bond, Helen K. *Caiaphas: The Friend of Rome and Judge of Jesus?* Louisville, KY: Westminster John Knox, 2004.

Borgen, Peder. "God's Agent in the Fourth Gospel." In *Interpretation of John*, edited by John Ashton, 67–78. Philadelphia: Fortress, 1986.

Boring, M. Eugene. *An Introduction to the New Testament: History, Literature, Theology*. Louisville, KY: Westminster John Knox, 2012.

Bornkamm, Günther. "Towards the Interpretation of John's Gospel: A Discussion of the Testament of Jesus by Ernst Käsemann." In *The Interpretation of John*, edited by John Ashton, 79–98. Issues in Religion and Theology 9. Philadelphia: Fortress, 1986.

Brant, Jo-Ann A. "Beauty, Sorrow and Glory in the Gospel of John." In *Beauty and the Bible: Toward a Hermeneutics of Biblical Aesthetics*, edited by Richard J. Bautch and Jean-François Racine, 83–99. SemeiaSt 73. Atlanta: Society of Biblical Literature, 2013.

———. *John*. Paideia Commentaries on the New Testament. Grand Rapids, MI: Baker Academic, 2011.

Brown, Raymond E. *The Community of the Beloved Disciple: The Lives, Loves and Hates of an Individual Church in the New Testament Times*. New York: Paulist, 1979.

———. *The Death of the Messiah: From Gethsemane to the Grave*. 2 Vols. ABRL. New York: Doubleday, 1994.

———. *The Gospel according to John* (I-II). AB 29 and 29A. Garden City, NY: Doubleday, 2006.

———. *An Introduction to the New Testament*. ABRL. New York: Doubleday, 1997.

———. "'Other Sheep Not of This Fold': The Johannine Perspective on Christian Diversity in the Late First Century." *JBL* 97 (1978) 5–22.

Brueggemann, Walter. *The Land: Place as Gift, Promise, and Challenge in Biblical Faith*. Philadelphia: Fortress, 1977.

Bruner, Frederick D. *The Gospel of John: A Commentary*. Grand Rapids, MI: Eerdmans, 2012.

Bultmann, Rudolf. *The Gospel of John*. Translated by George R. Beasley-Murray, R. W. N. Hoare, and J. K. Riches. Philadelphia: Fortress, 1974.

———. *The Gospel of John: A Commentary*. Translated by George R. Beasley-Murray. Philadelphia: Westminster, 1971.

———. *Theology of the New Testament*. Translated by Kendrick Grobel. 2 Volumes. New York: Charles Scribner's Sons, 1955.

Burge, Gary M. "Territorial Religion, Johannine Christology and the Vineyard of John 15." In *Jesus of Nazareth, Lord and Christ: Essays on the Historical Jesus and New Testament Christology*, edited by Joel B. Green and Max Turner, 384–96. Grand Rapids, MI: Eerdmans, 1994.

Caird, G. B. "The Glory of God in the Fourth Gospel: An Exercise in Biblical Semantics." *NTS* 15 (1969) 265–77.

Carey, G. "The Lamb of God and the Atonement Theories." *TynBul* 32 (1981) 97–122.

Carroll, John T., and Joel B. Green, eds. *The Death of Jesus in Early Christianity*. Peabody: Hendrickson, 1995.

Carson, D. A. *The Gospel According to John*. Grand Rapids, MI: Eerdmans, 1991.

Carter, Warren. "Constructions of Violence and Identities in Matthew." In *Violence in the New Testament*, edited by S. Matthews and E. L. Gibson, 81–108. London: T. & T. Clark, 2005.

———. *John and Empire: Initial Explorations*. New York: T. & T. Clark, 2008.

———. *Pontius Pilate: Portraits of a Roman Governor*. Interfaces. Collegeville, MN: Liturgical, 2003.

———. *The Roman Empire and the New Testament: An Essential Guide*. Abingdon Essential Guides. Nashville: Abingdon, 2006.

Casey, Edward. *Getting Back into Place: Towards a Renewed Understanding of the Place-World*. Bloomington: Indiana University Press, 1993.

———. *The Fate of Place: A Philosophical History*. Berkeley: University of California Press, 1997.

Cassidy, Richard J. *John's Gospel in New Perspective: Christology and the Realities of Roman Power*. Maryknoll, NY: Orbis, 1992.

Chancey, Mark A. *Greco-Roman Culture and the Galilee of Jesus*. Cambridge, UK: Cambridge University Press, 2005.

———. *The Myth of a Gentile Galilee*. SNTSMS 118. Cambridge, UK: Cambridge University Press, 2002.

Charlesworth, James H. "The Priority of John? Reflections of the Essenes and the First Edition of John," in *Für und wieder die Priorität des Johannesevangeliums*, edited by Peter L. Hofrichter, 73–114. TTS 9. Hildesheim: Georg Olms, 2002.

Cicero. *On the Orator*. Translated by E. W. Sutton. LCL 348. Cambridge, MA: Harvard University Press, 1939.

———. *Pro Rabirio*. Translated by H. Grose Hodge. LCL 252. Cambridge, MA: Harvard University Press, 1959.

———. *The Verrine Orations*. Translated by L. H. G. Greenwood. LCL 293. Cambridge, MA: Harvard University Press, 1960.

Cilia, Lucio. *La Morte di Gesu e L'Unita' degli Uomini (Gv 11:47–53. 12:32): Contributo allo Studio della Soteriologia Giovannea*. RivBSup 24. Bologna: Dehoniane, 1991.

Cima, Maddalena e E.Talamo, *Gli horti di Roma Antica*. Milan: Mondadori Electa, 2008.

Cohen, Anthony P. *The Symbolic Construction of Community*. New York: Tavistock and Ellis Horwood, 1985.

Coloe, Mary L. *God Dwells with Us: Temple Symbolism in the Fourth Gospel*. Collegeville, MN: Liturgical, 2001.

———. "The Nazarene King: Pilate's Title as the Key to John's Crucifixion." In *The Death of Jesus in the Fourth Gospel*, edited by G. van Belle, 839–48. BETL 200. Leuven: Leuven University Press and Uitgeverij Peeters, 2007.

Creswell, Tim. *In Place/Out of Place: Geography, Ideology and Transgression*. Minneapolis University of Minnesota Press, 1996.

Crossan, Dominic. *Who Killed Jesus? Exposing the Roots of Anti-Semitism in the Gospel Story of the Death of Jesus*. San Francisco: HarperCollins, 1995.

Culpepper, R. Alan. *Anatomy of the Fourth Gospel: A Study in Literary Design*. Philadelphia: Fortress, 1987.

———. *The Gospel and Letters of John*. Interpreting Biblical Texts. Nashville: Abingdon, 1998.

———. "The Gospel of John as a Document of Faith in a Pluralistic Society." In *What is John? Readers and Readings of the Fourth Gospel*, edited by F. F. Segovia, 121–25. SBLSymS 3. Atlanta: Scholars, 1996.

———. "The Theology of the Johannine Passion narrative: John 19:16–30." *Neot* 31 (1997) 21–37.

Cuss, Dominique. *Imperial Cult and Honorary Terms in the New Testament*. Fribourg: Fribourg University Press, 1974.

Dahl, Nils Alstrup. *The Crucified Messiah and Other Essays*. Minneapolis, MN: Augsburg, 1974.

Danker, Frederick W., ed. *Greek-English Lexicon of the New Testament and other Christian Literature*. 3rd edition. Based on Walter Bauer's *Griechisch-deutsche Worterbuch zu den Schriften des Neuen Testaments und der fruhchristlichen Literatur*, 6th edition. Chicago: University of Chicago Press, 2000.

BIBLIOGRAPHY

Dauer, Anton. *Die Passionsgeschichte im Johannesevangelium: Eine traditionsgeschichtliche und theologische Untersuchung zu Joh. 18, 1–19, 30.* SANT 30. Munchen: Kösel-Verlag, 1972.

Davidson, Steed V. *Empire and Exile: Postcolonial Readings of the Book of Jeremiah.* New York: T. & T. Clark, 2011.

Davies, W. D. *The Territorial Dimension of Judaism: With a Symposium and Further Reflections.* Minneapolis: Fortress, 1992.

DeConick, April D. *The Thirteenth Apostle: What the Gospel of Judas Really Says.* London and New York: Continuum, 2007.

Deissman, Adolf. *Light from the Ancient East: The New Testament Illustrated by Recently Discovered Texts of Graeco-Roman World.* Translated by Lionel R. M. Strachan, 1927. Reprint, Peabody, MA: Hendrickson, 1995.

Dennis, John A. *Jesus' Death and the Gathering of True Israel: The Johannine Appropriation of Restoration Theology in the Light of John 11:47–52.* WUNT 217. Tübingen: Mohr Siebeck, 2006.

———. "Jesus' Death in John's Gospel: A Survey of Research from Bultmann to the Present with Special Reference to the Hyper-Texts." *CBR* 4 (2006) 331–63.

———. "The 'Lifting up of the Son of Man' and the Dethroning of the 'Ruler of this World': Jesus' Death as the Defeat of the Devil in John 12:31–32." In *The Death of Jesus in the Fourth Gospel*, edited by G. van Belle, 677–91. BETL 200. Leuven: Leuven University Press and Uitgeverij Peeters, 2007.

Derrida, Jacques. *Positions.* Translated by Alan Bass. Chicago: University of Chicago Press, 1981.

deSilva, A. David. *An Introduction to the New Testament: Contexts, Methods and Ministry Formation.* Downers Grove, IL: InterVarsity, 2004.

Devereaux, Mary. "Beauty and Evil: The Case of Leni Riefenstahl's Triumph of the Will," in *Aesthetics and Ethics: Essays at the Intersection*, edited by Jerrold Levinson, 227–56. Cambridge Studies in Philosophy and the Arts. Cambridge, UK: Cambridge University Press.

Devillers, L. "La croix de Jésus et les Ioudaioi (John 19:16): *Crux interpretum* ou clé sotériologique?" In *The Death of Jesus in the Fourth Gospel*, edited by G. van Belle, 385–407. BETL 200. Leuven: Leuven University Press and Uitgeverij Peeters, 2007.

Dietrich, Manfried. "Das biblische Paradies und der babylonische Templegarten: Überlegungen zur Lange des Gartens Eden." In *Das biblische Weltbild und seine altorientalischen Kontexte*, edited by Bernd Janowski and Beate Ego, 281–323. FAT 32. Tübingen: Mohr Siebeck, 2001.

Dietzfelbinger, C. "Sühnetod im Johannesevangelium?" In *Evangelium–Schriftausegung–Kirche*, edited by J. Adna, et.al., 65–76. Göttingen: Vandenhoeck & Ruprecht, 1997.

Dio Cassius. *Roman History.* Translated by Earnest Cary. LCL 32. Cambridge, MA: Harvard University Press, 1955.

Dio Chrysostom. *Discourses.* Translated by H. Lamar Crosby. LCL 385. Cambridge, MA: Harvard University Press, 1959.

Dionysius. *Roman Antiquities.* Translated by Earnest Cary. LCL 319. Cambridge, MA: Harvard University Press, 1937.

Dodd, C. H. *Historical Tradition in the Fourth Gospel.* Cambridge, UK: Cambridge University Press, 1963.

———. *The Interpretation of the Fourth Gospel.* Cambridge, UK: Cambridge University Press, 1953.

————. "The Prophecy of Caiaphas John xi 47–53." *NeoPat* 6 (1962) 134–43.

Donahue, John R., ed. *Life in Abundance: Studies of John's Gospel in Tribute to Raymond E. Brown*. Collegeville, MN: Liturgical, 2005.

Douglas, Mary. *Purity and Danger*. London: Routledge & Kegan, 1966.

Du Bois, W. E. B. *W.E B. Du Bois Speaks: Speeches and Addresses 1920–1963*. Edited by Philip S. Foner. New York: Pathfinder, 1970.

Dube, W. Musa. "Reading for Decolonization (John 4:1–42)." In *John and Postcolonialism: Travel, Space and Power*, edited by Musa W. Dube and Jeffrey L. Staley, 51–75. The Bible and Postcolonialism 7. New York: Sheffield Academic, 2002.

————. "Savior of the World, but not of This World: A Postcolonial Reading of Spatial Construction in John." In *The Postcolonial Bible*, edited by R. S. Sugirtharajah, 118–35. Sheffield: Sheffield Academic Press, 1998.

Dube, W. Musa, and Jeffrey L. Staley. "Descending from and Ascending into Heaven: A Postcolonial Analysis of Travel, Space and Power in John." In *John and Postcolonialism: Travel, Space and Power*, edited by Musa W. Dube and Jeffrey L. Staley, 1–10. The Bible and Postcolonialism 7. New York: Sheffield Academic, 2002.

Duke, Paul D. *Irony in the Fourth Gospel*. Atlanta: John Knox, 1985.

Eck, Ernest van. *Galilee and Jerusalem in Mark's Story of Jesus: A Narratological and Social-Scientific Reading*. HTSSS 7. Pretoria: Kital, 1995.

————. "Jesus and Violence: An Ideological-Critical Reading of the Tenants in Mark 12:1–12 and Thomas 65." In *Coping with Violence in the New Testament*, edited by Pieter G. R. de Villers and Jan Willem van Henten, 10–31. STAR 16. Leiden: Brill, 2012.

Elden, Stuart. "Politics, Philosophy, Geography: Henri Lefebvre in Recent Anglo-American Scholarship." *Antipode* 33 (2001) 809–25.

————. "What about Huddersfield?" *Radical Philosophy* 84 (1997) 47–48.

Eliade, Mircea. *The Cosmos and History: The Myth of the Eternal Return*. Translated by Willard R. Trask. New York: Harper Torch, 1959.

————. *The Sacred and the Profane: The Nature of Religion*. Translated by Willard R. Trask. New York: Harcourt Brace, 1959.

Elliot, Neil. "An Imperial Message of the Cross." In *Paul and Empire: Religion and Power in Roman Imperial Society*, edited by Richard Horsley, 167–83. Harrisburg, PA: Trinity, 1997.

Elsen-Novák, Gabriele, and Mirko Novák. "Ich bin der wahre Weinstock und mein Vater ist der Weingärtner: Zur Semiotik des Weinstocks in Joh 15:1–8 aus Sicht der Altorientalistik." In *Picturing the New Testament*, edited by Annette Weissenrieder, et.al., 183–206. WUNT 193. Tübingen: Mohr Siebeck, 2005.

Evans, Craig A. "The Twelve Thrones of Israel: Scripture and Politics in Luke 22:24–30." In *Luke and Scripture: The Function of Sacred Tradition in Luke Acts*, edited by Craig A. Evans and James A. Sanders, 154–70. Minneapolis: Fortress, 1993.

Fitzmyer, Joseph A. "Crucifixion in Ancient Palestine, Qumran Literature, and the New Testament." *CBQ* 40 (1978) 498–507.

————. "The Palestinian Background of 'Son of God' as a Title for Jesus." In *Texts and Contexts: Biblical Texts in their Textual and Situational Contexts. Essays in Honor of Lars Hartman*, edited by T. Fornberg and D. Hellholm, 567–77. Oslo: Scandinavian University Press, 1995.

Forestell, Terence J. *The Word of the Cross: Salvation as Revelation in the Fourth Gospel*. AnBib 57. Rome: Biblical Institute Press, 1974.

Fortna, Robert T. *The Fourth Gospel and its Predecessor.* Philadelphia, PA: Fortress, 1988.

Frey Jörg. "'…das sie meine Herrlichkeit schauen' (John 17:24) Zu Hintergrund, Sinn und Funktion der johanneischen Rede von der δόξα Jesu." *NTS* 54 (2008) 375–97.

———. "Die '*theologia crucifixi*' in des Johannesevangeliums." In *Kreuzestheologie im Neuen Testament*, edited by A. Dettwiler and J. Zumstein, 169–238. WUNT 151. Tübingen: Mohr Siebeck, 2002.

Freyne, Sean. *Galilee and Gospel: Collected Essays.* WUNT 125. Tübingen: Mohr Siebeck, 2000.

———. *Galilee, Jesus and the Gospels: Literary Approaches and Historical Investigations.* Philadelphia: Fortress, 1988.

———. "Urban-Rural Relations in First-Century Galilee: Some suggestions from the Literary Sources." In *Galilee in Late Antiquity*, edited by L. I. Levine, 75–91. New York: Jewish Theological Seminary of America, 1992.

Fuss, D. *Essentially Speaking: Feminism, Nature and Difference.* New York: Routledge, 1991.

Galasterer, H. "A Man, a Book, and a Method: Sir Ronald Syme's *Roman Revolution* after Fifty Years." In *Between Republic and Empire*, edited by Kurt A. Raaflaub and Mark Toher, 1–20. Berkeley, CA: University of California Press, 1990.

Gates Jr., H. L. "Critical Feminism." *Critical Inquiry* 17 (1991) 457–70.

Giddens, Anthony. *The Constitution of Society: Outline of the Theory of Structuration.* Cambridge: Polity, 1984.

Gieschen, Charles A. "The Death of Jesus in the Gospel of John: Atonement for Sin?" *CTQ* 72 (2008) 243–61.

Glancy, Jennifer A. "Torture: Flesh, Truth and the Fourth Gospel." *BibInt* 13 (2005) 107–36.

Glare, P. G. W., ed. *Oxford Latin Dictionary.* Combined edition, reproduced with corrections. Oxford: Clarendon, 1996.

Glass, Zipporah G. "Building toward 'Nation-ness' in the Vine: A Postcolonial Critique of John 15:1–8." In *John and Postcolonialism: Travel, Space and Power*, edited by Musa W. Dube and Jeffrey L. Staley, 153–69. The Bible and Postcolonialism 7. Sheffield: Sheffield Academic, 2002.

Green, Joel B., and M. D. Baker, *Recovering the Scandal of the Cross: Atonement in the New Testament and Contemporary Contexts.* Downers Grove, IL: InterVarsity, 2000.

Green, Joel B. *The Gospel of Luke.* Grand Rapids, MI: Eerdmans, 1997.

Grigsby, B. H. "The Cross as an Expiatory Sacrifice in the Fourth Gospel." *JSNT* 15 (1982) 51–80.

Groom, Nigel. *The New Perfume Book.* London: Blackie, 1997.

Haenchen, Ernst. "Jesus von Pilatus (Joh. 18:28–19:15)." TLZ 85 (1960) 93–102.

———. *Das Johannesevangelium: Ein Kommentar.* Edited by U. Busse. Tübingen: Mohr-Paul Siebeck, 1980.

———. *The Johannine Question.* Tübingen: Mohr Siebeck, 1994.

———. *John: A Commentary on the Gospel of John.* 2 volumes. Translated by Robert W. Funk. Hermeneia. Philadelphia: Fortress, 1984.

Harvey, A. E. *Jesus on Trial: A Study in the Fourth Gospel.* Atlanta: John Knox, 1977.

Haufe, G. "τόπος." In *EDNT* 3, edited by Horst Balz and Gerhard Schneider, 366–67. Grand Rapids, MI: Eerdmans 1993.

Heil, John Paul. *Blood and Water: The Death and Resurrection of Jesus in John 18–21.* CBQMS 27. Washington, DC: Catholic Biblical Association of America, 1995.

Hengel, Martin. *Crucifixion in the Ancient World and the Folly of the Message of the Cross.* Minneapolis: Augsburg Fortress, 1977.

———. *The Johannine Question.* London: SCM, 1989.

Hill, David. "'My Kingdom is not of this World' (John 18:36): Conflict and Christian Existence in the World according to the Fourth Gospel." *IBS* 9 (1987) 54–62.

Hofius, O. "Die Sammlung der Heiden zur Herde Israels (John 10.16. 11:51f)." *ZNW* 58 (1967) 289–91.

Homer. *Odyssey.* Translated by A. T. Murray. LCL 104. Cambridge, MA: Harvard University Press, 1919.

Horrell, G. David, ed. *Social-Scientific Approaches to New Testament Interpretation.* Edinburg: T. & T. Clark, 1999.

Horsley, Richard A., ed. *In the Shadow of Empire: Reclaiming the Bible as a History of Faithful Resistance.* Louisville, KY: Westminster John Knox, 2008.

———. *Jesus and Empire: The Kingdom of God and the New World Disorder.* Minneapolis: Fortress, 2003.

———. *Jesus and the Spiral of Violence: Popular Jewish Resistance in Roman Palestine.* Minneapolis, MN: Augsburg Fortress, 1993.

———. *Oral Performance, Popular Tradition, and Hidden Transcript in Q. Semeia* 60. Atlanta: Society of Biblical Literature, 2006.

Hoskyns, E. C. *The Fourth Gospel.* 2nd edition. Edited by F. N. Davey. London: Faber and Faber, 1947.

Hoskyns, E. C., and F. N. Davey. *Crucifixion-Resurrection: The Pattern of Theology and Ethics in the New Testament.* London, SPCK, 1981.

Hubbard, P. R. K., and G. Valentine, ed. *Key Thinkers on Space and Place.* London: Sage, 2004.

Jenson, Philip Peter. *Graded Holiness: A Key to the Priestly Conception of the World.* JSOTSup 106. Sheffield: Sheffield Academic, 1992.

Jeong, Ho-Won. *Peace and Conflict Studies: An Introduction.* Hants, Eng.: Ashgate, 2000.

Josephus. *Against Apion.* Translated by H. St. J. Thackeray. LCL 186. Cambridge, MA: Harvard University Press, 1961.

———. *Jewish Antiquities.* Translated by Ralph Marcus and Allen Wikgren. LCL 242. Cambridge, MA: Harvard University Press, 1963.

———. *Jewish War.* Translated by H. St. J. Thackeray, et. al. LCL 203. Cambridge, MA: Harvard University Press, 1961.

Karakolis, C. "'Across the Kidron Brook' (John 18:1)." In *The Death of Jesus in the Fourth Gospel,* edited by G. Van Belle, 751–60. BETL 200. Leuven: Leuven University Press and Uitgeverij Peeters, 2007.

Käsemann, Ernst. *Jesu Letzter Wille nach Johannes 17.* Tübingen: J. C. B. Mohr, 1966.

———. *The Testament of Jesus: Study of the Gospel of John in the Light of Chapter 17.* Translated by Krodel Gerhard. London: SCM, 1968.

Katongole, Emmanuel. *The Sacrifice of Africa: A Political Theology for Africa.* Grand Rapids, MI: Eerdmans, 2011.

Kealey, Seán P. "Political Jesus." *ITQ* 61 (1995) 89–98.

Kimelman, R. "*Birkat ha-minim* and the Lack of Evidence for an Anti-Christian Jewish Prayer in Late Antiquity." In *Jewish and Christian Self-Definition,* edited by E. P. Sanders, 2:226–44, 2:391–403. Philadelphia: Fortress, 1981.

Klawans, Jonathan. *Impurity and Sin in Ancient Judaism.* Oxford: Oxford University Press, 2000.

————. "The Impurity of Immorality in Ancient Judaism." *JJS* 48 (1997) 1–16.

————. *Purity, Sacrifice, and the Temple: Symbolism and Supersessionism in the Study of Ancient Judaism*. Oxford: Oxford University Press, 2006.

Knöppler, Thomas. *Sühne im Neuen Testament: Studien zum urchristlichen Verständnis der Heilsbedeutung des Todes Jesus*. WMANT 88. Neukirken–Vluyn: Neukirchener Verlag, 2001.

————. *Die theologia crucis des Johannesevangelium: Das Verständnis des Todes Jesu im Rahmen der Johanneischen Inkarnations—und Erhöhungschristologie*. WMANT 69. Neukirken: Neukirchener, 1994.

Koester, Craig R. "The Death of Jesus and the Human Condition: Exploring the Theology of John's Gospel." In *Life in Abundance: Studies of John's Gospel in Tribute to Raymond E. Brown*, edited by John R. Donahue, 141–57. Collegeville, MN: Liturgical, 2005.

————. "The Passion and Resurrection according to John." *Word and World* 11 (1991) 84–91.

————. "'The Savior of the World' (John 4:42)." *JBL* 109 (1990) 665–80.

————. *Symbolism in the Fourth Gospel: Meaning, Mystery, Community*. Minneapolis: Fortress, 1995

————. "Why Was the Messiah Crucified? A Study of God, Jesus, Satan, and Human Agency in Johannine Theology." In *The Death of Jesus in the Fourth Gospel*, edited by G. van Belle, 169–238. BETL 200. Leuven: Leuven University Press and Uitgeverij Peeters, 2007.

Koester, Helmut. *Introduction to the New Testament*. 2nd Edition. New York: Walter de Gruyter, 2000.

————. "Τόπος." In *TDNT* VIII, edited by Gerhard Kittel and Gerhard Schneider, 187–208. Grand Rapids, MI: Baker, 1982.

Kovacs, Judith L. "Now Shall the Ruler of This World Be Driven out: Jesus' Death as a Cosmic Battle in John 12:20-36."*JBL* 114 (1995) 227–47.

Kundsin, Karl. *Topologische Überlieferungsstoffe im Johannes-Evangelium: Eine Untersuchung*. FRLANT 22. Göttingen: Vandehoeck & Ruprecht, 1925.

Kurichianil, J. "The Glory and the Cross: Jesus' Passion and Death in the Gospel of John." *Indian Theological Studies* 20 (1983) 5–15.

Kysar, Robert. *The Fourth Evangelist and His Gospel: An Examination of Contemporary Scholarship*. Minneapolis: Augsburg, 1975.

————. *John, the Maverick Gospel*. 3rd edition. Louisville, KY: Westminster John Knox, 2007.

————. *Voyages with John: Charting the Fourth Gospel*. Waco: Baylor University Press, 2005.

L'Eplattenier, C. "La Passion dans l'évangile de Jean." *FV* 81 (1982) 25–30.

Lampe, G. W. H., ed. *A Patristic Greek Lexicon*. Oxford: Clarendon, 1961.

Lang, Anthony F., Jr., ed. *Political Theory and International Affairs: Hans J. Morgenthau on Aristotle's "The Politics."* Westport, CT: Praeger, 2004.

Lefebvre, Henri. *The Production of Space*. Cambridge, MA: Blackwell, 1991.

Liddell, Henry G., and Robert A. Scott. *A Greek-English Lexicon*. 9th edition. Revised by S. H. Jones with the assistance of Roderick McKenzie. Revised supplement edited by P. G. W. Glare with the assistance of A. A. Thompson. Oxford: Clarendon, 1996.

Liew Tat-Siong, Benny. "Ambiguous Admittance: Consent and Descent in John's community of 'Upward' Mobility." In *John and Postcolonialism: Travel, Space and*

Power, edited by Musa W. Dube and Jeffrey L. Staley, 193–224. The Bible and Postcolonialism 7. New York: Sheffield Academic, 2002.

Lincoln, Andrew T. *The Gospel According to Saint John*. BNTC 4. New York: Continuum, 2005.

———. *Truth on Trial*. Peabody, MA: Hendrickson, 2000.

Lindars, B. *The Gospel of John*. NCB. London: Oliphants, 1972.

———. *Jesus Son of Man: A Fresh Examination of the Son of Man Sayings in the Gospels in the Light of Modern Research*. London: SPCK. Grand Rapids, MI: Eerdmans, 1983.

———. *John*. New Testament Guides. Sheffield: JSOT Press, 1990.

———. "The Passion in the Fourth Gospel." In *God's Christ and His People: Studies in honor of Nils Alstrup Dahl*, edited by J. Jervell and W. A. Meeks, 71-76. Oslo, Bergen: 1977.

Loader, W. G. *The Christology of the Fourth Gospel: Structure and Issues*. Frankfurt: Peter Lang, 1989.

Lohfink, G. "'Wenn wir ihn so weitermachen lassen...' (Joh 11:45–53)." *Orientierung* 48 (1984) 62–63.

Lohse, Eduard. *Märtyrer und Gottesknecht: Untersuchungen zur urchristlichen Verkündigung vom Sühntod Jesu Christi*. FRLANT 64. Göttingen: Vandenhoeck & Ruprecht, 1963.

Lopez, Kathryn Muller. "Standing Before the Throne of God: Critical Spatiality in Apocalyptic Scenes of Judgment." In *Constructions of Space II: the Biblical City and Other Imagined Spaces*, edited by Jon L. Berquist and Claudia V. Camp 139–55. New York: T. & T. Clark, 2008.

Louw, J. P., E. A. Nida, et.al. *Greek-English Lexicon of the New Testament Based on Semantic Domains*. New York: United Bible Societies, 1989.

Malatesta, Edward. *St. John's Gospel: 1920–1965: A Cumulative and Classified Bibliography of Books and Periodical Literature on the Fourth Gospel*. AnBib 32. Rome: Pontifical Biblical Institute, 1967.

Malina, Bruce J. *Christian Origins and Cultural Anthropology: Practical Models for Biblical Interpretation*. Atlanta, GA: John Knox, 1986.

———. *The New Testament World, Insights from Cultural Anthropology*. 3rd edition. Louisville, KY: Westminster John Knox, 2001.

———. *The Social Gospel of Jesus: The Kingdom of God in Mediterranean Perspective*. Minnesota: Fortress, 2001.

Malina, Bruce J., and Richard L. Rohrbaugh. *Social Science Commentary on the Gospel of John*. Minneapolis: Fortress, 1998.

Mardaga, Hellen. "The Repetitive Use of ὑψόω in the Fourth Gospel." *CBQ* 74 (2012) 101–17.

Maritz, Petrus. "The Glorious and Horrific Death of Jesus in John 17: Repetition and Variation of Imagery related to John's Portrayal of the Crucifixion." In *The Death of Jesus in the Fourth Gospel*, edited by G. Van Belle, 693–710. BETL 200. Leuven: Leuven University Press and Uitgeverij Peeters, 2007.

Martial. *Epigrams*. Translated by D. R. Shackleton Bailey. LCL 94. Cambridge, MA: Harvard University Press, 1993.

Martyn, Louis J. *History and Theology in the Fourth Gospel*. 3rd edition. Louisville, KY: Westminster John Knox, 2003.

Marzotto, Damiano. *L'Unità Degli Uomini nel Vangelo di Giovanni*. RivB 9. Brescia: Paideia, 1977.

Massey, Doreen. *Space, Place and Gender*. Minneapolis: University of Minneapolis Press, 1994.

Matera, Francis J. "'On Behalf of Others,' 'Cleansing,' and 'Return': Johannine Images for Jesus' Death." *LS* 13 (1988) 161–78.

Maunier, René. *The Sociology of Colonies: An Introduction to the Study of Race Contact*. Volume 1. Translated by E. O. Lorimer. London: Routledge, 1949.

McHugh, J. "The Glory of the Cross: The Passion According to St. John." *CR* 67 (1982) 117–27.

Meeks, Wayne A. "The Man from Heaven in Johannine Sectarianism." *JBL* 91 (1972) 44–72.

———. "The Man from Heaven in Johannine Sectarianism." In *The Interpretation of John*, edited by John Ashton, 141–73. Philadelphia: Fortress, 1986.

———. *The Prophet-King: Moses Traditions and the Johannine Christology*. NovTSup 60. Leiden: Brill, 1967.

———. Review of *the Testament of Jesus: A Study of the Gospel of John in the Light of Chapter 17, by Ernst Käsemann*, USQR 24 (1968–1969) 414–20.

Metzger, Bruce M. *A Textual Commentary on the Greek New Testament*. 2nd edition. 1994. Reprint, Minneapolis: Fortress, 2001.

Metzner, Rainer. *Kaiphas Der Hohepriester jenes Jahres: Geschichte und Deutung*. Leiden: Brill, 2010.

———. *Das Verständnis der Sünde in Johannesevangelium*. WUNT 122. Tübingen: Mohr Siebeck, 2000.

Mirguet, François. "Voir la mort de Jésus: Quand le 'Voir' se fait récit." In *The Death of Jesus in the Fourth Gospel*, edited by G. van Belle, 469–79. BETL 200. Leuven: Leuven University Press and Uitgeverij Peeters, 2007.

Mishra, Pankaj. *From the Ruins of Empire: The Intellectuals who remade India*. New York: Farrar, Strauss and Giroux, 2012.

Moloney, J. Francis. *The Gospel According to John*. Sacra Pagina 4. Collegeville, MN: Liturgical, 1998.

———. *The Johannine Son of Man*. Biblioteca di Scienze Religiose 14. Rome: LAS, 1976.

———. "Johannine Theology." In *NJBC*, edited by Raymond E. Brown, et. al., 1417–26. Englewood Cliffs, NJ: Prentice-Hall, 1990.

———. *Signs and Shadows: Reading John 5–12*. Minneapolis, MN: Fortress, 1996.

Moore, Stephen D. *Empire and Apocalypse: Postcolonialism and the New Testament*. The Bible in the Modern World. Sheffield: Sheffield Phoenix, 2006.

———. "The Romans Will Come and Destroy Our Place and Our Nation: Representing Empire in John." In *The Bible in Theory: Critical and Postcritical Essays*, edited by Tom Thatcher, 327–52. SBLRBS 57. Atlanta: Society of Biblical Literature, 2010.

Morgan-Wynne, J. E. *The Cross in the Johannine Writings*. Eugene, OR: Pickwick Publications, 2011.

Morgenthau, Hans J. *Politics among Nations: The Struggle for Power and Peace*. Boston: McGraw Hill Higher Education, 2006.

Mosala, I. J. *Biblical Hermeneutics and Black Theology in South Africa*. Grand Rapids, MI: Eerdmans, 1989.

Motyer, Stephen. *Your Father the Devil? A New Approach to John and 'the Jews'*. Paternoster Biblical and Theological Monographs. Carlisle, UK: Paternoster, 1997.

Moulton, W. F and A. S. Geden. *Concordance to the Greek New Testament*. 6th edition. London: T. & T. Clark, 2002.

Mudimbe, V. Y. *The Invention of Africa: Gnosis, Philosophy and the Order of Knowledge.* Bloomington: Indiana University Press, 1998.

Müller, Th. *Das Heilsgeschehen im Johannesevangelium: Eine exegetische Studie, zugleich der Versuch einer Antword an Rudolf Bultmann.* Zurich: Gotthelf, 1961.

Müller, U. B. "Die Bedeutung des Kreutzestodes Jesu im Johannesevangelium: Erwägungen zur Kreuzestheologie im Neuen Testament." *KD* 21 (1975) 49–71.

Neusner, Jacob. *A Life of Yohanan ben Zakkai Ca. 1–80 CE.* 2nd edition. SPB. Leiden: Brill, 1970.

———. *A Life of Yohanan ben Zakkai. From Politics to Piety: The Emergence of Pharisaic Judaism.* Englewood Cliffs, NJ: Prentice-Hall, 1973.

Neyrey, Jerome H. *The Gospel of John.* New Cambridge Bible Commentary. New York: Cambridge University Press, 2007.

———. *An Ideology of Revolt: John's Christology in Social Science Perspective.* Philadelphia: Fortress, 1988.

———. "The 'Noble Shepherd' in John 10: Cultural and Rhetorical Background." *JBL* 120 (2001) 267–91.

———. "Spaces and Places, Whence and Whither, Homes and Rooms: 'Territory' in the Fourth Gospel." *BTB* 32 (2002) 60–75.

———. "The Symbolic Universe of Luke Acts: 'They Turn the World Upside Down.'" In *The World of Luke-Acts: Models for Interpretation*, edited by Jerome H. Neyrey. Peabody: Hendrickson, 1991.

Nicholson, G. C. *Death as Departure: The Johannine Descent–Ascent Schema.* SBLDS 63. Chico, CA: Scholars, 1983.

Nielsen, H. K. "John's understanding of the Death of Jesus," in *New Readings in John: Literary and Theological Perspectives: Essays from the Scandinavian Conference on the Fourth Gospel*, edited by J. Nissen and S. Pedersen, 232–54. JSNTSup 182. Sheffield: Sheffield Academic, 1999.

Nielsen, Jesper Tang "The Narrative Structure of Glory and Glorification in the Fourth Gospel." *NTS* 56 (2010) 343–66.

O'Day, Gail R. "The Gospel of John: Introduction, Commentary and Reflections." In *New Interpreters Bible* 9, edited by Leander E. Keck, 491–865. Nashville: Abingdon, 1995.

Obermann, Andreas. *Die Christologische Erfüllung der Schrift im Johannes-evangelium.* WUNT 83. Tübingen: Mohr Siebeck, 1996.

Okure, T. *The Johannine Approach to Mission: A Contextual Study of John 4:1–42.* WUNT 31. Tübingen: Mohr Siebeck, 1988.

Olsson, Birger. *Structure and Meaning in the Fourth Gospel: A Text-Linguistic Analysis of John 2:1–11 and 4:1–42.* ConBNT 6. Lund: C. W. K. Gleerup, 1974.

Ottenjeijm, Eric. "Impurity between Intention and Deed: Purity Disputes in first Century Judaism and in the New Testament." In *Purity and Holiness: The Heritage of Leviticus*, edited by M. J. H. M. Poorthuis and J. Schwartz, 121–47. Leiden: Brill, 2000.

Overman, Andrew J. *Matthew's Gospel and Formative Judaism: The Social World of the Matthean Community.* Minneapolis: Fortress, 1990.

Pancaro, S. "The People of God in John's Gospel." *NTS* 16 (1970) 114–29.

Park, Sang-Kyu. "Spatial Eschatology: A Reading of the New Temple of God in the Fourth Gospel." Ph.D. diss., Graduate Theological Union, 2011.

Pasquale, Giovanni di, and Fabrizio Paolucci, eds. *Il giardino antico da Babilonia a Roma: Scienza, arte e natura.* Istituto e Museo di Storia della Scienza di Firenze. Livorno: Sillabe, 2007.

Perschbacher, W. J., ed. *The New Analytical Greek Lexicon*. Peabody, MA: Hendrickson, 1990.

Philo. *Philonis Alexandrini in Flaccum*. Oxford: Oxford University Press, 1939.

Piper, R. A. "Pilate and the death of Jesus in the Fourth Gospel." In *The Death of Jesus in the Fourth Gospel*, edited by G. van Belle, 121–62. BETL 200. Leuven: Leuven University Press and Uitgeverij Peeters, 2007.

Plautus. *Miles Gloriosus*. Edited by Mason Hammond, et. al. LCL 60. Cambridge, MA: Harvard University Press, 1997.

Polybius. *Histories*. Translated by W. R. Paton. LCL 159. Cambridge, MA: Harvard University Press, 1927.

Pseudo-Quintilian. *The Lesser Declamations*. Translated by D. R. Shackleton Bailey. LCL 500. Cambridge, MA: Harvard University Press, 2006.

Punt, Jeremy. "Violence in the New Testament and the Roman Empire: Ambivalence, Othering, Agency." In *Coping with Violence in the New Testament*, edited by Pieter G. R. de Villers and Jan Willem van Henten, 23–39. STAR 16. Leiden: Brill, 2012.

Rein, Matthias. *Die Heilung des Blindgeborenen (Joh 9): Tradition und Redaktion*. WUNT 2/73. Tübingen: Mohr Siebeck, 1995.

Reinhartz, Adele. "The Colonizer as Colonized: The Intertextual dialogue between the Gospel of John and Canadian Identity." In *John and Postcolonialism: Travel, Space and Power*, edited by Musa W. Dube and Jeffrey L. Staley, 170–92. The Bible and Postcolonialism 7. New York: Sheffield Academic, 2002.

———. "The Johannine Community and its Jewish Neighbors: A Reappraisal." In *What is John? Literary and Social Readings of the Fourth Gospel*, edited by Fernando F. Segovia, 111–38. SBLSymS 3. Atlanta: Scholars, 1998.

Rensberger, David. *Johannine Faith and Liberating Community*. Philadelphia: Westminster Press, 1988.

———. "The Politics of John: The Trial of Jesus in the Fourth Gospel." *JBL* 103/3 (1984) 395–411.

Resseguie, James L. *The Strange Gospel: Narrative Design and Point of View in John*. Leiden: Brill, 2001.

Reynolds, Benjamin E. *The Apocalyptic Son of Man in the Gospel of John*. WUNT 2/249. Tübingen: Mohr Siebeck, 2008.

Richey, L. B. *Roman Imperial Ideology and the Gospel of John*. CBQM 43. Washington DC: The Catholic Biblical Association of America, 2007.

Ritva H. Williams. "Purity, Dirt, Anomalies, and Abominations." In *Understanding the Social World of the New Testament*, edited by Neufeld, Dietmar and Richard E. DeMaris, 207–19. London: Routledge 2010.

Robinson, A. T. John. *The Priority of John*. Edited by J. F. Coakley. London: SCM, 1985.

Rose, Gillian. "Place and Identity: A Sense of Place." In *A Place in the World? Places, Culture and Globalization*, vol. 4, edited by Doreen Massey and Pat Jess, 88–134. The Shape of the World. Oxford: Oxford University Press, 1995.

———. "Thirdspace." In *Dictionary of Human Geography*, edited by Johnston Gregory, et.al., 827. Oxford: Blackwell, 2000.

Sabbe, M. "The Johannine Account of the Death of Jesus and its Synoptic Parallels (John 19:16b–42)." *EThL* 70 (1994) 34–64.

Sack, Robert David. *Human Territoriality: Its Theory and History*. Cambridge Studies in Historical Geography 7. Cambridge: Cambridge University Press, 1986.

Salier, Willis H. *The Rhetorical Impact of the Semeia in the Gospel of John*. WUNT/186. Tübingen: Mohr Siebeck, 2004.

Sanders, E. P. *The Historical Figure of Jesus*. London: Penguin, 1993.

Scarry, Elaine. *The Body in Pain: The Making and Unmaking of the World*. Oxford: Oxford University Press, 1985.

Schlatter, Adolf von. *Der Evangelist Johannes: Wie er spricht, denk und glaubt*. Stuttgart: Clawer, 1960.

Schlier, H. "Jesus und Pilatus nach dem Johannesevangelium." In *Die Zeit der Kirche*, edited by H. Schlier, 56–74. 4th edition. Freiburg: Herder, 1966.

———. *The Relevance of the New Testament*. Freiburg: Herder and Herder, 1968.

Schmidt, K. L. "'ἔθνος' in the New Testament." In *TDNT II*, edited by Gerhard Kittel and Gerhard Friedrich, 369–72. Grand Rapids, MI: Eerdmans, 1978.

Schnackenburg, Rudolf. *The Gospel according to Saint John*. 3 vols. Trans. Cecily Hastings, Francis McDonagh, David Smith and Richard Foley. New York: Crossroad, 1982.

Schneiders, Sandra M. *The Johannine Resurrection Narrative: An Exegetical and Theological Study of John 20 as a Synthesis of Johannine Spirituality*. Unpublished Dissertation for Doctor of Sacred Theology submitted at the Pontifical Gregorian University in 1975. Rome: University Microfilms International, 1983.

———. *The Revelatory Text: Interpreting the New Testament as Sacred Scripture*. Collegeville, MN: Liturgical, 1999.

———. "The Resurrection (of the Body) in the Fourth Gospel: A Key to Johannine Spirituality." In *Life in Abundance: Studies of John's Gospel in Tribute to Raymond E. Brown*, edited by John R. Donahue, 168–98. Collegeville, MN: Liturgical, 2005.

———. *Written That You May Believe: Encountering Jesus in the Fourth Gospel*. New York: Crossroad, 2003.

Schnelle, Udo. "Cross and Resurrection in the Gospel of John." In *The Resurrection of Jesus in the Gospel of John*, edited by C. R. Koester and R. Bieringer, 127–51. WUNT 1/222. Tübingen: Mohr Siebeck, 2008.

———. *Theology of the New Testament*. Trans. M. Eugene Boring. Grand Rapids, MI: Baker Academic, 2009.

Scholer, John Mitchel. Review of *John's Gospel in New Perspective: Christology and the Realities of the Roman Power*, by Richard J. Cassidy, *Int* 48 (1994) 210.

Scholtissek, Klaus. *In ihm sein und bleiben: Die Sprache der Immanenz in den Johanneischen Schriften*. HBS 21. Freiburg: Herder, 2000.

Schroer, M. *Räume, Orte, Grenzen: Auf dem Weg zu einer Soziologie des Raums*. Frankfurt a.M.: Suhrkamp, 2006.

Schubert, K. "Biblical Criticism Criticized: With Reference to the Markan Report of Jesus' extermination before the Sanhedrin." In *Jesus and the Politics of his Day*, edited by E. Bammel and C. F. D. Moule, 385–402. Cambridge: Cambridge University Press, 1984.

Schulz, Siegried. *Das Evangelium nach Johannes*. NTD 4. Göttingen: Vandenhoeck & Ruprecht, 1963.

Schürer, E. *The History of the Jewish People in the Age of Jesus Christ (175 BC–AD 135)*. Rev. G. Vermes and F. Millar. Edinburgh: Clark, 1973.

Scott, James C. *Domination and the Arts of Resistance: Hidden Transcripts*. New Haven: Yale University Press, 1990.

Segovia, F. Fernando. "The Gospel of John." In *A Postcolonial Commentary on the New Testament Writings*, edited by Fernando S. Segovia and R. S. Sugirtharajah, 156–94. The Bible and Postcolonialism 13. London/New York: T. & T. Clark, 2007.

———. "Johannine Studies and the Geopolitical Reflections upon Absence and Irruption." In *What We Have Heard from the Beginning: The Past, Present and Future of Johannine Studies*, edited by Tom Thatcher, 281–306. Waco, TX: Baylor University Press, 2007.

———. "The Journey(s) of the Word of God: A Reading of the Plot of the Fourth Gospel." In *The Fourth Gospel from a Literary Perspective*, edited by R. A. Culpepper and F. F. Segovia, 23–54. *Semeia* 53. Atlanta: Scholars, 1991.

———. "Postcolonial and Diasporic Criticism in Biblical Studies: Focus, Parameters, Relevance." *Studies in World Christianity* 5 (1999) 177–96.

Seneca. *Moral Essays*. Translated by John W. Basore. LCL 310. Cambridge, MA: Harvard University Press, 1948.

Senior, Donald. "The Death of Jesus as a Sign: A Fundamental Johannine Ethic." In *The Death of Jesus in the Fourth Gospel*, edited by G. Van Belle, 271–91. BETL 200. Leuven: Leuven University Press and Uitgeverij Peeters, 2007.

———. *The Passion of Jesus in the Gospel of John*. Collegeville, MN: Liturgical, 1991.

Sherk, Robert K., ed. *The Roman Empire: Augustus to Hadrian*. Cambridge: Cambridge University Press, 1988.

Shields, Rob. *Lefebvre, Love and Struggle: Spatial Dialectics*. London: Routledge, 1999.

———. *Places on the Margins*. London: Routledge, 1991.

Skinner, Matthew L. *The Trial Narratives: Conflict, Power and Identity in the New Testament*. Louisville, KY: Westminster John Knox, 2010.

Sleeman, Matthew. *Geography and the Ascension Narrative in Acts*. Cambridge: Cambridge University Press, 2009.

Smallwood, Mary E. "High Priests and Politics in Roman Palestine." *JTS* (1962) 14–34.

———. *Jews under Roman Rule from Pompey to Diocletian: A Study in Political Relations*. SJLA 20. Leiden: Brill, 2001.

Smith, D. Moody. *The Theology of the Fourth Gospel*. Cambridge, UK: Cambridge University Press, 1995.

Smith, D. M., Jr. "Johannine Christianity: Some Reflections on its Character and Delineation." *NTS* 21 (1975) 222–48.

Smith, Jonathan Z. "The Influence of Symbols on Social Change: A Place on Which to Stand: Symbols and Social Change." *Worship* 44 (1970) 457–74.

———. *To Take Place: Toward Theory in Ritual*. Chicago: University of Chicago, 1987.

Smith, Morton. "Palestinian Judaism in the First Century," in *Israel: Its Role in Civilization*, edited by Moshe Davis, 74–77. New York: Jewish Theological Seminary of America, 1956.

Smith, Neil and Cindi Katz. "Grounding Metaphor: Towards a Spatialized Politics." In *Place and the Politics of Identity*, edited by Michael Keith and Steve Pile, 67–83. New York: Routledge, 1993.

Smith, Susan J. "The Cultural Politics of Difference." In *Human Geography Today*, edited by Doreen Massey, John Allen and Philip Sarre, 129–50. Oxford: Polity Press, 1999.

Soja, Edward W. *Postmodern Geographies: The Reassertion of Space in Critical Social Theory*. London: Verso, 1989.

———. "Third Space: Expanding the Scope of the Geographical Imagination," in *Human Geography Today*, edited by Doreen Massey, John Allen and Philip Sarre, 260–77. Oxford: Polity, 1999.

———. *Third Space: Journeys to Los Angeles and Other Real and Imagined Spaces.* Cambridge, MA: Blackwell, 1996.

Sophocles, *Oedipus at Colonus.* Translated by F. Storr. LCL 21. Cambridge, MA: Harvard University Press, 1912.

Spears, Rufus J. *Princeps a diis electus: The Divine Election of the Emperor as a Political Concept at Rome.* Papers and Monographs of the American Academy in Rome 26. Rome: American Academy in Rome, 1977.

Spicq, Ceslaus. *Agape dans le Nouveau Testament.* 3 Volumes. Paris: Gabalda, 1958–59.

Staley, Jeffrey L. "'Dis Place, Man': A Postcolonial Critique of the Vine (the Mountain and the Temple) in the Gospel of John." In *John and Postcolonialism: Travel, Space and Power,* edited by Musa W. Dube and Jeffrey L. Staley, 32–50. The Bible and Postcolonialism 7. New York: Sheffield Academic, 2002.

———. "The Politics of Place and the Place of Politics in the Gospel of John." In *What is John? II: Literary and Social Readings of the Fourth Gospel,* edited by Fernando F. Segovia, 265–77. SBLSymS 7. Atlanta, GA: Scholars, 1996.

Stavrakopoulou, Francesca. "Exploring the Garden of Uzza: Death, Burial and Ideologies of Kingship." *Bib* 87 (2006) 1–21.

Stegner, Wallace. *Where the Bluebird Sings to the Lemonade Springs: Living and Writing in the West.* New York: Penguin 1992.

Strabo. *Geography.* Translated by Horace Leonard Jones. LCL 49. Cambridge, MA: Harvard University Press, 1917.

Strathmann, H. "λαός" in the New Testament." In *TDNT* IV, edited by Gerhard Kittel and Gerhard Friedrich, 50–57. Grand Rapids, MI: Eerdmans, 1978.

Suetonius. *Lives of the Caesars.* Translated by J. C. Rolfe. LCL 31. Cambridge, MA: Harvard University Press, 1940.

Swanson, Tod D. "To Prepare a Place: Johannine Christianity and the Collapse of Ethnic Territory." *JAAR* 62 (1994) 241–63.

———. "To Prepare a Place: Johannine Christianity and the Collapse of Ethnic Territory." In *John and Postcolonialism: Travel, Space and Power,* edited by R. S. Sugirtharajah, 11–31. The Bible and Postcolonialism 7. New York: Sheffield Academic, 2002.

Tacitus. *Agricola. Germania. Dialogus.* Translated by A. M. Hutton et al. LCL 35. Cambridge, MA: Harvard University Press, 1998.

Talbert, Charles H. "The Myth of a Descending-Ascending Redeemer in Mediterranean Antiquity." In *The Development of Christology during the First Hundred Years and other Essays on Early Christian Christology,* edited by Charles H. Talbert, 83–111. NovTSup 140. Leiden: Brill, 2011.

Taylor, Lily Ross. *The Divinity of the Roman Emperor.* Middletown, CT: American Philological Association, 1931.

Thatcher, Tom. *Greater Than Caesar: Christology and Empire in the Fourth Gospel.* Minneapolis: Fortress, 2009.

Thompson, Marie Meye. *The Incarnate Word: Perspectives of Jesus in the Fourth Gospel.* Peabody, MA: Hendrickson, 1988.

Thucydides. *History of the Peloponnesian Wars.* Harmonds, Eng.: Penguin Books, 1974.

Thüsing, W. *Die Erhöhung und Verherrlichung Jesu im Johannesevangelium.* 3rd edition. NTAbh 21. Münster: Aschendorff, 1979.

Toenges, Elke. "The Image of God as Father as a Response to Political Crises in the First Century BCE." In *Religious Responses to Political Crisis,* edited by Henning Graf Reventlow and Yair Hoffman, 94–108. New York: T. & T. Clark, 2008.

Tomei, Maria Antonietta. *Museo Palatino*. English edition. Roma: Electa, 1997.

Tomson, Peter J. "Transformations of Post-70 Judaism: Scholarly Reconstructions and their Implications for our Perception of Matthew, Didache, and James." In *Matthew, James, and Didache: Three Related Documents in their Jewish and Christian Settings*, edited by H. van de Sandt and J. K. Zangenberg, 91–121. SBLSymS 45. Atlanta: Scholars, 2008.

Tonstad, Sigve K. "'the Father of Lies,' 'the Mother of Lies,' and the Death of Jesus (John 12:20–33)." In *The Gospel of John and Christian Theology*, edited by Richard Bauckham and Carol Mosser, 193–208. Grand Rapids, MI: Eerdmans, 2008.

Trumbower, Jeffrey A. *Born From Above: Anthropology of the Gospel of John*. HUT 20. Tübingen: Mohr Siebeck, 1992.

Tsutserov, Alexander. *Glory, Grace, and Truth: Ratification of the Sinai Covenant according to the Gospel of John*. Eugene, OR: Pickwick, 2009.

Tuan, Yi-Fu. *Space and Place: The Perspective of Experience*. Minneapolis: University of Minneapolis Press, 1977.

Turner, M. "Atonement and the Death of Jesus in John—Some Questions to Bultmann and Forestell." *EQ* 62:2 (1990) 99–122.

Twelftree, Graham H. "Exorcisms in the Fourth Gospel and the Synoptics." In *Jesus in Johannine Tradition*, edited by Robert T. Fortna and T. Thatcher, 135–53. Louisville, KY: Westminster John Knox, 2001.

Um, Stephen T. *The Theme of Temple Christology in John's Gospel*. London: T. & T. Clark International, 2006.

Umoh, Camillus. *The Plot to Kill Jesus: A Contextual Study of John 11:47–53*. Europaische Hochschulschriften xxiii. Frankfurt a.M.: Peter Lang, 2000.

Van Belle, Gilbert. "The Death of Jesus and the Literary Unity of the Fourth Gospel." In *The Death of Jesus in the Fourth Gospel*, edited by G. Van Belle, 3–64. BETL 200. Leuven: Leuven University Press and Uitgeverij Peeters, 2007.

———. *Johannine Bibliography, 1966–1985: A Cumulative Bibliography on the Fourth Gospel*. Collectanea Biblica et Religiosa Antiqua 1. Brussels: Wetenschappelijk Comitè Voor Godsdienst-wetenschappen Koninklijke Academic Voor Wetenschappen, Letteren En Schone Kunsten Van België, 1988.

Van de Sandt, H. "The Purpose of Jesus' Death: John 11:51–52 in the Perspective of the Did 9, 4." In *The Death of Jesus in the Fourth Gospel*, edited by G. Van Belle, 635–45. BETL 200. Leuven: Leuven University Press and Uitgeverij Peeters, 2007.

Verheyden, Joseph. "De la Potterie on John 19:13." In *The Death of Jesus in the Fourth Gospel*, edited by G. Van Belle, 817–37. BETL 200. Leuven: Leuven University Press and Uitgeverij Peeters, 2007.

Von Wahlde, Urban C. *The Gospel and Letters of John*. Volume 2. ECC. Grand Rapids, MI: Eerdmans, 2010.

———. "The Johannine 'Jews': A Critical Survey." *NTS* 28 (1982) 33–60.

Weil, Simone. "The Love of God and Affliction." In *The Simone Weil Reader*, edited by George A. Panichas, 439–68. New York: David McKay, 1977.

Weissenrieder, Annette. "Contested Spaces in 1 Corinthians 11:17–33 and 14:30." In *Contested Spaces: Houses and Temples in Roman Antiquity and the New Testament*, edited by David L. Balch and Annette Weissenrieder, 59–107. WUNT 285. Tübingen: Mohr Siebeck, 2012.

Williams, Raymond. *Keywords: A Vocabulary of Culture and Society*. New York: Oxford University Press, 1985.

Wróbel, Miroslaw Stanislaw. *Who are the Father and His Children in John 8:44? A Literary, Historical and Theological Analysis of John 8:44 and its Context*. CahRB 63. Paris: J. Gabalda, 2005.

Zumstein, J. "L'interprétation johannique de la mort du Christ," in *The Four Gospels: Festschrift Frans Neirynck*, edited by F. Van Segbröck, C. M. Tuckett, G. Van Belle, and J. Verheyden, 2119–38. BETL 100. Leuven: Leuven University/Peeters, 1992.

Name/Subject Index

Scripture Index